Words

Are

My

Matter

Nonfiction works by Ursula K. Le Guin:

Essays and Talks

Dancing at the Edge of the World: Thoughts on Words, Women, Places
The Language of the Night: Essays on Fantasy and Science Fiction
Steering the Craft: A Twenty-First-Century Guide to Sailing the Sea of Story
The Wave in the Mind: Talks and Essays on the Writer, the Reader, and the Imagination
Cheek By Jowl

Poetry

Wild Angels
Walking in Cornwall (chapbook)
Tillai and Tylissos (chapbook with Theodora Kroeber)
Hard Words
In the Red Zone (chapbook with Henk Pander)
Wild Oats and Fireweed
No Boats (chapbook)
Blue Moon Over Thurman Street (with Roger Dorband)
Going Out With Peacocks
Sixty Odd
Out Here: Poems and Images from Steens Mountain Country (with Roger Dorband)
by Ursula K. Le Guin (Author), Roger Dorband
Incredible Good Fortune
Finding My Elegy: New and Selected Poems
Late in the Day: Poems 2010–2014

Words Are My Matter

Writings About Life
and Books, 2000–2016
with
A Journal
of a
Writer's Week

Ursula K. Le Guin

Small Beer Press
Easthampton, MA

Words Are My Matter: Writings About Life and Books, 2000–2016 with A Journal of a Writer's Week Copyright © 2016 by Ursula K. Le Guin (ursulakleguin.com). All rights reserved. Page 319 functions as an extension of the copyright page.

Small Beer Press
150 Pleasant Street #306
Easthampton, MA 01027
smallbeerpress.com
weightlessbooks.com
info@smallbeerpress.com

Distributed to the trade by Consortium.

First Edition 1 2 3 4 5 6 7 8 9 0

Library of Congress Cataloging-in-Publication Data

Names: Le Guin, Ursula K., 1929- author.
Title: Words are my matter : writings about life and books, 2000-2016 with a
   journal of a writer's week / Ursula K. Le Guin.
Description: First edition. | Easthampton, MA : Small Beer Press, 2016. |
   Includes bibliographical references.
Identifiers: LCCN 2016029895 (print) | LCCN 2016035410 (ebook) | ISBN
   9781618731340 (alk. paper) | ISBN 9781618731210
Classification: LCC PS3562.E42 A6 2016b (print) | LCC PS3562.E42 (ebook) |
   DDC 818/.5409--dc23
LC record available at https://lccn.loc.gov/2016029895

Text set in Centaur.
Printed on 50# Natures Natural 30% PCR Recycled Paper by the Maple Press in York, PA.

Contents

The Mind Is Still

The mind is still. The gallant books of lies
are never quite enough.
Ideas are a whirl of mazy flies
    over the pigs' trough.

Words are my matter. I have chipped one stone
for thirty years and still it is not done,
that image of the thing I cannot see.
I cannot finish it and set it free,
    transformed to energy.

I chip and stutter but I do not sing
the truth, like any bird.
Daily I come to Judgment stammering
    the same half-word.

So what's the matter? I can understand
that stone is heavy in the hand.
Ideas flit like flies above the swill.
I crowd with other pigs to get my fill.
    The mind is still.

(1977)

Foreword

I seldom have as much pleasure in reading nonfiction as I do in a poem or a story. I can admire a well-made essay, but I'd rather follow a narrative than a thought, and the more abstract the thought the less I comprehend it. Philosophy inhabits my mind only as parables, and logic never enters it at all. Yet my grasp of syntax, which seems to me the logic of a language, is excellent. So I imagine that this limitation in my thinking is related to my abysmal mathematical incompetence, my inability to play chess or even checkers, perhaps my incomprehension of key in music. There seems to be a firewall in my mind against ideas expressed in numbers and graphs rather than words, or in abstract words such as Sin or Creativity. I just don't understand. And incomprehension is boredom.

So the nonfiction I read is mostly narrative—biography, history, travel, and science in its descriptive aspect: geology, cosmology, natural history, anthropology, psychology, etc., the more specific the better. And not only narrativity but the quality of the writing is of the first importance to me. Rightly or not, I believe a dull, inept style signals poverty or incompleteness of thought. I see the accuracy, scope, and quality of Darwin's intellect directly expressed in the clarity, strength, and vitality of his writing—the beauty of it.

This means I've set myself an awfully high standard when it comes to writing nonfiction. And if it isn't narrative, it's going to be hard work, and hard for me to judge as good or bad. Writing fiction or poetry is natural to me. I do it, want to do it, am fulfilled in doing it, the way a dancer dances or a tree grows. Story or poem is spun directly out of my entire self. And so I consider myself without question the primary judge of its accuracy, honesty, and quality. Writing talks or essays, however, is always more like doing schoolwork. It's going to be assessed for style and content, and rightly so. Nobody knows better than I do what my stories are about, but my essays may be judged by people who know a lot more than I do about what I'm talking about.

Fortunately, studying French and other Romance literatures, I got good training in scholarship and in writing critical prose, which gave me some confidence. Unfortunately, I also showed a gift for the snow job—not the kind that buries fake facts under a blizzard of statistics, but the stylistic snow job, expressing incomplete ideas with such graceful confidence that they are perfectly convincing until examined. After all, a fluent style isn't altogether dependent on the thoughts it expresses—it can be used to skate over gaps in knowledge and conceal rickety joints between ideas. When I'm writing nonfiction I have to be very aware of my tendency to let the words take their own course, leading me softly, happily, away from fact, away from rigorous connection of ideas, toward my native country, fiction and poetry, where truths are expressed and thoughts connected in an entirely different way.

As I got old and my total store of energy began to shrink, I began to travel about to give speeches less often and less far, and was less willing to take on a big talk or essay topic that would eat up weeks or months of research, planning, writing, and rewriting. So there are fewer talks and essays in this book than in my earlier nonfiction collections, and proportionately more book reviews.

A book review is usually pretty short, under a thousand words, and naturally limited in topic; it has certain requirements of description, but allows a lot of leeway as to pronouncing judgment—even though it involves the writer's conscience pretty directly. It's an interesting and demanding form. And one can say a good deal in a review that has to do with wider matters, literary and otherwise.

I like writing reviews except when I dislike the book I'm reviewing. When it comes to reading reviews, of course the best is one that sends me right to the bookstore, but I also treasure a hatchet job well-written and well-deserved. The pleasure of reading a killer review of a bad book is guiltless. The pleasure of writing one, however, is darkened for me by all kinds of compunctions, fellow-feeling for the author, shame at enjoying inflicting shame. . . . All the same, so long as I've tried to understand what the author tried to do, and have no illusions of my critical infallibility, condoning inferiority isn't an option open to me. For this reason the only real killer review in this book presented me with an intense problem. I had considerable respect for the author but thought the book almost incredibly bad. I had no idea how to review it. I appealed to my friend the novelist Molly Gloss—what to do? She suggested that I simply tell the plot. It was an excellent solution. Supply enough hemp, and the problem vanishes.

As for what writing an essay or talk demands—the expense of time and energy on research, thinking out, rethinking—this of course varies according to the subject. One of the longer pieces in this book, "Living in a Work of Art," was not written as most of them were as a talk to a group or on commission by a periodical (though it ended up happily in *Paradoxa*). It was something I wanted to write, purely on the principle of E. M. Forster's lady who said, "How do I know what I think till I see what I say?" It didn't take very much research, and once it got going it was a pleasure to write. When I can use prose as I do in writing stories as a direct means or form of thinking, not as a way of saying something I know or believe, not as a vehicle for a message, but as an exploration, a voyage of discovery resulting in something I didn't know before I wrote it, then I feel that I am using it properly. So that one is probably my favorite of these pieces.

I am often asked to deliver a message, and quite capable of doing so. But I seldom find it easy or particularly pleasant. One of the shortest pieces in the book is my speech on receiving the National Book Foundation medal in 2014. I was informed in June that this honor had been awarded me, so long as I'd come to New York to get it and make an acceptance speech lasting not more than seven minutes. I accepted, with much hesitation. From June until November, I worked on that little talk. I rethought and replanned it, anxiously, over and over. Even on a poem I've never worked so long and so obsessively, or with so little assurance that what I was saying was right, was what I ought to say. I was daunted, too, by the ingratitude of insulting the people who printed my books and were giving me an award. Who was I to spit in the publishers' punch bowl at the annual industry party?

Well, I was, in fact, the one to do it. So I did it.

I've never been so nervous before a speech since junior high school commencement. I've never been so surprised by an audience reaction (though the Amazon table sat predictably, glumly, mute). The viral flurry on the internet and my ensuing fifteen Warhol minutes of celebrity status were encouraging: people do care about books, some of them worry about capitalism. How much good it did in the long run is another question. But at least I ended up feeling that getting what I had to say said right in six minutes was entirely worth six months of work.

This confirms my sense that I have been allowed to use my life well, in work that was worth the time spent on it. Many people might see my two principal occupations as incompatible: being a middle-class American intellectual/wife/housewife/mother of three children, and being a writer. I won't say that doing both jobs at once was easy, but I can report, from very late in the life in question, that I found some inevitable conflict but no incompatibility between the two. Little abnegation was demanded, and no sacrifice of life for art or art for life. On the contrary, each nourished and supported the other so deeply that, looking back, they all seem one thing to me.

Talks, Essays, and Occasional Pieces

These are, really, all occasional pieces, addressed on various occasions to various audiences. Their subjects range through animals in books, invented languages, sleep, the house I grew up in, anarchism, how to read a poem, and a poem about a plinth. The most useful way to arrange them was chronologically. Many of them were revised slightly for this book; their original versions can be found in the original publication or on my website.

Only two of them are overtly political; but as we learned from Robin Morgan and others, the personal and the political are inseparable. A good many of them present a defense, sometimes a fairly belligerent defense, of certain aspects of literature—imaginative fiction, genre, women's writing, reading as distinct from experiencing media.

All through the past fifteen years there's been a steady and increasing shift of critical interest and understanding towards imaginative fiction and away from a rigid view of realism as the only fiction worthy the name of literature. I'm delighted to know that my arguments in defense of genre were becoming unnecessary even as I made them.

Gender in literature, however, remains a vexed issue. Books by women continue to be marginalised or segregated, receive fewer "major" literary awards, and are more subject to terminal inattention following the writer's death. So long as we hear about "women's writing" but not about "men's writing"—because the latter is assumed to be the norm— the balance is not just. The same signal of privilege and prejudice is reflected in the common use of the word feminism and the almost total absence of its natural counterpart, masculinism. I long for the day when neither word is necessary.

The Operating Instructions

A talk given at a meeting of Oregon Literary Arts in 2002.

A poet has been appointed ambassador. A playwright is elected president. Construction workers stand in line with office managers to buy a new novel. Adults seek moral guidance and intellectual challenge in stories about warrior monkeys, one-eyed giants, and crazy knights who fight windmills. Literacy is considered a beginning, not an end.

. . . Well, maybe in some other country, but not this one. In America the imagination is generally looked on as something that might be useful when the TV is out of order. Poetry and plays have no relation to practical politics. Novels are for students, housewives, and other people who don't work. Fantasy is for children and primitive peoples. Literacy is so you can read the operating instructions. I think the imagination is the single most useful tool mankind possesses. It beats the opposable thumb. I can imagine living without my thumbs, but not without my imagination.

I hear voices agreeing with me. "Yes, yes!" they cry. "The creative imagination is a tremendous plus in business! We value creativity, we *reward* it!" In the marketplace, the word creativity has come to mean the generation of ideas applicable to practical strategies to make larger profits. This reduction has gone on so long that the word creative can hardly be degraded further. I don't use it any more, yielding it to capitalists and academics to abuse as they like. But they can't have imagination.

Imagination is not a means of making money. It has no place in the vocabulary of profit-making. It is not a weapon, though all weapons originate from it, and their use, or non-use, depends on it, as with all tools and their uses. The imagination is an essential tool of the mind, a fundamental way of thinking, an indispensable means of becoming and remaining human.

We have to learn to use it, and how to use it, like any other tool. Children have imagination to start with, as they have body, intellect, the capacity for language: things essential to their humanity, things they need to learn how to use, how to use well. Such teaching, training, and practice should begin in infancy and go on throughout life. Young human beings need exercises in imagination as they need exercise in all the basic skills of life, bodily and mental: for growth, for health, for competence, for joy. This need continues as long as the mind is alive.

When children are taught to hear and learn the central literature of their people, or, in literate cultures, to read and understand it, their imagination is getting a very large part of the exercise it needs.

Nothing else does quite as much for most people, not even the other arts. We are a wordy species. Words are the wings both intellect and imagination fly on. Music, dance, visual arts, crafts of all kinds, all are central to human development and well-being, and no art or skill is ever useless learning; but to train the mind to take off from immediate reality and return to it with new understanding and new strength, nothing quite equals poem and story.

Through story, every culture defines itself and teaches its children how to be people and members of their people—Hmong, !Kung, Hopi, Quechua, French, Californian. . . . We are those who arrived at the Fourth World. . . . We are Joan's nation. . . . We are the sons of the Sun. . . . We came from the sea. . . . We are the people who live at the center of the world.

A people that doesn't live at the center of the world, as defined and described by its poets and storytellers, is in a bad way. The center of the world is where you live fully, where you know how things are done, how things are done rightly, done well.

A child who doesn't know where the center is—where home is, *what* home is—that child is in a very bad way.

Home isn't Mom and Dad and Sis and Bud. Home isn't where they have to let you in. It's not a place at all. Home is imaginary.

Home, imagined, comes to be. It is real, realer than any other place, but you can't get to it unless your people show you how to imagine it—whoever your people are. They may not be your relatives. They may never have spoken your language. They may have been dead for a thousand years. They may be nothing but words printed on paper, ghosts of voices, shadows of minds. But they can guide you home. They are your human community.

All of us have to learn how to invent our lives, make them up, imagine them. We need to be taught these skills; we need guides to show us how. Without them, our lives get made up for us by other people.

Human beings have always joined in groups to imagine how best to live and help one another carry out the plan. The essential function of human community is to arrive at some agreement on what we need, what life ought to be, what we want our children to learn, and then to collaborate in learning and teaching so that we and they can go on the way we think is the right way.

Small communities with strong traditions are often clear about the way they want to go, and good at teaching it. But tradition may crystallise imagination to the point of fossilising it as dogma and forbidding new ideas. Larger communities, such as cities, open up room for people to imagine alternatives, learn from people of different traditions, and invent their own ways to live.

As alternatives proliferate, however, those who take the responsibility of teaching find little social and moral consensus on what they should be teaching—what we need, what life ought to be. In our time of huge populations exposed continuously to reproduced voices, images, and words used for commercial and political profit, there are too many people who want to and can invent us, own us, shape and control us through seductive and powerful media. It's a lot to ask of a child to find a way through all that alone.

Nobody can do anything very much, really, alone.

What a child needs, what we all need, is to find some other people who have imagined life along lines that make sense to us and allow some freedom, and listen to them. Not hear passively, but listen.

Listening is an act of community, which takes space, time, and silence. Reading is a means of listening.

Reading is not as passive as hearing or viewing. It's an act: you do it. You read at your pace, your own speed, not the ceaseless, incoherent, gabbling, shouting rush of the media. You take in what you can and want to take in, not what they shove at you fast and hard and loud in order to overwhelm and control you. Reading a story, you may be told something, but you're not being sold anything. And though you're usually alone when you read, you are in communion with another mind. You aren't being brainwashed or co-opted or used; you've joined in an act of the imagination.

I know no reason why our media could not create a similar community of the imagination, as theater has often done in societies of the past, but they're mostly not doing it. They are so controlled by advertising and profiteering that the best people who work in them, the real artists, if they resist the pressure to sell out, get drowned out by the endless rush for novelty, by the greed of the entrepreneurs.

Much of literature remains free of such co-optation, in part because a lot of books were written by dead people, who by definition are not greedy. And many living poets and novelists, though their publishers may be crawling abjectly after bestsellers, continue to be motivated less by the desire for gain than by the wish to do what they'd probably do for nothing if they could afford it, that is, practice their art—make something well, get something right. Literature remains comparatively, and amazingly, honest and reliable.

Books may not be "books," of course, they may not be ink on wood pulp but a flicker of electronics in the palm of a hand. Incoherent and commercialised and worm-eaten with porn and hype and blather as it is, electronic publication offers those who read a strong new means of active community. The technology is not what matters. Words are what matter. The sharing of words. The activation of imagination through the reading of words.

The reason literacy is important is that literature *is* the operating instructions. The best manual we have. The most useful guide to the country we're visiting, life.

What It Was Like

A talk given at a meeting of Oregon NARAL in January 2004.

My friends at NARAL asked me to tell you what it was like before *Roe vs. Wade*. They asked me to tell you what it was like to be twenty and pregnant in 1950 and when you tell your boyfriend you're pregnant, he tells you about a friend of his in the army whose girl told him she was pregnant, so he got all his buddies to come and say, "We all fucked her, so who knows who the father is?" And he laughs at the good joke.

They asked me to tell you what it was like to be a pregnant girl—we weren't "women" then—a pregnant college girl who, if her college found out she was pregnant, would expel her, there and then, without plea or recourse. What it was like, if you were planning to go to graduate school and get a degree and earn a living so you could support yourself and do the work you loved—what it was like to be a senior at Radcliffe and pregnant and if you bore this child, this child which the law demanded you bear and would then call "unlawful," "illegitimate," this child whose father denied it, this child which would take from you your capacity to support yourself and do the work you knew it was your gift and your responsibility to do: What was it like?

I can hardly imagine what it's like to live as a woman under Fundamentalist Islamic law. I can hardly remember now, fifty-four years later, what it was like to live under Fundamentalist Christian law. Thanks to *Roe vs. Wade*, none of us in America has lived in that place for half a lifetime.

But I can tell you what it *is* like, for me, right now. It's like this: If I had dropped out of college, thrown away my education, depended on my parents through the pregnancy, birth, and infancy, till I could get some kind of work and gain some kind of independence for myself and the child, if I had done all that, which is what the anti-abortion people want me to have done, I would have borne a child for them, for the anti-abortion people, the authorities, the theorists, the fundamentalists; I would have borne a child for them, their child.

But I would not have borne my own first child, or second child, or third child. My children.

The life of that fetus would have prevented, would have aborted, three other fetuses, or children, or lives, or whatever you choose to call them: my children, the three I bore, the three wanted children, the three I had with my husband—whom, if I had not aborted the unwanted one, I would never have met and married, because he would have been a Fulbright student going to France on the *Queen Mary* in 1953 but I would not have been a Fulbright student going to France on the *Queen Mary* in 1953. I would have been an "unwed mother" of a three-year-old in California, without work, with half an education, living off her parents, not marriageable, contributing nothing to her community but another mouth to feed, another useless woman.

But it is the children I have to come back to, my children Elisabeth, Caroline, Theodore, my joy, my pride, my loves. If I had not broken the law and aborted that life nobody wanted, they would have been aborted by a cruel, bigoted, and senseless law. They would never have been born. This thought I cannot bear. I beg you to see what it is that we must save, and not to let the bigots and misogynists take it away from us again. Save what we won: our children. You who are young, before it's too late, save your children.

Genre: A Word Only a Frenchman Could Love

A talk given at the Public Library Association Preconference on Genre, in Seattle, February 2004, revised in 2014.

The concept of genre is a valid one. We need a method for sorting out and defining varieties of narrative fiction, and genre gives us a tool to begin the job. But there are two big problems in using the tool. The first is that it's been misused so often that it's hard to use it rightly—like a good screwdriver that's all bent out of shape because some dork tried to pry paving stones apart with it.

Genre is a generic word—naturally!—for "a kind or style, especially of art or literature," says the *OED*, and more specifically a term for paintings of a certain type and subject matter: "scenes and subjects of common life."

Now, "scenes and subjects of common life" nicely covers the subject matter of the realistic novel, the literary equivalent of genre painting. But when the term made its way into literature, it came to mean anything but the realistic and the commonplace. It was oddly enough applied to fictions whose subject matter is some degrees removed from common life—Westerns, murder mysteries, spy thrillers, romances, horror stories, fantasies, science fiction, and so on.

The subject matter of realism is broader than that of any genre except fantasy; and realism was the preferred mode of twentieth-century modernism. By relegating fantasy to kiddylit or the trash, modernist critics left the field to the realistic novel. Realism was central. The word genre began to imply something less, something inferior, and came to be commonly misused, not as a description, but as a negative value judgment. Most people now understand "genre" to be an inferior form of fiction, defined by a label, while realistic fictions are simply called novels or literature.

So we have an accepted hierarchy of fictional types, with "literary fiction," not defined, but consisting almost exclusively of realism, at the top. All other kinds of fiction, the "genres," are either listed in rapidly descending order of inferiority or simply tossed into a garbage heap at the bottom. This judgmental system, like all arbitrary hierarchies, promotes ignorance and arrogance. It has seriously deranged the teaching and criticism of fiction for decades, by short-circuiting useful critical description, comparison, and assessment. It condones imbecilities on the order of "If it's science fiction it can't be good, if it's good it can't be science fiction."

And judgment by genre is particularly silly and pernicious now that the idea of genre itself is breaking down.

That's the other problem with our good tool; the screwdriver is melting, the screws are all screwy. Much of the best fiction doesn't fit into the genres any more, but combines, crosses, miscegenates, transgresses, and reinvents them. Seventy years ago Virginia Woolf questioned the possibility of writing realistic fiction honestly. Many honest writers have given up the attempt.

Terms such as "magical realism" or "slipstream" are taken from the literatures to which they're suited and slapped hastily across great widening cracks in the conventional structure of narrative. They disguise more than they reveal, and are useless as description. Major novelists appear outside any recognised category—tell me what kind of fiction it is that José Saramago writes. It is not realism; no, it certainly isn't; but it very certainly is literature.

The breakdown is occurring even across a major boundary, that between fiction and nonfiction. Jorge Luis Borges said that he considered all prose literature to be fiction. Fiction, for Borges, thus includes history, journalism, biography, memoir, Cervantes' *Don Quixote*, Pierre Menard's *Don Quixote*, the works of Borges, *Peter Rabbit*, and the Bible. It seems a large category, but it may prove more intellectually practicable than any attempt to salvage useless distinctions.

And yet the categories established by genre are not only perpetuated, cemented in, by the stereotyped thinking of reviewers, by the ingrained habits and superstitions of publishers, and by the shelving and descriptive practices of booksellers and libraries; they also are—have been and still are—useful, perhaps necessary, to the appreciation of fiction. If you don't know what kind of book you're reading and it's not a kind you're used to, you probably need to learn how to read it. You need to learn the genre.

Useless and harmful as a value category, genre is a valid descriptive category. It may be most useful historically, for defining twentieth-century works; in the postmodern era the genres begin to melt and flow. But where definition by genre applies and is applied fairly, it is valuable both to readers and to writers.

For example: A writer sets out to write science fiction but isn't familiar with the genre, hasn't read what's been written. This is a fairly common situation, because science fiction is known to sell well, but, being "subliterary," is supposed to be not worth study. It's just Sci-Fi—what's to learn? Plenty. A genre is a genre by virtue of having a field and focus of its own, its appropriate and particular tools and rules and techniques for handling the material, its traditions, and its experienced, appreciative readers. Ignorant of all this, our novice is about to reinvent the wheel, the space ship, the space alien, and the mad scientist, with cries of innocent wonder. The cries will not be echoed by the readers. Readers familiar with the genre have met the space ship, the alien, and the mad scientist before. They know much more about them than the writer does.

In the same way, critics who set out to talk about a fantasy novel in ignorance of the history and extensive theory of fantasy literature will make fools of themselves, because they don't know how to read the book. They have no contextual information to tell them what its tradition is, where it's coming from, what it's trying to do, what it does. This was liberally proved when the first Harry Potter book came out and literary reviewers ran around shrieking about its incredible originality. This originality was an artifact of the reviewers' blank ignorance of its genres, children's fantasy and the British boarding-school story, plus the fact that they hadn't read a fantasy since they were eight. It was pitiful. It was like watching a TV gourmet chef eat a piece of buttered toast and squeal, "But this is delicious! Unheard of! What genius invented it?"

When *The Hobbit* and its sequels were published, ignorance as a critical qualification was celebrated every time a literary pundit exhibited his sophistication by performing the time-hallowed Ceremony of the Ritual Sneers at Tolkien. Happily, that custom is fast dying out.

All in all we need to rethink genre in order to reform the practices of critics and reviewers and the assumptions of readers, and to bring the description of fiction into some kind of relation to reality. I admit that the temptation to pull a Borges is very strong—to just say, All Fiction is Genre and all Genre is Literature! And I do say it when I lose patience.

But what's the use in saying it when you know that you're running your head right against the solid obstruction of category labeling and shelving practice, from the conception of the book, the contract, the cover, to the bookstores and libraries? How can you tell reviewers to stop shoving books into outmoded categories where they don't fit when the publishers themselves absolutely insist on the category labels—and when many, perhaps most of the authors would scream bloody murder if they didn't get the genre label and cover and category that keeps their book from getting lost among all the other books in all the other genres?

Marketing rules, OK? I have no illusions that intelligence could possibly replace marketing in this or any other matter. Commercial genrification has its reasons. They are intelligible reasons, though not intelligent ones.

Consumerism also rules. If the books aren't categorised, if they aren't shelved by genre, if they don't have a little label saying SF or M or YA, a whole lot of customers and library users will come storming the counter or the desk or the online book dealer, shouting, Where is my Fiction Fix? I want a Fantasy, I can't read all that realistic stuff! I want a Mystery, I can't read all that plotless stuff! I want a Masterpiece of Grim Realism, I can't read all that imaginary stuff! I want Mindless Fluff, I can't read all that literary stuff! Etc.

Genre addicts want books to be easy the way fast food is easy. They want to go to the big online commercial fiction dealer who knows what they like to read and offers cheap fixes, or go to the library shelf and stick out their hand and get a free fix. Did you ever notice handwritten initials next to the previously published titles on the flyleaf of a series mystery at the library—sometimes a whole row of them down the leaf? They're so people will know they've read that one already; looking at the story itself wouldn't tell them anything, since it's exactly like all the other books in that series by that author. This signifies reader addiction. The most harm I can see in it is that it may keep addicts from reading good stuff, though they might not read the good stuff anyway, because they've been scared into thinking that literature can't include anything about horses, space ships, dragons, dreams, spies, monsters, animals, aliens, or dark, handsome, taciturn men who own large houses in remote bits of England. Fitzwilliam Darcy, they need you! But they've been scared away from Darcy, or never allowed a glimpse of him. Instead, the commercial fiction machine feeds their hunger for story with junk food—commercial, mechanical, formula fiction.

Any genre, including realism, can be formulised and made commercial. Genre and formula are two different things, but the assumption that they are the same thing allows the lazy-minded critic and professor to ignore and dismiss all genre literature.

A genre label on a book is usually an appeal to a safe but limited audience. Publishers go for safe, and so they like genre labels for high-risk authors. But with low-risk big-name authors, the assumption has been that their literary reputation would be damaged by the admission that one or more of their books belongs to a genre. Some "literary" novelists have performed amazing contortions to preserve their pure name from the faintest taint of genre pollution. I am tempted to imitate them, backwards. How am I to protect my unspotted name as a Sci-Fi Writer from the scorn of those who may notice that I have shamelessly published realistic fiction?

Easy. Consider my book *Searoad*, which makes ironic use of some realist tropes—but of course I don't write Re-Fi, as its fat fans in three-piece-suit costumes call it. Realism is for lazy-minded, semi-educated people whose atrophied imagination allows them to appreciate only the most limited and conventional subject matter. Re-Fi is a repetitive genre written by unimaginative hacks who rely on mere mimesis. If they had any self-respect they'd be writing memoir, but they're too lazy to fact-check. Of course I never *read* Re-Fi. But the kids keep bringing home these garish realistic novels and talking about them, so I know that it's an incredibly narrow genre, completely centered on one species, full of worn-out clichés and predictable situations—the quest for the father, mother-bashing, obsessive male lust, dysfunctional suburban families, etc., etc. All it's good for is being made into mass-market movies. Given its old-fashioned means and limited subject matter, realism is quite incapable of describing the complexity of contemporary experience.

There are many bad books. There are no bad genres.

Of course there are genres that are unappealing to individual readers. A reader who liked or valued all kinds of narrative equally would be undiscriminating to the point of imbecility. Some people honestly can't read fantasy with any pleasure. I honestly can't read porn, horror, or most political thrillers with pleasure. I have friends who cannot read *any* fiction with pleasure; they need what they can consider or pretend to be facts. These differences point, again, to the underlying validity of the concept of literary genre.

But they do not justify any judgment of literature by genre.

There are commercial subcategories, such as some series mysteries, gross-out books for children concerning snot, and strict formula romances, which are so narrowly prescribed, so rigidly diminished in emotional and intellectual scope, that a genius would go mad trying to write one of serious merit. But if you sneer at romance as an intrinsically inferior fictional category, may I invite you to read the works of Charlotte and Emily Brontë?

Judgment of literature by category or genre is worthless.

So what are we going to do now? What use is the concept of genre if you can't damn whole categories of fiction with it so that you never have to bother learning how to read them, and if the fiction writers are going to keep crossing over, ignoring boundaries, miscegenating, interbreeding like a barnful of cats while publishers and booksellers and librarians cling desperately to the old, false, rigid divisions because they're commercially unrisky and they make it easy for people to find certain types of books without being exposed to any alien forms of literature that might possibly take over their minds and put new ideas into them?

Perhaps in the almost pathless confusion of the internet, and in the fact that we now have two major ways of publishing and reading books, the problem of genre has already begun to find its solution.

"Things Not Actually Present": On Fantasy, with a Tribute to Jorge Luis Borges

A talk given at a meeting of Oregon Literary Arts in January 2005.

The unabridged *Oxford English Dictionary* is a wonderful book. It's not quite Borges's Book of Sand, yet it is inexhaustible. All we have ever said and can ever say is in it, if we can only find it. I think of the *OED* as my wise aunt. So I went to Auntie, with my magnifying glass, and said, "Auntie! Please tell me about fantasy, because I want to talk about it, but I am not sure what I am talking about."

"Fantasy, or Phantasy," Auntie replies, clearing her throat, "is from the Greek *phantasia*, lit. 'a making visible.'" And she shows me how "fantasy" in the late Middle Ages meant "the mental apprehension of an object of perception," the mind's act of linking itself to the external world, but later came to mean just the reverse: an hallucination, a false perception, or the habit of deluding oneself. And she tells me that the word fantasy also came to mean the imagination itself, "the process, the faculty, or the result of forming mental representations of things not actually present." And again, those representations, those imaginations, can be true ones, or false. They can be the insights and foresights that make human life possible, or the delusions and follies that bedevil and endanger our lives.

So the word fantasy remains ambiguous, standing between the false, the foolish, the shallows of the mind, and the mind's deep, true connection with the real.

Auntie has very little to say about fantasy as a kind of literature. So I have to say it. In the Victorian and modernist periods, writers of fantasy were often apologetic about what they did, offering it as mere whimsy, a sort of bobble-fringing to *real* literature, or passing it off, sneakily, as Lewis Carroll did, as being "for children" and therefore beneath serious notice. Writers of fantasy are often less modest now that what they do is recognised as literature, or at least as a genre of literature, or at least as a subliterary genre, or at least as a commercial product.

Fantasy has, in fact, become quite a business. There are people who turn out unicorns by the yard. Capitalism flourishes in Elfland.

But when one night in Buenos Aires in 1937 three friends sat talking together about fantastic literature, it wasn't yet a business. Even less so one night in a villa in Geneva in 1816, when four friends sat talking together and telling ghost stories. They were Mary Godwin, Percy Shelley, Lord Byron, and Mr. Polidori; and they told awful tales to one another, and Mary was scared. "We will each write a ghost story!" cried Byron. So Mary went away and thought about it, and a few nights later she had a nightmare in which a "pale student" used strange arts and machineries to arouse from unlife the "hideous phantasm of a man."

And so, alone of the friends, she wrote her ghost story, *Frankenstein: A Modern Prometheus*, which is the first great modern fantasy. There are no ghosts in it; but fantasy, as the *OED* observes, is more than ghoulie-mongering. Because ghosts haunt one corner of the vast domain of fantastic literature, people familiar with that corner of it call the whole thing ghost stories, or horror stories; just as others call it Fairyland after the part of it they love best or hate worst, and others call it science fiction, and others call it stuff and nonsense. But the nameless being given life by Frankenstein's or Mary Shelley's arts and machineries is not a ghost, not a fairy; science-fictional he may be; stuff and nonsense he is not. He is a creature of fantasy, archetypal, deathless. Once raised he will not sleep again, for his pain will not let him sleep, the unanswered moral questions that woke with him will not let him rest in peace.

When there began to be money in the fantasy business, plenty of money was made out of him in Hollywood, but even that did not kill him.

Very likely his story was mentioned on that night in 1937 in Buenos Aires when Silvina Ocampo and her friends Jorge Luis Borges and Adolfo Bioy Casares fell to talking, so Casares tells us, "about fantastic literature . . . discussing the stories which seemed best to us." And they enjoyed it so much they collected the stories into a *Book of Fantasy*, which exists now in both Spanish and English. It is a wild mishmash, horror story and ghost story and fairy tale and science fiction all together. A piece we might think we know almost too well, such as "The Cask of Amontillado," regains its strangeness when read among works from the Orient and South America and distant centuries, by Kafka, Swedenborg, Cortázar, Akutagawa, Niu Chiao. The book reflects the taste and curiosity of Borges, who was himself a member of the international tradition of fantasy which includes Rudyard Kipling and H. G. Wells.

Perhaps I should not say tradition, since it has so little recognition in critical circles, and is distinguished in college English departments mainly by being ignored; but I believe there is a company of fantasists that Borges belonged to even as he transcended it, and that he honored even as he transformed it. By saying fantasy is for children (which of course some of it is) and dismissing it as commercial and formulaic (which of course some of it is), many academics and most literary critics feel justified in ignoring it all. Yet looking at such writers as Italo Calvino, Gabriel García Márquez, and José Saramago, I see our narrative fiction going slowly and massively, as a deep current, in one direction: and that direction is towards the reinclusion of fantasy as an essential element of fiction. Or put it this way: fiction—writing it, reading it—is an act of the imagination.

Fantasy is, after all, the oldest kind of narrative fiction, and the most universal.

Fiction offers the best means of understanding people different from oneself, short of experience. Actually, fiction can be lots better than experience, because it's a manageable size, it's comprehensible, while experience just steamrollers over you and you understand what happened decades later, if ever. Fiction is terrific at giving factual, pyschological, and moral understanding.

But realistic fiction is culture-specific. The language, the unspoken assumptions, all the details of ordinary life that are the substance and strength of realistic fiction, may be utterly obscure to the reader of another time and place. And reading a realistic story that takes place in another century or another country involves an act of displacement, of translation, which many readers are unable or unwilling to attempt.

Fantasy need not have this problem. People tell me they don't read fantasy "because it's all just made up," but the material of fantasy is far more permanent, more universal, than the social customs realism deals with. Whether a fantasy is set in the real world or an invented one, its substance is psychic stuff, human constants, imageries we recognise. It seems to be a fact that everybody, everywhere, even if they haven't met one before, recognises a dragon.

Until fairly recently, the societies in and for which realistic fiction was written were limited and homogeneous. The realistic novel could describe such societies. But that limited language is in trouble now. To describe society since the mid twentieth century—global, multilingual, infinitely interlinked—we need the global, intuitional language of fantasy. García Márquez wrote his histories of his own nation in the fantastic images of magical realism because it was the only way he could do it.

The central moral dilemma of our age, and of this very moment now, is the use or non-use of annihilating power. This choice was posed most cogently in fictional terms by the purest of fantasists. Tolkien began *The Lord of the Rings* in 1937 and finished it about ten years later. During those years, Frodo withheld his hand from the Ring of Power, but the nations did not.

So, in so much contemporary fiction, the most revealing and accurate descriptions of our daily life are shot through with strangeness, or displaced in time, or set on imaginary worlds, or dissolved into the phantasmagoria of drugs or of psychosis, or rise from the mundane suddenly into the visionary and then come out the other side.

So the magical realists of South America and their counterparts in India and elsewhere are valued for their accuracy, their truthfulness to the way things are.

And so Jorge Luis Borges, who chose to identify himself with a tradition considered marginal, not the mainstream of realism and modernism that dominated literature in his youth and maturity, remains a writer central to our literature. His poems and stories, his images of reflections, libraries, labyrinths, forking paths, his books of tigers, of rivers, of sand, of mysteries, of changes, are everywhere honored, because they are beautiful, because they are nourishing, because they fulfill the most ancient, urgent function of words: to form for us "mental representations of things not actually present," so that we can form a judgment of what world we live in and where we might be going in it, what we can celebrate, what we must fear.

A Response, by Ansible, from Tau Ceti

This piece first appeared in The New Utopian Politics of Ursula K. Le Guin's *The Dispossessed, edited by Laurence Davis and Peter Stillman, Lexington Books, 2005. It is a general response to the articles in that book. I revised it slightly for this book in 2014.*

I've spent a good deal of vehemence objecting to the reduction of fiction to ideas. Readers, I think, are often led astray by the widespread belief that a novel springs from a single originating "idea," and then are kept astray by the critical practice of discussing fiction as completely accessible to intellect, a rational presentation of ideas by means of an essentially ornamental narrative. In discussing novels that clearly deal with social, political, or ethical issues, and above all in discussing science fiction, supposed to be a "literature of ideas," this practice is so common—particularly in teaching and academic texts—that it has driven me to slightly lunatic extremes of protest.

In reaction to it, I find myself talking as if intellect had nothing to with novel-writing or novel-reading, speaking of composition as a pure trance state, and asserting that all I seek when writing is to allow my unconscious mind to control the course of the story, using rational thought only to reality-check when revising.

All this is perfectly true, but it's only half the picture. It's because the other half of the picture is so often the only one shown and discussed that I counter-react to the point of sounding woowoo.

When critics treat me—even with praise—as a methodical ax-grinder, I am driven to deny that there's any didactic intention at all in my fiction. Of course there is. I hope I have avoided preaching, but the teaching impulse is often stronger than I am. Still, I'd rather be praised for my efforts to resist it than for my failures.

Even in quite sophisticated criticism, the naïve conflation of what a character (particularly a sympathetic one) says with what the author believes will goad me into denying that I agree with what the character says, even when I do. How else can I assert the fact that a character's voice is never to be taken for the author's? *Je suis Mme Bovary*, said Flaubert, groaning as usual. I say: *J'aime Shevek mais je ne suis pas Shevek.* I envy Homer and Shakespeare, who by being only semi-existent evade such impertinent assimilations. They retain effortlessly the responsible detachment which I must consciously, and never wholly successfully, labor to achieve.

So *The Dispossessed*, a science-fiction novel not only concerned with politics, society, and ethics but approaching them via a definite political theory, has given me a lot of grief. It has generally, not always but often, been discussed as a treatise, not as a novel. This is its own damn fault, of course—what did it expect, announcing itself as a utopia, even if an ambiguous one? Everybody knows utopias are to be read not as novels but as blueprints for social theory or practice.

But the fact is that, starting with Plato's *Republic* in Philosophy I-A when I was seventeen, I read utopias as novels. Actually, I still read everything as novels, including history, memoir, and the newspaper. I think Borges is quite correct, all prose is fiction. So when I came to write a utopia of course I wrote a novel.

I wasn't surprised that it was treated as a treatise, but I wondered if the people who read it as a treatise ever wondered why I had written it as a novel. Were they as indifferent as they seemed to be to what made it a novel—the inherent self-contradictions of novelistic narrative that prevent simplistic, single-theme interpretation, the novelistic "thickness of description" (Geertz's term) that resists reduction to abstracts and binaries, the embodiment of ethical dilemma in a drama of character that evades allegorical interpretation, the presence of symbolic elements that are not fully accessible to rational thought?

You will understand, perhaps, why I approached this collection of essays about *The Dispossessed* with my head down and my shoulders hunched. Experience had taught me to expect a set of intellectual exercises which, even if not accusing me of preaching, moralising, political naïveté, compulsive heterosexuality, screeching feminism, or bourgeois cowardice, even if interested in or supportive of what the book "says," would prove essentially indifferent to how it says it.

If fiction is how it says what it says, then useful criticism is what shows you how fiction says what it says.

To my grateful surprise, that's what this collection does. These essays are not about an idea of the book. They are about the book.

Perhaps I can express my gratitude best by saying that reading them left me knowing far better than I knew before how I wrote the book and why I wrote it as I did. By seldom exaggerating the intentionality of the text, they have freed me from exaggerating its non-intentionality, allowing me once more to consider what I wanted to do and how I tried to do it. They have restored the book to me as I conceived it, not as an exposition of ideas but as an embodiment of idea—a revolutionary artifact, a work containing a potential permanent source of renewal of thought and perception, like a William Morris design, or the Bernard Maybeck house I grew up in.

These critics show me how the events and relationships of the narrative, which as I wrote the book seemed to follow not an arbitrary but not a rationally decided course, do constitute an architecture which is fundamentally aesthetic and which, *in being so,* fulfills an intellectual or rational design. They enable me to see the system of links and echoes, of leaps and recurrences, that make the narrative structure work. This is criticism as I first knew it, serious, responsive, and jargon-free. I honor it as an invaluable aid to reading, my own text as well as others'.

Though I had pretty well saturated my mind with utopian literature, with the literature of pacifist anarchism, and with "temporal physics" (insofar as it existed) before I wrote the book, my knowledge of relevant theoretical thinking was very weak. When I read recurrent citations in these essays—Hegel above all, Bakhtin, Adorno, Marcuse, and many more—I hunch up a bit again. I am embarrassed. My capacity for sustained abstract thought is somewhat above that of a spaniel. I knew and know these authors only by name and reputation; the book was not written under their influence, and they can't be held responsible, positively or negatively, for anything in my text. At most (as with the "shadow" in Carl Jung and in *A Wizard of Earthsea*) it is interesting to observe parallels or intersections of thought.

On the other hand, I was glad to see my thought experiment tested against the writers who did contribute to its formation—above all Lao Tzu, Kropotkin, and Paul Goodman.

A good many of the writers in this book treat *The Dispossessed* as if it stood quite alone in my work. This ahistorical approach seems odd, since the book has been around so long, and isn't an anomaly among my other works. It was followed in 1982 by a fairly lengthy discussion of utopias ("A Non-Euclidean View of California as a Cold Place to Be"), which forms a clear link to a second, if radically different, utopian novel, *Always Coming Home* (1985). It's hard for me to put these out of my mind when thinking about *The Dispossessed*. Both offer a chance to compare some of the things I did in the earlier novel with things I said in the essay or did in the later novel—testing for consistency, change of mind, progress, regress, aesthetic and intellectual purpose. And also, the unanimity with which these writers refuse to read *The Dispossessed* as a single-theme, monistic, closed-minded text makes me long to see some of them take on *Always Coming Home*, which has often been read, or dismissed unread, as a naïvely regressive picture of a sort of Happy Hunting Ground for fake Indians. The narrative experimentation and the postmodernist self-conscious fictionality which some of these essayists point to in *The Dispossessed* are carried a great deal further in *Always Coming Home*. I for one am curious as to why I play these particular tricks only when writing utopias, or anyhow semi-utopias with flies in them. In some of these essays I began to catch a glimpse of why, and I'd very much like to learn more.

I found nothing really to correct—nothing I thought simply wrong, a misreading—in all these pages. I would point out that Hainish guilt is not unmotivated or mysterious; in other stories one finds that the Hainish, everybody's ancestors, have a terribly long history which is, like all human histories, terrible. So Ketho, who comes in at the end, is indeed cautious in his search for hope. But whether he finds it or not the book does not say. And here I felt in a few of the essays a slight tendency to wishful thinking. The book doesn't have a happy ending. It has an open ending. As pointed out in at least one of the essays, it's quite possible that both Shevek and Ketho will be killed on arrival by an angry mob. And it's only too likely that Shevek's specific plans and hopes for his people will come to little or nothing. That would not surprise Ketho.

In speaking of the end of the book I must once again thank its first reader and first critic, Darko Suvin, who brought to my anarchist manuscript the merciless eye of a Marxist and the merciful mind of a friend. It had twelve chapters then, and a neat full-circle ending. Twelve chapters? he cried, enraged. It should be an odd number! And what is this—closure? You are not allowed to close this text! Is the circle open or not?

The circle is open. The doors are open.

In order to have doors to open, you have to have a house.

To those who helped me build my drafty and imaginary house, and to those who have brought to it their generous comment and keen perception, making its rooms come alive with resounding and unending arguments, I am grateful. Be welcome, ammari.

The Beast in the Book

A talk given at the Conference on Literature and Ecology in Eugene, Oregon, June 2005, revised in 2014.

The oral literatures of hunter-gatherer peoples consist largely of myths, in many of which the protagonists are chiefly or solely animals.

The general purpose of a myth is to tell us who we are—who we are as a people. Mythic narrative affirms our community and our responsibilities, and is told in the form of teaching-stories both to children and adults.

For example, many Native North American myths concern a First People, called by animal species names, whose behavior is both human and animal; among them are creators, tricksters, heroes, and villains; and what they are doing, usually, is getting the world ready for the "people who are coming," that is, us, us humans, us Yurok or Lakota or whomever. Out of context, the meaning of stories from these great mythologies may be obscure, and so they get trivialised into just-so stories—how the woodpecker got his red head, and so on. In the same way, the Jataka tales of India are retold as mere amusements, with no hint of their connection to the ideas of dharma, reincarnation, and the Buddha-nature. But a child who "gets" the story may "get" a sense of those deep connections without even knowing it.

The oral and written literatures of preindustrial civilisations are, of course, about everything under the sun, but all those I know contain a powerful and permanent element of animal story, largely in the form of folktale, fairy tale, and fable, again told both to children and adults. In these, the humans and animals mingle, cheek by jowl.

In postindustrial civilisation, where animals are held to be irrelevant to adult concerns except insofar as they are useful or edible, animal story is mostly perceived as being for children. Young children hear or read stories from the earlier eras, both animal myths and animal fables and tales, retold and illustrated for them, because animal stories are considered suitable for children, and surely also because many children want them, seek them, demand them. There is also a large modern literature of animal stories, written sometimes for children, sometimes not, though the kids usually get hold of it. Although non-satirical writing about animals is automatically dismissed by literary critics as trivial, authors continue to write animal stories. They are writing in response to a real and permanent demand.

Why do most children and many adults respond both to real animals and to stories about them, fascinated by and identifying with creatures which our dominant religions and ethics consider mere objects for human use: no longer working with us, in industrial societies, but mere raw material for our food, subjects of scientific experiments to benefit us, entertaining curiosities of the zoo and the TV nature program, pets kept to improve our psychological health?

Perhaps we give animal stories to children and encourage their interest in animals because we see children as inferior, mentally "primitive," not yet fully human: so we see pets and zoos and animal stories as "natural" steps on the child's way up to adult, exclusive humanity—rungs on the ladder from mindless, helpless babyhood to the full glory of intellectual maturity and mastery. Ontogeny recapitulating phylogeny in terms of the Great Chain of Being.

But what is it the kid is after—the baby wild with excitement at the sight of a kitten, the six-year-old spelling out *Peter Rabbit*, the twelve-year-old weeping as she reads *Black Beauty*? What is it the child perceives that her whole culture denies?

I will skip over a lot of discussion and example to a few books I want to talk about in this context. Three of the great works of children's literature and animal literature are Hugh Lofting's *Doctor Dolittle*, Rudyard Kipling's *Jungle Books*, and T. H. White's *The Sword in the Stone*, the first book of *The Once and Future King*. (May I say here that I am talking about books, not about movies "based on" the books.) These books are about the relationship of human beings and animals. In each it is different, and each explores it in depth.

Such language may sound a bit fancy in talking of *Doctor Dolittle*, but Hugh Lofting's unpretentious fantasy deserves its classic status. As in *The Wind in the Willows*, animals and people interact without the slightest plausibility and without the slightest hesitation. This is because the animals act like people, mostly, but they act better than most people. None of them does anything cruel or immoral. Gub-Gub is very piggy, to be sure, and the Lion has to be scolded by his wife before he'll help the other animals, but this is the Peaceable Kingdom, where the lion will truly lie down with the lamb. The Doctor helps animals by sheltering and healing them, they begin to help him in return, and that is the theme and the basis of almost everything in the story.

The Doctor says, "So long as the birds and the beasts and the fishes are my friends, I do not have to be afraid." This sentence has been spoken in many, many languages over many thousands of years. Every people in the world understood this theme of mutual aid, of the Animal Helper, until we drove the animals out of our streets and skyscrapers. I think every child in the world still understands it. To be friends with the animals is to be a friend and a child of the world, connected to it, nourished by it, belonging to it.

Lofting's morality is entirely sweet and sunny. In Kipling's Mowgli stories, the connections between human and animal are complex and ultimately tragic. Mowgli is a link between his village people and the people of the jungle, and like all go-betweens, all liminal figures, he is torn between the two sides, torn apart. There is no common ground between the village and the jungle; they have turned their back on each other. In every language of the animals Mowgli can say, "We be of one blood, ye and I!"—but can he truly say it in Hindi? And yet that is his mother's tongue, his mother's blood. Whom must he betray?

The wolf child, the wild boy, both in rare and painful reality and in Kipling's dream-story, can never, in the end, be at home. The ache of exile from Eden is there even in the first story, "Mowgli's Brothers," ever stronger in "Letting in the Jungle" and "The Spring Running." Those are heartbreaking stories. Yet from the *Jungle Books* we may also carry with us all our lives the blessing of those lazy hours and breathless adventures when boy and wolf, bear, black panther, python, speak and think and act in joyous community: the mystery and beauty of belonging, totally belonging to the wildness of the world.

T. H. White's *The Sword in the Stone*, though about King Arthur, is crowded with animals. In the first chapter King Arthur-to-be, currently known as the Wart, takes out a goshawk, loses him, and meets Merlyn's owl Archimedes:

> "Oh, what a lovely owl!" cried the Wart.
>
> But when he went up to it and held out his hand, the owl grew half as tall again, stood up as stiff as a poker, closed its eyes so that there was only the smallest slit to peep through . . . and said in a doubtful voice:
>
> "There is no owl."
>
> Then it shut its eyes entirely and looked the other way.
>
> "It's only a boy," said Merlyn.
>
> "There is no boy," said the owl hopefully, without turning round.

Merlyn undertakes Arthur's education, which consists mostly of being turned into animals. Here we meet the great mythic theme of Transformation, which is a central act of shamanism, though Merlyn doesn't make any fuss about it. The boy becomes a fish, a hawk, a snake, an owl, and a badger. He participates, at thirty years per minute, in the sentience of trees, and then, at two million years per second, in the sentience of stones. All these scenes of participation in nonhuman being are funny, vivid, startling, and wise.

When a witch puts Wart into a cage to fatten him up, the goat in the next cage plays Animal Helper and rescues them all. All animals rightly trust Wart, which is proof of his true kingship. That he goes along on a boar hunt does not vitiate this trust: to White, true hunting is a genuine relationship between hunter and hunted, with implacable moral rules and a high degree of honor and respect for the prey. The emotions aroused by hunting are powerful, and White draws them all together in the scene of the death of the hound Beaumont, killed by the boar, a passage I have never yet read without crying.

At the climax of the book, Wart can't draw the sword of kingship from the stone anvil by himself. He calls to Merlyn for help, and the animals come.

There were otters and nightingales and vulgar crows and hares, and serpents and falcons and fishes and goats and dogs and dainty unicorns and newts and solitary wasps and goat-moth caterpillars and corkindrills and volcanoes and mighty trees and patient stones . . . all, down to the smallest shrew mouse, had come to help on account of love. Wart felt his power grow.

Each creature calls its special wisdom to the boy who has been one of them, one with them. The pike says, "Put your back into it," a stone says, "Cohere," a snake says, "Fold your powers together with the spirit of your mind"—and: "The Wart walked up to the great sword for the third time. He put out his right hand softly and drew it out as gently as from a scabbard."

T. H. White was a man to whom animals were very important, perhaps because his human relationships were so tormented. But his sense of connection with nonhuman lives goes far beyond mere compensation; it is a passionate vision of a moral universe, a world of terrible pain and cruelty from which trust and love spring like the autumn crocus, vulnerable and unconquerable. *The Sword in the Stone*, which I first read at thirteen or so, influenced my mind and heart in ways which must be quite clear in the course of this talk, convincing me that trust cannot be limited to mankind, that love cannot be specified. It's all or nothing at all. If, called to reign, you distrust and scorn your subjects, your only kingdom will be that of greed and hate. Love and trust and be a king, and your kingdom will be the whole world. And to your coronation, among all the wondrous gifts, an "anonymous hedgehog will send four or five dirty leaves with some fleas on them."

To end with, I will talk about two fables or fantasies, a new one and an old one.

Philip Pullman's *His Dark Materials* trilogy is a long, richly imagined, and deeply incoherent work, in which I'll try only to trace the part animals play. Despite appearances, it is a small part. The two cats in the story, who have a minor but important role, do what cats have often done in myth and fable: they cross between worlds. Otherwise they're just cats, realistically drawn. Animals are otherwise absent from the books, except for a tribe of polar bears who talk and build forts and use weapons, as humans do, but who don't have daemons, as humans do.

These daemons are animals in form, and the reason that the trilogy—particularly the first volume—seems to be full of animals is that every human being has one. Until you reach puberty your daemon may take any animal shape at any moment; with your sexual maturity your daemon settles into a permanent form, always of the other gender. Social class is a decisive influence: we are told that servants always have dog daemons, and we see that upper-class people's daemons are rare and elegant creatures such as snow leopards. Your daemon accompanies you physically and closely at all times, everywhere; separation is unbearably painful. Though they do not eat or excrete, daemons are tangible, and you can pet and cuddle with your own daemon, though you must not touch anybody else's. Daemons are rational creatures and speak fluently with their owners and with others. Wish-fulfillment is strong in this concept and gives it great charm: the ever-loyal, ever-present, dear companion, soulmate, comforter, guardian angel, and ultimately perfect pet. As with the beloved stuffed animal, you don't even have to remember to feed it.

But I think Pullman overloads the concept and then confuses it. He implies strongly that the daemon is a kind of visible soul, that to be severed from it is fatal, and his plot hinges on the cruelty and horror of this separation. But then he begins changing the rules: we find that witches can live apart from their daemons; in the second volume we are in our world, where nobody has visible or tangible daemons; back in her world, the heroine Lyra leaves her daemon on the wharves of hell, and though she misses him, she lives on perfectly competently, and in fact saves the universe, without him. Their reunion seems almost perfunctory.

In a fantasy, to change or break your own rules is to make the story literally inconsequential. If the daemons are meant to show that we are part animal and must not be severed from our animality, they can't do it, since the essence of animality is the body, the living body with all its brainless needs and embarrassing functions—exactly what the daemons do not have. They are spiritual beings, forms without substance. They are fragments or images of the human psyche, wholly contingent, having no independent being and therefore incapable of relationship. Lyra's much-emphasized love for her daemon is self-love. In Pullman's world human beings are dreadfully alone, since God has gone senile and there aren't any real animals. Except those two cats. Let us place our hope in the cats.

Lewis Carroll's *Through the Looking-Glass* begins with cats. Alice is talking to Dinah and the kittens, who can't talk back, so Alice does it for them, and then she climbs up onto the mantelpiece with one of the kittens and goes through the mirror. . . . As noted before, cats cross between worlds.

The looking-glass world, like the one down the rabbit hole, is a dream world, and therefore all the characters in them may be seen as aspects of Alice—fragments of psyche, but in a very different sense from Pullman's daemons. Their independence is notable. As soon as Alice gets through the glass into the garden, the flowers not only talk but talk back; they are extremely rude and passionate flowers.

As in folktale, all creatures are on an equal footing, mingling and arguing, even turning into each other—the baby becomes a piglet, the White Queen a sheep—transformation going both ways. Train passengers include humans, a goat, a beetle, a horse, and a gnat, which begins as a tiny voice in Alice's ear but presently is "about the size of a chicken." It asks if Alice dislikes insects, and she replies, with admirable aplomb, "I like them when they can talk. None of them ever talk, where I come from." Alice is a nineteenth-century British middle-class child with a strict moral code of self-respect and respect for others. Her good manners are sorely tried by the behavior of the dream creatures, whom we can see, if we choose, as acting out Alice's own impulses of rebellion, her passion, her wild willfulness. Violence is not permitted. We know that the Queen's "Off with her head!" is a threat not to be executed. And yet nightmare is never far off. The creatures of Alice's dreams come close to total uncontrol, to madness, and she must wake to know herself.

The Alice books are not animal stories, but there is no way I could leave them out of this talk; they are the purest modern literary instance of the animals of the mind, the dream beasts that every human society has known as ancestors, as spirit doubles, as omens, as monsters, and as guides. In them we have spiraled back round to the Dream Time, where human and animal are one.

This is a sacred place. That we got back to it by following a little Victorian girl down a rabbit hole is absolutely crazy and appropriate.

"People and animals are supposed to be together. We spent quite a long time evolving together, and we used to be partners," writes Temple Grandin in *Animals in Translation.*

We human beings have made a world reduced to ourselves and our artifacts, but we weren't made for it, and we have to teach our children to live in it. Physically and mentally equipped to be at home in a richly various and unpredictable environment, competing and coexisting with creatures of all kinds, our children must learn poverty and exile: to live on concrete among endless human beings, seeing a beast now and then through bars.

But our innate, acute interest in the animal as a fellow being, friend or enemy or food or playmate, can't be instantly eradicated. It resists deprivation. And imagination and literature are there to fill the void and reaffirm the greater community.

The Animal Helper motif of mutual aid across species, which we see clearly both in folktale and modern animal stories, tells that kindness and gratitude can't be limited to your own species, that all creatures are kin.

By the assimilation of animal to human and the mingling as equals that we see in folktale and in such books as *The Wind in the Willows* and *Doctor Dolittle*, the community of living creatures is shown as simple fact.

Transformation of man into beast, in folktales often a curse or unhappy spell, is in modern stories more likely to be enlarging and educational, and even, as in the Wart's last great journey, to offer a glimpse of mystical participation, of an ultimate and eternal communion.

The yearning for a Lost Wilderness which runs through so many animal tales is a lament for the endless landscapes and creatures and species that we have wasted and destroyed. These laments grow urgent now. We come ever closer to isolating ourselves, a solitary species swarming on a desert world. "Look on my works, ye mighty, and despair."

We go crazy in solitude. We are social primates, sociable beings. Human beings need to belong. To belong to one another, first, of course; but because we can see so far and think so cleverly and imagine so much, we aren't satisfied by membership in a family, a tribe, people just like us. Fearful and suspicious as it is, yet the human mind yearns towards a greater belonging, a vaster identification. Wilderness scares us because it is unknown, indifferent, dangerous, yet it is an absolute need to us; it is that animal otherness, that strangeness, older and greater than ourselves, that we must join, or rejoin, if we want to stay sane and stay alive.

The child is our closest link to it. The storytellers know that. Mowgli and young Wart reach out their hands, the right hand to us and the left hand to the jungle, to the wild beast in the wilderness, to the hawk and the owl and the panther and the wolf; they join us together. The six-year-old spelling out *Peter Rabbit*, the twelve-year-old weeping over *Black Beauty*—they have accepted what so much of their culture denies, and they too reach out their hands to rejoin us to the greater creation, keeping us where we belong.

Inventing Languages

Published as the foreword to The Encyclopedia of Fictional and Fantastic Languages, *ed. Conley and Cain, Greenwood Publishing, 2006, and revised in 2014.*

Most invented languages begin with invented names. Those who write fiction with an entirely imaginary setting—fantasy, or far-future or alien-world science fiction—must play Adam: they need names for the characters, creatures, and places of their fictive world.

Invented names are a quite good index of writers' interest in their instrument, language, and their ability to play it. In a crude stage of such naming, back in the pulp days of science fiction, invention was largely by convention. Heroes resisted invention entirely: whizzing through distant galaxies in the thirtieth century, they were still Buck and Rick and Jack. Aliens were Xbfgg and Psglqkjvk, unless they were princesses named Laweena or LaZolla.

If you're creating a world out of words and there are speaking creatures in it, you suggest a great deal—whether you mean to or not—by naming them. The old pulp-science-fiction naming conventions implied the permanent hegemony of manly, English-speaking men, the risible grotesqueness of non-English languages, and the inviolable rule that pretty princesses (the only women worth naming) have musical names ending in *a*. And the conventions dragged on endlessly in movie sci-fi, with a hero named Luke, an alien named Chewbacca, and a princess named Leia.

A more thoughtful and inventive approach to naming may offer less naïvely unexamined social and moral implications. Take Swift's horses in *Gulliver's Travels*, the Houyhnhnms. The best guide to how to say the name is provided by the Professor and Maria in T. H. White's *Mistress*

Masham's Repose; according to them it involves not moving your tongue while squealing through the back of your nose. I find that tossing your head and shaking it at the same time helps. It isn't easy. But Houyhnhnm isn't a contemptuously meaningless and unpronounceable clump of letters: on the contrary, it's a conscious attempt to spell how a horse might say who it is, and a deliberate challenge to the English speaker. If you're willing to learn to say that one word of the horses' language, you may be that much more able to think like a horse. Swift is not dismissing the nonhuman, but inviting us into to it.

Many, many children draw maps of strange countries and name them: Islandia, Angria. . . . With the name comes a hint of the color of the hills, the weather, the temper of the people there. Some children explore these lands, sometimes returning to them in imagination all their lives.

To make up a name of a person or a place is to open the way to the world of the language the name belongs to. It's a gate to Elsewhere. How do they talk in Elsewhere? How do we find out how they talk?

The best thing ever written on the subject is J. R. R. Tolkien's essay "A Secret Vice." It is a splendid and often very funny description, explanation, and defense of the creation of fictive languages. It discusses how such languages, when carried through to any extent, are mythopoeic: they bear in them an intrinsic mythology, a view of the world—even, as with Swift's horses, a new morality. Tolkien addresses the aesthetic motivation of such creations with characteristic vigor and insight. He says:

> The instinct for 'linguistic invention'—the fitting of notion to oral symbol, and *pleasure in contemplating the new relation established*, is rational, and not perverted. . . . . Certainly it is the contemplation of the relation between sound and notion which is the main source of pleasure. We see it in an alloyed form in the peculiar keenness of the delight scholars have in poetry or fine prose in a foreign language, almost before they have mastered that language.

What such scholars (and I would add poets, and any readers of a certain bent) find in reading a language new to them, he says, is the pleasure roused by "a great freshness of perception of the word-form."

Many critics and teachers of fiction are so deaf or indifferent to the sound of prose that they, and their students, may find this statement puzzling or trivial, or fail to see how it applies to their own language. I can only say that to me it holds an invaluable suggestion of how I come at my invention of fictions as a writer, and my appreciation of fiction as a reader. I seek the appropriateness of sound to sense.

I first discovered the particular pleasure of a "new relation established" between the two when I was eight or so. The kindly Swiss lady who was trying to teach me French picked up a little china whale from my desk and said, smiling, "Ah! Le Moby-Dick!" Lemobeedeek? Slowly the mysterious, senseless, charming noise revealed the whale: a revelation. Leviathan! Leviathan made new!

A few years later, when I first read Lord Dunsany's fantasies, the fine, playful relation of sound and sense in his made-up names gave me joy—the evil gnoles, for instance, or the doomed city Perdóndaris, through which flows the great river Yann. . . . Equally strong was the magic of half-guessed meaning in a language whose mystery was merely that I didn't know it.

> *Muy más clara que la luna*
> *sola una*
> *en el mundo tu nacistes . . .*

When I was thirteen that song in Hudson's *Green Mansions* held all romance in it, all the moon, all love and yearning . . . more than it could possibly have held if I had known Spanish. This, says Tolkien, is the advantage of seeing things at a distance. It is the great gift of hearing words as music.

Language is "for" communicating, but when we come to such phenomena as poetry and made-up names and languages, the function of communication and the construction of meaning become as impenetrable to intellect alone as the tune of a song. The writer has to listen. The reader has to hear. Pleasure in articulate sound, and in the symbolic use of it, is what moves the maker of a poem, and also the maker of a fictional language, even if her tongue is the only one that will ever speak it and her ear alone is tuned to it.

The undertaking of this book is, as its makers confess, ambitious: to gather all the imaginary languages into one Tower of Babel. So widespread and so public is the Secret Vice these days that the authors have had to omit from detailed consideration not only languages such as Esperanto, which though utopian are not fictional, but also the "constructed languages" that fill whole websites, and the "alien languages" presented in comics and video and role-playing games. A lot of people are busy making up new ways to speak. This encyclopedia comes in the nick of time to guide us into the myriad worlds thus suggested.

Rightly, it concentrates on languages that belong to an imagined race of speakers, a society, a world—genuinely fictive languages, not exclusive codes, and not games, even though some of them are immensely playful.

In the beginning is the word: one may imagine a language before imagining who speaks it. This is how it was, evidently, with Tolkien. A linguist playing with language for the joy of it, he found his invented languages bringing to life the mythology of a people, and thence an anthropology, a history, a topography, and all the vast epic of Middle Earth . It can also happen the other way round: the development of an imagined world beyond a certain point demands the development of a language to suit it. This was the case with my *Always Coming Home*. I thought a few dozen words of the language of the Kesh people would suffice to suggest their key concepts, and had already blithely written that "the difficulty of translation from a language that doesn't yet exist is considerable, but there's no need to exaggerate it." But when the composer Todd Barton began to write the music of the Valley for the book, he needed a Kesh text for the songs. I had to be an honest woman, sit down, and invent Kesh—at least enough of the grammar and syntax and vocabulary to get me through writing the poems which I had pretended to translate into English before they existed in Kesh. The difficulty of that process needs no exaggeration.

Usually it's not so convoluted. A few mysterious words can give the impression of a language, the flavor of it, which is all most novels need to do; all the inventor has to do is make the words linguistically plausible.

An incoherent language is a contradiction in terms. A language is, in a sense, its rules. It is a symbolic pact, a convention, a social contract. Whether it's the limited choice of sounds used (the phoneme pool), the combination of those sounds to make words, or the combination of those words in syntax, every aspect of any language is largely arbitrary, intensely regular, and perfectly characteristic. In English you *never* pronounce *u* the way the French do, and in French you *never* say *th* the way the English do. Mandarin would perish rather than agglutinate. The rules are so pervasive that you can identify a language by a single word— "Achtung!"

This self-consistence is convenient to the novelist. If she only needs a few words or names for local color, all she has to do is make up some that don't sound like the language she's writing in. Her inventions may have a strong lurking flavor of her native tongue, but probably only readers who come to it from other languages will taste it. Then she merely needs to ask herself: is this humanly sayable? This is where Xbfgg and Psglqkjvk fail the test, though Houyhnhmn passes it. And she should consider whether the invented words and names seem to come from the same language. For if one character is named Krzgokhbazthwokh and another Lia-tua-liuli, readers will reasonably assume that the two come from different parts of Elsewhere.

Noam Chomsky, as quoted in the introduction to this encyclopedia, appears to assume that the nefarious purpose of a made-up language is "to violate universal grammar." I doubt that many inventors of language have had any desire to violate universal grammar, if they have ever heard of it. Those who are serious about making their invention plausible and even usable naturally avoid any attempt to violate universal grammar—if in fact it's possible to do so. If a deep grammar is innate in us, supplying the fundamental structure of all human languages, to ignore or violate it would result not in an invented language but in mere unintelligibility.

As far as I can see, the rules we make up for our imaginary languages are all mere variations on the rules of the languages we know. Any appearance of linguistic terrorism turns out to be inept rule-making, or mere ignorance that there are rules. Professor Chomsky may sleep sound; fictional barbarians are not battering at the gates of his universal grammar.

Although it is possible that Borges, with his perverse, subversive, marvelous daring, at least knocked politely at those gates. The primordial languages of Tlön, he tells us, have no nouns; in one the noun is replaced by a cluster of adjectives, in another "there is no word corresponding to the word 'moon,' but there is a verb which in English would be 'to moon' or 'to moonate.'" And thus "The moon rose above the river" becomes "upward behind the onstreaming mooned": *Hlör u fang axaxaxas mlö*. But we must remember that the Ur-languages of Tlön, like Indo-European, are theoretical reconstructions of the early source of a whole family of languages. It may by now be necessary also to remember that none of the languages of Tlön, in fact, exist, because Tlön does not exist; unless, of course, as the end of the story "Tlön, Uqbar, Orbis Tertius" suggests, we are now living there.

Hlör u fang axaxaxas mlö is a particularly fine example of linguistic invention—of the mad variety of imaginary words and grammars gathered in this book, their proliferation into jungles of exuberant glossolalia—the laborious delight with which sane people translate utter, deliberate nonsense into English, and vice versa—the touching spectacle of poets blissfully writing poems in languages nobody ever heard or heard of. This is a side of humanity I like very much. These are people doing what only people can do, a peculiarly human and peculiar thing. They do it without malice, and without any gain or profit in sight except the increase of pleasure. If the pleasure can be shared—as it is, liberally, here—so much the better; but the thing is done, like most good things and all art, for the doing of it.

How to Read a Poem: "Gray Goose and Gander"

This piece appeared in Poetry Northwest, *in response to editor David Biespiel's call for contributions on the subject of how to read a poem. I revised it somewhat for publication here. I cannot retrieve the original date of publication from my files or any online source, but I place it here as a best guess, or perhaps on a whim.*

How to read a poem is aloud. There are eye-poems, of course—I'm fond of e. e. cummings—but to me they are all offshoots, technologically enabled derivatives of the heard poem. The words the eyes see are a notation, a score; the mind can only fully understand them through the ear. But, being words, they *say* the meaning of their music. Words sung to a tune make a song; when the words are the tune, you have a poem.

This can be a big deal, like the *Aeneid* or the *Canterbury Tales*, or a very small one, like this:

> *Gray goose and gander*
> *Waft your wings together*
> *And carry the good king's daughter*
> *Over the one-strand river.*

I read it first in *The Oxford Nursery Rhyme Book*, by Iona and Peter Opie, a source of endless joy to myself and the people who at various times have sat on my lap.

I'll try to describe the music and the meaning as I hear them, hoping to clarify my idea of how they work together, or rather are aspects of one thing.

The "tune" of the little poem is most obvious in its repeated sounds: the alliterations of the first letter of stressed syllables ($g - g - g$ / $w - w - g$ / $k - g - k$ in the first three lines); and, instead of full end-rhyme, four slant-rhymed words ending in unstressed *er*—a syllable pronounced variously in different regions, from *ah* to *uh* to (in my dialect) the sound of the *r* itself, a dull purr which can be extended indefinitely, like a vowel. However pronounced, it is a mild syllable, fading off into open silence. All the vowels and consonants of the poem tend toward softness, giving an effect, to my ear, of silvery hush and spaciousness.

As you might expect in an oral form like a nursery rhyme, the beat is strong, reinforced by alliterations. Using *S* for a stressed syllable and *u* for unstressed, I read the meter as:

> *S S u S u*
> *S u S u S u*
> *u S u u S S S u*
> *S u u S S S u*

You could call it trochaic trimeter with a lot of latitude, but I don't know that that gets us much of anywhere. There are lots of trochees in nursery rhymes—rocking rhythms—but it may be more useful to look at the line as the metric unit, or even the stanza, rather than the foot. In these poems worn down by generations of voices, like river stones by water, to the smoothest and most irreducible shape, each has arrived at its own essential rhythmic logic.

The abruptness of a trochaic opening suits the suddenness of the address, "Gray goose and gander" summoned out of nothing. And no sooner invoked than commanded, "Waft your wings together." The old word "waft" for "wave" needs no explanation to the youngest child; sound and context are enough.

Now the birds are aloft, and the rhythm changes: a pair of unstressed syllables lightens each line before it delivers the weight of three stressed syllables in a row, a trick you don't often meet in formal poems. The rocking-chair beat makes me want to put less stress on "king's" and "strand"—*good* king's *daugh*ter, *one*-strand *river*. But the complexity of both the meaning and the sound of the words keeps me from unstressing them, forcing me to say all three words slowly, with a mysterious, lingering weightiness.

And they are mysterious words. Who is the good king? Who is his daughter? From what folktale or cloudy history did they arrive? And why is the princess to be carried "over the one-strand river"—the river that has only one shore? Is it the ocean, or is it death?

No answer. Event is all. The glimpse is given. We can spend the rest of our life enriched by that brief music with its inexhaustible suggestion of flight above vast landscapes and a story we will never be told.

On David Hensel's Submission to the Royal Academy of Art

A top art gallery in Britain displayed a block of slate topped by a small piece of wood as a work of art, unaware that it was merely the plinth for a missing sculpture. The Royal Academy in London later admitted that it was confused because the plinth and sculpture—a human head by artist David Hensel—were sent to the museum separately. "Given their separate submission, the two parts were judged independently," museum officials said. "The head was rejected. The base was thought to have merit and accepted."

The Guardian, "The Week," June 30, 2006

"We know our art, we do not minth
our wordth," the Royal Jury said.
"A human noggin won't convinth.
A thlab of thlate ith far more great,
cauthing the true aeththetic winth.
Off with hith head!" the Jury said.
"Off with hith head, and on with hith plinth!"

On Serious Literature

Published on my website, then in Ansible, *then (without my permission and extremely briefly) on boingboing, and then in* Harper's, *all in 2007.*

"Michael Chabon has spent considerable energy trying to drag the decaying corpse of genre fiction out of the shallow grave where writers of serious literature abandoned it."

Ruth Franklin, *Slate*, May 8, 2007

Something woke her in the night. Was it steps she heard, coming up the stairs—somebody in wet training shoes, climbing the stairs very slowly ... but who? And why wet shoes? It hadn't rained. There, again, the heavy, soggy sound. But it hadn't rained for weeks, it was only sultry, the air close, with a cloying hint of mildew or rot, sweet rot, like very old finocchiona, or perhaps liverwurst gone green. There, again—the slow, squelching, sucking steps, and the foul smell was stronger. Something was climbing her stairs, coming closer to her door. As she heard the click of heel bones that had broken through rotting flesh, she knew what it was. But it was dead, dead! God damn that Chabon, dragging it out of the grave where she and the other serious writers had buried it to save serious literature from its polluting touch, the horror of its blank, pustular face, the lifeless, meaningless glare of its decaying eyes! What did the fool think he was doing? Had he paid no attention at all to the endless rituals of the serious writers and their serious critics— the formal expulsion ceremonies, the repeated anathemata, the stakes driven over and over through the heart, the vitriolic sneers, the endless, solemn dances on the grave? Did he not want to preserve the virginity of Yaddo? Had he not even understood the importance of the distinction between Sci-Fi and counterfactual fiction? Could he not see that Cormac

McCarthy—although everything in his book except the wonderfully blatant use of an egregiously obscure vocabulary was remarkably similar to a great many earlier works of science fiction about men crossing the country after a holocaust—could never under any circumstances be said to be a Sci-Fi writer, because Cormac McCarthy was a serious writer and so *by definition* incapable of lowering himself to commit genre? Could it be that Chabon, just because some mad fools gave him a Pulitzer, had forgotten the sacred value of the word mainstream? No, she would not look at the thing that had squelched its way into her bedroom and now stood over her, reeking of rocket fuel and kryptonite, creaking like an old mansion on the moors in a wuthering wind, its brain rotting like a pear from within, dripping little grey cells through its ears. But its call on her attention was, somehow, imperative, and as it stretched out its hand to her she saw on one of the half-putrefied fingers a fiery golden ring. She moaned. How could they have buried it in such a shallow grave and then just walked away, abandoning it? "Dig it deeper, dig it deeper!" she had screamed, but they hadn't listened to her, and now where were they, all the other serious writers and critics, when she needed them? Where was her copy of *Ulysses*? All she had on her bedside table was a Philip Roth novel she had been using to prop up the reading lamp. She pulled the slender volume free and raised it up between her and the ghastly golem—but it was not enough. Not even Roth could save her. The monster laid its squamous hand on her, and the ring branded her like a burning coal. Genre breathed its corpse breath in her face, and she was lost. She was defiled. She might as well be dead. She would never, ever get invited to write for *Granta* now.

Teasing Myself
Out of Thought

A talk given at the Blue River Gathering in Oregon, 2008, revised 2014.

Our hosts gave me some ideas for topics to start off our discussion: Where is a writer to find strength and hope in this world? What is a writer's calling in this time and place? What work will make a difference? And how might we create a community of purpose?

I'm embarrassed because I come out with the same response to each question. Where am I to find strength and hope in this world? In my work, in trying to write well. What's a writer's calling, now or at any time? To write, to try to write well. What work will make a difference? Well-made work, honest work, writing well written. And how might we create a community of purpose? I can't say. If our community of purpose as writers doesn't lie in our shared interest in and commitment to writing as well as we can, then it must lie in something outside our work—a goal or end, a message, an effect, which may be most desirable, but which makes the writing merely a means to an end that lies outside the work, the vehicle of a message. And this is not what writing is to me. It is not what makes me a writer.

Kids are taught writing in school as a means to an end. Most writing is indeed a means to an end: love letters, information of all kinds, business communications, instructions, tweets. Much writing embodies, is, a message.

So the kids ask me, "When you write a story, do you decide on the message first or do you begin with the story and put the message in it?"

No, I say, I don't. I don't do messages. I write stories and poems. That's all. What the story or the poem means to you—its "message" to you—may be entirely different from what it means to me.

The kids are often disappointed, even shocked. I think they see me as irresponsible. I know their teachers do.

They may be right. Maybe all writing, even literature, is not an end in itself but a means to an end other than itself. But I couldn't write stories or poetry if I thought the true and central value of my work was in a message it carried, or in providing information or reassurance, offering wisdom, giving hope. Vast and noble as these goals are, they would decisively limit the scope of the work; they would interfere with its natural growth and cut it off from the mystery which is the deepest source of the vitality of art.

A poem or story consciously written to address a problem or bring about a specific result, no matter how powerful or beneficent, has abdicated its first duty and privilege, its responsibility to itself. Its primary job is simply to find the words that give it its right, true shape. That shape is its beauty and its truth.

A well-made clay pot—whether it's a terra-cotta throwaway or a Grecian urn—is nothing more and nothing less than a clay pot. In the same way, to my mind, a well-made piece of writing is simply what it is, lines of words.

As I write my lines of words, I may try to express things I think are true and important. That's what I'm doing right now in writing this essay.

But expression is not revelation, and this essay, though there's art in the writing of it, is less a work of art than a message.

Art reveals something beyond the message. A story or poem may reveal truths to me as I write it. I don't *put* them there. I *find* them in the story as I work.

And other readers may find other truths in it, different ones. They're free to use the work in ways the author never intended. Think of how we read Sophocles or Euripides. For three thousand years, we've been reading the Greek tragedies, putting our souls into them and discovering in them lessons in human passion, pleas for justice, inexhaustible meanings— far beyond what the author's conscious intention of religious or moral teaching, of warning or solace or community celebration, could ever provide. Those works were written out of that mystery, the deep waters, the wellspring of art.

Keats is on my side in this, if I understand his principle of negative capability, and so is Lao Tzu, who observed that the use of the pot is where the pot is not. A poem of the right shape will hold a thousand truths. But it doesn't *say* any of them.

I am not talking "Art for Art's sake," because that unfortunate slogan implies that art is solipsistic, its effect on its audience of no account. That's a mistake. Art does change people's minds and hearts.

And an artist is a member of a community: the people who may see, hear, read her work. My first responsibility is to my craft, but if what I write may affect other people, obviously I have a responsibility to them too. Even if I don't have a clear idea of what the meaning of my story is and only begin to glimpse it as I write—still, I can't pretend it isn't there.

So, as the bright-eyed and accusatory children ask me, "If you know something, shouldn't you just say it?"

Can truth only be implicit? Why does the pot you make have to be empty, why can't you fill it with goodies for us?

Well, first, for a totally practical reason: because "telling it slant" works much better than overt moralising does. It is more effective.

But there's a moral reason too. What my reader gets out of my pot is what she needs, and she knows her needs better than I do. My only wisdom is knowing how to make pots. Who am I to preach?

No matter how humble the spirit it's offered in, a sermon is an act of aggression.

"The great Way is very simple; merely forgo opinion," says the Taoist, and I know it's true—but there's a preacher in me who just longs to cram my lovely pot with my opinions, my beliefs, with Truths. And if my subject's a morally loaded one, such as Man's relationship to Nature—well, that Inner Preacher's just itching to set people straight and tell them how to think and what to do, yes, Lord, amen!

I have more trust in my Inner Teacher. She is subtle and humble because she hopes to be understood. She contains contradictory opinions without getting indigestion. She can mediate between the arrogant artist self who mutters, "I don't give a damn if you don't understand me," and the preacher self who shouts, "Now hear this!" She doesn't declare truth, but offers it. She takes a Grecian urn and says, "Look closely at this, study it, for study will reward you; and I can tell you some of the things that other people have found in this pot, some of the goodies you too may find in it."

Since, like most artists, I long to share with others what my art has taught me, I need my Inner Teacher; but I can never fully trust her either. After all, she's the one who taught the kids to expect a message. Her instinct is to "be clear," be explicit. Mine is to try to go past explication into a larger clarity. My job is to keep the meaning completely embodied in the work itself, and therefore alive and capable of change. I think that's how an artist can best speak as a member of a moral community: clearly, yet leaving around her words that area of silence, that empty space, in which other and further truths and perceptions can form in other minds. That space is where such words as these are spoken:

> *Thou still unravish'd bride of quietness,*
> *Thou foster-child of Silence and slow Time . . .*
> *Thou, silent form, dost tease us out of thought*
> *As doth eternity . . .*

Living in a Work of Art

First published in Paradoxa *in 2008, in an issue about my work (volume 21, edited by Sylvia Kelso).*

The extraordinary Palace of Fine Arts near the San Francisco marina—you can see it from the freeway to the Golden Gate: a giant orange upheld and surrounded by very large, very pensive ladies—was contributed to the San Francisco World's Fair of 1915 by the architect Bernard Maybeck. Exposition buildings weren't expected to be permanent, and Maybeck, a great experimenter with materials, built the Palace out of chicken wire and plaster or some such set of ephemeral ingredients. But it was so lovely in its utter originality, and so beloved by the people of the city, that it wasn't knocked down with the rest of the fair. When after six or seven decades it finally began to crumble away, the city rebuilt it, repainting its dome the improbable gold they assure us was the original color.

Born in New York, trained at the École des Beaux-Arts in Paris, Maybeck lived and worked in the Bay Area from 1890 till his death in 1957. His best-known buildings date from before the Second World War. He built churches, the most famous of which is the Christian Science church in Berkeley, and at least one of his buildings for the University of California still stands, the old Women's Gym; but he was principally a domestic architect. The house I grew up in is known in the Maybeck canon as the Schneider house. The Schneider family lived in it eighteen years. My family, the Kroebers, lived in it from 1925 to my mother's death in 1979, fifty-four years. There are a couple of pictures of the house in the excellent book *Bernard Maybeck: Artisan, Architect, Artist,* by Kenneth H. Cardwell.

It seems to me that, while Frank Lloyd Wright remains more or less a holy idol, and various old styles such as Carpenter Gothic, Queen

Anne, and Arts and Crafts go in and out of fashion, we haven't given much real thought for decades now to domestic architecture. Are any beautiful houses built now in any but an imitation of some older style? The high-rise apartment building, the split-level "ranch," the little-box development house, the McMansion in its grandiose banality, reveal the poverty of our thought about buildings for people to live in.

Maybeck was certainly in some ways a visionary, and his personality so marked his buildings that one can often identify "a Maybeck" at a glance; but he had a premodern understanding of the connection between dwelling place and dweller. It would be extremely silly to call a Maybeck house a "machine for living." In 1908, the year after he built the house I grew up in, he wrote:

> The house after all is only the shell and the real interest must come from those who are to live in it. If this is done carefully and with earnestness it will give the inmates a sense of satisfaction and rest and will have the same power over the mind as music or poetry or any healthy activity in any kind of human experience.

This consideration of the interaction of the house and its inhabitants is no less sophisticated and complex for being unfashionably modest. It asserts that the builder of the house has a relationship with the (future) dwellers in the house (whether he knows them or not), and that that relationship implies a responsibility towards them on the part of the architect—or so I interpret Maybeck's "earnestness." We are familiar with the idea that an architect should consider the natural environs and the social setting and make his building appropriate to them. We are not as used to this idea that the house should also be appropriate to the individuals who will inhabit it; indeed we are not used to our architects thinking about individuals at all.

Maybeck evidently would not have thought himself justified in seeing his relationship to individual inhabitants as subordinate to a theory he wished to illustrate or a "statement" he wished to make. I have been in Frank Lloyd Wright houses which clearly exhibit Wright's idea of architecture as self-expression; their inhabitants have no part in them but to accept and obey the whims and mandates of the Master. Maybeck's approach was quite different. Though he was as interested as Wright in the aesthetic value of the work, to him aesthetic meaning was not a final declaration made by the architect, but the result of an ongoing dialogue between builder and dwellers. In its *inhabitation* a house's beauty would be active and fulfilled.

So the house I grew up in was remarkably beautiful, delightfully comfortable, and almost entirely practical. Maybeck had quirks, though, which not only make his style highly characteristic, but sometimes lend it real oddity. Our house, for example, originally had no stairs to the basement.

"Maybeck was moody about stairs," my mother said. She claimed that he had also left them off one of his University of California buildings, or added them outside because they didn't look right inside, or something of the sort. I wonder if it was basements that Maybeck was moody about, rather than stairs. He was a designer of joyously inventive staircases, as many houses in Berkeley still prove.

The main staircase of our house was a fine rise of wide, dark steps to a landing, where it met a very narrow back flight angling up in two turns from the pantry to the landing. Straight on up from the back stairs, or a 180-degree turn on the landing, brought you to the final flight: six quite narrow steps up to the second floor. (Furniture movers who had ascended the first flight with high hopes here met their doom.) A fine, short, broad banister rail beside this last flight made a single but imperative statement of slant; everything else was at right angles. Looked at from above, the short straight waterfall of the top flight broke into two, a narrow sidestream angling down from the broad turn and fall of the main stair-river. The loftiness of the ceiling over the landing and the complexity of the joining angles of walls and ceiling beams was a pleasure to the eye. It was literally uplifting to look at those high surfaces and high spaces, lit by the north light that came through a French door giving on a little decorative balcony at the level of the upper turn of the back stairs, which were so narrow they got triangular at the turns.

If this sounds complicated, I mean it to. The whole staircase arrangement was organically complicated, like the arrangements inside a living creature. It was fascinatingly complex, yet (unlike the balcony) expressed the purest structural necessity. And it consisted entirely of redwood. Air and redwood. Light and air and redwood. And shadows.

The house, with its notable beauty of material and proportion, was eminently habitable. Its proportions were human proportions. Proportion failed only at the top of the basement stairs—for a flight of steps had been installed, I think by the Schneiders, so that you wouldn't have to go outside and all the way around two sides of the house from either the front door or the kitchen door to get into the basement by its outside door. As the house was built into a hilltop slope, the ceiling over these steps was quite low; so if, standing in the tall, narrow hall at the foot of the back stairs, you flung open the door to the basement and started boldly down, you hit your head on a beam. King Somebody of Scotland was killed by hitting his head on a beam. My father told us this as a solemn warning, and put marks in white paint on the lintel, which he repainted every decade or so. We all crouched when we started down to the basement. I myself grew tall enough only to scrape the top of my head occasionally on the murderous beam, but whenever I opened that door I thought about the King of Scotland.

Aside from that, I can't remember anything out of proportion or uncomfortable or unfriendly about that house. It could be terrifying at night, but I will get to that later. Even in daylight it was shadowy in places, like a forest. Maybeck speaks somewhere in his writings of "dark heights," and our house had such dark heights. It was built entirely of redwood inside and out, and redwood darkens with age, but it was full of tall windows and glass-paned doors.

Because the walls and ceilings and spaces were so interesting in themselves, it seemed to require little furnishing. When I was a child we had no rugs downstairs, just the wide bare floors, and most of our furniture was shabby: odd chairs, wicker stools, a horsehair and mahogany sofa that was easier to slide off than to sit on, my mother's mother's bed with the bullet embedded in the footboard, and so on. The dining table was one of our few elegant pieces, because it had been built with and for the house—a single broad redwood board, rather low as tables go, that sat eight comfortably and ten with a squeeze. It was somewhat battered, since redwood is soft and scars easily, but if you beeswaxed it diligently, it got a fine, deep glow, like a chestnut horse. There were cabinets built in corners here and there, in good Arts and Crafts style, some with paned glass fronts; and a seat like a window seat ran along the inner living-room wall, at right angles to the huge firebrick hearth and chimney. That was comfortable. So were the little stone seats built out from the hearth, where you could sit almost inside the fireplace and get really warm.

Except in the few, always threatened groves protected for tourists, there are no sequoias left like those from which that dining-room table was cut, or with which the whole house with its great rafters and wide, long, clear boards was built. *Sequoia sempervirens* were common in many northern parts of California, and their wood was as commonly used for building houses. It was cheap then, and it has remarkable virtues as lumber, resistance to dry rot and weather among them. Our house in the Napa Valley, a humble ordinary farmhouse of the 1870s, was built of redwood—painted and papered as if it were mere pine or fir. Maybeck's generation realised the extraordinary beauty of the wood, and used it bare and grand. What they didn't realise was the exhaustibility of the sequoias. I don't think anyone thought much about that in 1907. None of us thought much about it till the fifties. Then, as the price of redwood went up and up, and the Save the Redwoods people fought their endless struggle against the lumber companies and the politicians, we began to look up at those wide, sweet boards and beams with a guilty, grateful awe.

They were untreated, but sanded to a silken finish. Cardwell describes the color of a natural redwood interior very well: "The pink tone of new lumber mellows rapidly to a rich red-brown which is highlighted by an iridescent gold caused by the refraction of natural or incandescent light falling on the spring wood of the boards."

The house was not only built throughout of redwood but had several *Sequoia sempervirens* planted just northwest of it; they were very large and grand by the time I first remember them. The west front stood high above the street over a steep slope and a double flight of stone-walled steps. The whole exterior was in the general style of a mountain chalet, with peaked roofs, deep eaves, and wooden balconies jutting out on all four sides and from both stories. The beams and struts supporting the eaves and balconies made bold diagonals against the sky and against the batten walls—the lower story with horizontal battens, the upper with vertical. This sounds ornate in words, but the simplicity of the dark wood and the massive, splendid proportions of the house itself subordinated all its roof angles and balconies to the tall, rather stern and noble whole. Decorative elements, like that tiny north balcony, kept the nobility from being either boring or overwhelming. The house both soared up from its commanding position at the top of a hill-street and echoed the slope of the hills as a whole in the long western downsweep of the main roof. In every aspect it was superbly suited and fitted to its landscape and community.

It became, with the years, ever more suited and fitted to its occupants.

One of the bedroom balconies, intended as a sleeping porch, was roofed and enclosed with windows to make a sunny, narrow playroom for the four children of my family; I don't know whether the Schneiders or we did that. We did a lot of things to that house. It was built for a family with only one child—Cardwell calls it "a modest house constructed on a modest budget." There were seven of us in it by 1930, and we must have been pretty crowded until my father added a wing to the east side: four rooms, two baths, two fireplaces, and a spacious attic. (The attic of the original house was a dreadful dark crawlspace, unusable except by black widows and bats.)

Nobody, I suppose, would dream of building on to a Maybeck house these days; the Great Man syndrome tells us that the Master's work is sacrosanct. I can only say that the wing designed by my father and his carpenter-builder, a Welshman named John Williams, fits seamlessly onto the house; no visitor I ever took round realised it wasn't part of Maybeck's original design. In proportions, the size and shape of windows, and so on, it matches the original, though without deep eaves or balconies, and without the fine details of iron latches, etc., in the William Morris style, which would have been out of fashion in the thirties and hard to find.

This large addition perfected the comfortableness of the house for us, perhaps for the children most of all—lots of rooms, corridors to race through, space to crowd into, space to be alone in, sunny corners, an enormous attic where we set up the electric train and the armies of toy soldiers.

My mother always said that women didn't like that house and men did. I think this was one of my mother's theories. The house did have a hunting-lodge quality, a certain rough, roomy starkness, which might be seen as having a virile appeal to men and not to chintz-loving women; but then, we didn't know many chintz-loving women. The women and girls I knew who knew the house loved it.

The kitchen, perhaps, wasn't the modern housewife's ideal—not many kitchens built in 1907 were. It was rather narrow, but there is convenience in being able to turn from the stove to the chopping board to the sink to the fridge in a few steps. It did have the one element that to me is essential in a kitchen, that is, a window over the sink. The window looked out into the north garden and the boughs of a crab-apple that blossomed wonderfully in spring. There were plenty of good kitchen cabinets and drawers, and a wall of shelves to keep and display china, with sliding wood-framed glassed doors from waist level up to the ceiling. Those tall doors were well made, like everything belonging to the house; they continued to slide admirably all the decades we lived there. The pantry, off the narrow hall at the foot of the back stairs, across from the King of Scotland's door, was the kind with a screened opening to the outside to keep it cool; it was a tiny dark room full of shelves, smelling of apples and old pfeffernusse and other pantry things. I would go into the pantry sometimes just to smell it.

Its smell was partly redwood. The wood is aromatic; you can't easily catch the scent in a single piece as you can in a piece of cedar or fresh-cut pine, but an enclosed space built of it has a characteristic fragrance, dearly welcome to the nose to which it smells like home. To come into our house after a long absence was to know again how immediately and profoundly the nose is connected to the emotions.

Because it has nothing to do with sight or touch or hearing, the space in which smell takes place seems to me to be dark or at least shadowy; still; and without boundaries, therefore very large: mysterious and benign. In this it resembles the very earliest and most primitive impressions that I find in my memory of the house itself.

I said, above, "the north garden," which sounds rather grand; and in fact, the original garden must have been grand. The house stood just south of the center line of a double lot, and its steep hillside garden filled both lots. It was laid out by John McLaren, the designer of Golden Gate Park. It had a rose plot and a fountain. It was formal, as the house was not. I do not remember this garden. I can just remember some flower beds and the fountain, which didn't fount, but dripped a little. The redwoods and the ground juniper and a pair of English yews in front of the house, a fine camphor tree south of it, a big abelia, and a couple of very William-Morris weeping willows were elements of it that remained through my childhood. I don't know whether the Schneiders kept the garden up or let it go; we certainly let it go. Part of it became a badminton court, and the rest of it straggled along the way gardens of large families tend to do. I laid out acreage for my Britains toy farm set between the old roses, and played in the secret passages under the huge cumquat bushes, until my parents decided to build two houses on the north lot as rental properties. The crab-apple tree remained in its glory, and both new houses had crowded, flowery little gardens, so our view while washing the dishes remained charming. The garden of our house was thus reduced to manageable size; and as we children grew up, my parents had time to potter in it, and my father planted and tended roses and dahlias, which he loved.

I realise I may be causing real pain in describing the desecration of a unique Maybeck chalet and McLaren garden by an uncouth anthropologist, a Welsh carpenter, and a swarm of brats. I am sorry if this is so. It seems to me that we used both the house and the garden the best way we could. We used every inch of the house. We adapted ourselves to it and it to ourselves. We lived in it intensely and completely. We adored it and abused it as children do their mother. It was our house and we were its family. I think this is exactly what Maybeck had in mind when he built it. I hope so. He lived farther up the hill, in one of his chicken-wire houses. I have a faint recollection of a visit from him; I must have been very small, because I remember looking up at the gentle curve of his belly, and he was a very short man. It seems to me his trousers were fastened differently from other men's trousers, with a single central button placed somewhere high, but I can't get the image clear. His presence was mysterious and benign.

I keep talking about comfort, practicality and impracticality, stairs, smells, and so on, when what I want to talk about is beauty; but I don't know how to. It seems you can only describe beauty by describing something else, the way you can only see the earliest star after sunset by not looking directly at it.

Surely, if you have lived in one house from birth to maturity, you're going to find the house entangled with your psyche. This may depend somewhat on gender; women are said to identify themselves more with their house, or their house with themselves, than most men do. The old ranch house in the Napa Valley was and is extremely dear to me, as is the house in Portland I have lived in for nearly fifty years now. But the Berkeley house was fundamental. If I recall my childhood, I recall that house. It is where everything happened. It is where I happened.

And the space it allowed me to happen in was truly extraordinary— that is what I am trying to talk about. It was unusually beautiful. Not just pretty and pleasant: much more than that. Maybeck's artistic standard was very high. Everything around us indoors, under the scurf and scruff of children's stuff and the mess of daily living, every surface and area, was nobly proportioned, handsome and generous in material and workmanship, grave, genial, and spacious.

Cardwell says of the house, "Its ample feeling was developed by Maybeck's skill in relating one volume to another, as well as by his astute placement of voids in the walls that define them." The finest of those voids, I think, was created by the single massive redwood-cased pillar that supported the massive main beam of the living-room ceiling; you met it as you came from the rather dark entry hall into the large light living room, sunlit all afternoon. You were aware of the empty spaces around that pillar. You were aware of the movement of the air around it (indeed, the house was rather drafty, but in California that doesn't much matter). You were aware of the clear, firm intention of the pillar itself. The house depends on me, it said, and I am dependable.

The many windows and the several sets of French doors admitted the extraordinary light of the Bay Area, which combines inland sunshine with sea-reflected radiance. Each window had a view, either of pleasant Berkeley gardens or, to south and west, the magnificent sweep of San Francisco Bay and its cities and bridges. Each window in itself was a pleasure, low-silled, but always tall enough to include the sky.

A house so carefully and deliberately planned and intended to give pleasure has got to have an influence on a person living in it, and perhaps most of all on a child, because for a little child the house is pretty much the world. If that world has been deliberately made beautiful, a familiarity with and expectation of beauty, on the human scale and in human terms, may develop in the child. As Maybeck said, such daily experience "will have the same power over the mind as music or poetry." But the experience of music or poetry is brief, occasional. To a child living in it, the experience of the presence of a house is permanent and inclusive.

I fear I may seem to be describing a little princess growing up in a palace. That's not it. A palace may be beautiful or may not. Beauty's not its business. The business of a palace is to express power, wealth, importance. The modern McMansion is far more palatial in that sense than any Maybeck. When Maybeck built a palace, it wasn't for kings and princesses to live in or as a statement of grandeur and wealth, it was to house and celebrate the public art display of a popular exposition. His buildings declare power only in the integrity and honesty of their design. The only purpose the Maybeck house might be said to share with a palace is the expression of order.

When the relationship of everything in the structure around you is harmonious, when the relationships are vigorous, peaceful, and orderly, one may be led to believe that there is order in the world, and that human beings can attain it.

What I am circling around here is the very difficult question of the expression of moral feeling, and the advancement of moral feeling, through aesthetic means.

Just growing up in a beautiful environment is not going to shape a child's mind favorably. The human, social factor outweighs nature decisively. The extraordinary natural splendor of the Bay Area is probably not a very large factor in the development of kids growing up in poverty in the Oakland slums, though it may offer them some relief from decay and disorder. Even apart from social degradation and industrial ugliness, people who live way out in the country among lovely, varied scenery don't seem to have more breadth of soul or nobility of purpose than those who never saw anything in their life but dreary scrubland. For the beauty of nature as such to brighten and enlarge the mind, I think a child needs either an unusual gift of observation, or a gradual training in observation and aesthetic perception, that will deepen with maturity.

There is evidence that young children kept in a single room or a narrow apartment arrive at school with stunted intellectual, spatial, and social skills, mentally handicapped by the physical and visual limitations of the space they grew in. It is hard to doubt that the cramped, ugly, filthy, noisy, disorganised surroundings of slums and poor barrios foster depression and anger in children who live in them, and limit and darken their perception of the world as a whole. All the same, their awareness of human interdependence and mutual responsibility may be far more intense than that of the middle-class child brought up with a room of her own.

Neither natural beauty nor deliberately created beauty is enough to foster moral perception and discrimination. But I think it possible that early and continuous experience of aesthetic beauty may foster an expectation of order and harmony that may in turn lead to an active desire for moral clarity. I have trouble distinguishing the ethical from the aesthetic. Both my ethical and my aesthetic responses tend to be immediate to the point of suddenness; hesitant only in cases of real novelty or complexity; and stubborn, though capable of being educated and improved. They are so much alike that I am often uncertain whether I'm responding ethically or aesthetically. "That's right: that's wrong."

Such spontaneous certainty seems shallow, but it is not: it is deep and deeply irrational, rising from old, tangled, multitudinous roots, reaching down to the depths of me. As soon as I try to justify it, to find its reason, I'm in deep. When I ask myself why I think the Gehry museum in Seattle is wrong and why I think the Palace of Fine Arts in San Francisco is right, I am involved in the same immensely laborious, ultimately unsatisfactory processes as in explaining why I think abortion on demand is right or why I think torture is wrong. And I do not feel a real difference in kind—or even of importance—between the ethical and the aesthetic inquiry. But to pursue that statement further would require some understanding of philosophy, and I have none.

I will not pursue abortion, torture, or Gehry either, but will come back to the house I lived in. I think the house was built to an aesthetic ideal or concept which was indistinguishable from—or which I cannot distinguish from—a moral ideal or concept. Is it not fair to say that every building has a morality, in this sense, and not merely a metaphorical one, in the honesty and integrity of its design and materials, or the dishonesty expressed in incompetence, incoherence, shoddiness, fakery, snobbery?

I think I absorbed this morality of the building as I did the smell of redwood or the sense of complex space.

I think the moral conception of the building was as admirable as its aesthetic conception, from which it is, to me, inseparable.

"There is no Beauty which hath not some Strangeness in the Proportion," Francis Bacon said, which may or may not be wholly true, but which is a useful idea. Our house had a great deal of strangeness in it.

Does anybody play Sardines any more? For Sardines, you have to have a large house, quite a lot of people, and darkness. One person is It. Everybody but It waits noisily in one room, long enough for It to find a hiding place somewhere else—under a bed, in the broom closet, in the bathtub, anywhere It pleases. Then the lights go off, and separately, in silence, everyone hunts for It. When you find It, you say nothing: you simply join It in the hiding place. If that's a broom closet there may be room for quite a few; if it's under a bed, there are problems. One by one other hunters find the site, and squash themselves into the sardine can, and suffocate giggles, and try not to move, until at last the final hunter finds them and they all burst free at once. It's a good game. Our house, with its endless nooks and corners, was a perfect Sardines house.

That would be a benevolent side of its largeness, darkness, and unexpected spaces. Another aspect was revealed to anybody staying alone in it at night.

The first of our family to do so was a cousin of mine who spent the night there before my father and mother moved in. He tried to sleep in the big bedroom at the top of the stairs. He leapt up because he quite clearly heard somebody coming up the stairs, step after step. He went to the top landing to challenge the intruder, but he could not see anybody at all. He went back to bed. More people climbed the stairs. People walked across the floor of the room towards him, creak, creak, and still he could not see them. He ended up sleeping out on one of the balconies with the door shut, hoping the people would stay inside the house.

Redwood floors have a kind of delayed resilience; compressed by a footfall, they snap back . . . after a while . . . hours perhaps. Once you understand the phenomenon, it is more or less endurable. As an adolescent I rather liked to hang over the deep well of the staircase and listen to the invisible people ascending it, or later, to lie in my small room and listen to myself walking around up in the attic, the floor repeating every step I had taken there that afternoon.

But when I was a young child, the explanations were not very helpful to me. I slept then in the big bedroom at the top of the stairs; and the house, deep in the night, was scary. It was limitlessly large and deeply dark. There was room in it for many and mysterious beings. I had night terrors for years after seeing *King Kong* at age six, but could handle them pretty well, so long as I knew people were in the house. The first time I was ever left alone in it, I went into a slow panic. I tried to be brave, but little by little the shadows and the creakings were too much for me. My older brothers were just across the street, and when I leaned from a window and wailed aloud, they came at once and were most comforting and remorseful. I wept apologetically, feeling very foolish. Why was I afraid of my own dear house? How could it have become so strange to me?

It had a strangeness in it; that is, I think, the truth.

Beauty is a very difficult word: I have already complained about not being able to approach it straight on. People don't use the word as freely as they used to, and many artists—painters, sculptors, photographers, architects, poets—reject it entirely; they deny that there is any common standard by which to judge it; they diminish it to mean prettiness and so righteously despise it; or they deliberately abandon it for truth, or self-expression, or edginess, or other values they prize more highly.

I don't pretend to be able to argue with such refusals of beauty when I can't even offer a generally acceptable definition of the word. But I think it behooves artists to consider what the word means to them, no matter what it means to others. How do they interpret the aesthetic component of what they do, its importance, its weight? What, besides that component, makes it appropriate to call their work art? What, besides the search to make something beautiful, makes an artist? There are perhaps as many answers to those questions now as there are artists, and nothing gives me the right to ask them of others; but I do feel the obligation to ask them of myself, and answer as honestly as I can.

Novelists probably talk less than any other kind of artist about beauty, because the word is seldom used to describe what they make. As a novelist, however, I have always found it an important word in thinking about my work, and in describing that of other novelists. For instance, *Pride and Prejudice* is, to me, an absolutely beautiful work of art. If exquisite accuracy of language, perfection of proportion, of gait, of rhythm, in the service of powerful intelligence and insight and strong moral feeling, forming a complete and vital whole—if that isn't beautiful, what is? If that makes sense to you, you may be willing to let me use the word beauty in describing novels of very different kinds, such as *Little Dorrit, War and Peace, To the Lighthouse,* or *The Lord of the Rings,* or to think of novels which you'd be willing to call beautiful.

Now, if *Pride and Prejudice* were a house, I think it would be a nobly proportioned, delightfully livable, not very large English house of the eighteenth century.

I don't know what novel our Maybeck house could be compared to, but it would contain darkness and radiant light; its beauty would arise from honest, bold, inventive construction, from geniality and generosity of spirit and mind, and would also have elements of fantasy and strangeness.

Writing this, I wonder if much of my understanding of what a novel ought to be was taught to me, ultimately, by living in that house. If so, perhaps all my life I have been trying to rebuild it around me out of words.

Staying Awake

Published in Harper's *in February 2008, and reprinted in* The Wild Girls *(PM Press, 2011). In a time of super-accelerated technological change, how fast references get dated and universal assumptions become ridiculous! I was tempted to update this piece, but didn't. A text speaks to the time in which it was written, but it may also speak usefully to later times by revealing changes, continuities, and our inability to predict anything other than, as Benjamin said, death and taxes.*

Some people lament the disappearance of the spotted owl from our forests, others sport bumper stickers boasting that they eat fried spotted owls. It appears that books, too, are a threatened species, and reactions to that news are similarly various. In 2002 a National Endowment for the Arts survey announced, with considerable hand-wringing, that fewer than half of adult Americans polled said they had read a work of literature that year. (Strangely, the NEA excluded nonfiction from "literature," so that you could have read *The Decline and Fall of the Roman Empire*, *The Voyage of the Beagle*, Elizabeth Gaskell's biography of Charlotte Brontë, and the entire *Letters* and *Diaries* of Virginia Woolf and yet be counted as not having read anything of literary value.) In 2004 an NEA poll revealed that 43 percent of Americans polled hadn't read a book all year, and last November, in its report "To Read or Not to Read," the NEA lamented the decline of reading, warning that non-readers do less well in the job market and are less useful citizens in general. This moved Motoko Rich of the *New York Times* to write a Sunday feature in which she inquired of various bookish people why anyone should read at all. The Associated Press ran their own poll and announced last September that 27 percent of their respondents had spent the year bookless, a better figure than the NEA's, but the tone of the AP piece was remarkable for its complacency. Quoting a project manager for a telecommunications company in Dallas who said, "I just get sleepy when I read," the AP correspondent, Alan Fram, commented, "a habit with which millions of Americans doubtless can identify."

Self-satisfaction with the inability to remain conscious when faced with printed matter seems questionable. But I also want to question the assumption—whether gloomy or faintly gloating—that books are on the way out. I think they're here to stay. It's just that not all that many people ever did read them. Why should we think everybody ought to now?

For most of human history, most people couldn't read at all. Literacy was not only a demarcator between the powerful and the powerless, it was power itself. Pleasure was not an issue. The ability to maintain and understand commercial records, the ability to communicate across distance and in code, the ability to keep the word of God to yourself and transmit it only at your own will and in your own time—these are formidable means of control over others and aggrandizement of self. Every literate society began with literacy as a constitutive prerogative of the (male) ruling class.

Literacy very gradually filtered downward, becoming less sacred as it became less secret, less directly potent as it became more popular. The Romans ended up letting slaves, women, and such rabble read and write, but they got their comeuppance from the religion-based society that succeeded them. In the Dark Ages, a Christian priest could read at least a little, but most laymen didn't, and many women couldn't—not only didn't but couldn't: reading was considered an inappropriate activity for women, as in some Muslim societies today.

In Europe, one can perceive through the Middle Ages a slow broadening of the light of the written word, which brightens into the Renaissance, and shines out with Gutenberg. Then, before you know it, slaves are reading, and revolutions are made with pieces of paper called Declarations of this and that, and schoolmarms replace gunslingers all across the Wild West, and people are mobbing the steamer delivering the latest installment of a new novel to New York, crying, "Is Little Nell dead? Is she dead?"

I see a high point of reading in the United States from around 1850 to about 1950—call it the century of the book—the high point from which the doomsayers see us declining. As the public school came to be considered fundamental to democracy, and as libraries went public and flourished, reading was assumed to be something we shared in common. Teaching from first grade up centered on "English," not only because immigrants wanted their children fluent in it, but because literature—fiction, scientific works, history, poetry—was a major form of social currency.

To look at schoolbooks from 1890 or 1910 can be scary; the level of literacy and general cultural knowledge expected of a ten-year-old was rather awesome. Such texts, and lists of the novels kids were expected to read in high school up to the 1960s, lead one to believe that Americans really wanted their children not only to be able to read, but to do it, and not to fall asleep doing it.

Literacy was not only the front door to any kind of individual economic advancement and class status, it was an important social activity. The shared experience of books was a genuine bond. A person reading seems to be cut off from everything around them, almost as much as the person shouting banalities into a cellphone as they ram their car into your car—that's the private aspect of reading. But there is a large public element, too, which consists in what you and others *have read*.

As people these days can maintain nonthreatening, unloaded, sociable conversation by talking about who murdered whom on the latest hit TV police procedural or mafia show, so strangers on the train or coworkers on the job in 1840 could talk perfectly unaffectedly together about *The Old Curiosity Shop* and whether poor Little Nell was going to cop it. Since public school education was strong on poetry and various literary classics, a lot of people would recognize and enjoy a reference to Tennyson, or Scott, or Shakespeare—shared properties, a social meeting ground. A man might be less likely to boast about falling asleep at the sight of a Dickens novel than to feel left out of things by not having read it.

The social quality of literature is still visible in the popularity of bestsellers. Publishers get away with making boring, baloney-mill novels into bestsellers via mere PR, because people need bestsellers. It is not a literary need. It is a social need. We want books everybody is reading (and nobody finishes) so we can talk about them.

If we brought books over from England by ship these days, crowds would have swarmed on the docks of New York to greet the final volume of *Harry Potter*, crying, "Did she kill him? Is he dead?" The Potter boom was a genuine social phenomenon, like the worship of rock stars, and the whole subculture of popular music, which offers adolescents and young adults both an exclusive in-group and a shared social experience.

Books are social vectors, but publishers have been slow to see it. They barely even noticed book clubs until Oprah goosed them. But then, the stupidity of the contemporary corporation-owned publishing company is fathomless: they think they can sell books as commodities.

Moneymaking entities controlled by obscenely rich executives and their anonymous accountants have acquired most previously independent publishing houses with the notion of making quick money by selling works of art and information. I wouldn't be surprised to learn that such people get sleepy when they read. Within the corporate whales are many luckless Jonahs who were swallowed alive with their old publishing house—editors and such anachronisms, people who read wide awake. Some of them are so alert they can scent out promising new writers. Some of them have their eyes so wide open they can even proofread. But it doesn't do them much good. For years now, most editors have had to waste most of their time on an unlevel playing field, fighting Sales and Accounting.

In those departments, beloved by the CEOs, a "good book" means a high gross and a "good writer" is one whose next book can be guaranteed to sell better than the last one. That there are no such writers is of no matter to the corporationeers, who don't comprehend fiction even if they run their lives by it. Their interest in books is self-interest, the profit that can be made out of them—or occasionally, for the top executives, the Murdochs and other Merdles, the political power they can wield through them; but that is merely self-interest again, personal profit.

And not only profit, but growth. If there are stockholders, their holdings must increase yearly, daily, hourly. The AP article ascribed "listless" or "flat" book sales to the limited opportunity for expansion. But until the corporate takeovers, publishers did not expect expansion;

they were quite happy if their supply and demand ran parallel, if their books sold steadily, "flatly." How can you make book sales expand endlessly, like the American waistline?

Michael Pollan explains in *The Omnivore's Dilemma* how you do it with corn. When you've grown enough corn to fill every reasonable demand, you create unreasonable demands—artificial needs. So, having induced the government to declare corn-fed beef to be the standard, you feed corn to cattle, who cannot digest corn, tormenting and poisoning them in the process. And you use the fats and sweets of corn by-products to make an endless array of soft drinks and fast foods, addicting people to a fattening yet inadequate diet in the process. And you can't stop these processes, because if you did profits might become "listless," even "flat."

This system has worked only too well for corn, and indeed throughout American agriculture and manufacturing, which is why we increasingly eat junk and make junk while wondering why tomatoes in Europe taste like tomatoes and foreign cars are well engineered.

You can cover Iowa border to border with Corn #2, but with books, you run into problems. Standardization of the product and its production can take you only so far, because there is some intellectual content to even the most brainless book. People will buy interchangeable bestsellers, formula thrillers, romances, mysteries, pop biographies, and hot-topic books up to a point, but their product loyalty is defective. A book has to be read, it takes time, effort—you have to be awake to do it. And so you want some reward. The loyal fans bought *Death at One O'Clock* and *Death at Two O'Clock* . . . yet all of a sudden they won't buy *Death at Eleven O'Clock* even though it follows exactly the same surefire formula as all the others. The readers got bored. What is a good growth-capitalist publisher to do? Where can he be safe?

He can find some safety in exploiting the social function of literature. That includes the educational, of course—schoolbooks and college texts, favorite prey of corporations—as well as the bestsellers and popular books of fiction and nonfiction that provide a common current topic and a bond among people at work and in book clubs. Beyond that, I think corporations have been foolish to look for safety or reliable growth in publishing.

Even during what I have called the century of the book, when it was taken for granted that many people read and enjoyed fiction and poetry, how many people in fact had or could make much time for reading once they were out of school? During those years most Americans worked hard and worked long hours. Weren't there always many who never read a book at all, and never very many who read a lot of books? We don't know how many, because we didn't have polls to worry us about it.

If people make time to read, it's because it's part of their jobs, or because other media aren't readily available or they aren't much interested in them—or because they enjoy reading. Lamenting over percentages induces a moralizing tone: it is bad that we don't read; we should read more; we must read more. Concentrating on the drowsy fellow in Dallas, perhaps we forget our own people, the hedonists who read because they want to. Were such people ever in the majority?

I like knowing that a hard-bitten Wyoming cowboy carried a copy of *Ivanhoe* in his saddlebag for thirty years, and that the mill girls of New England had Browning Societies. There are readers like that still. Our schools are no longer serving them (or anybody else) well, on the whole; yet some kids come out of even the worst schools clutching a book to their heart.

Of course books are now only one of the "entertainment media," but when it comes to delivering actual pleasure, they're not a minor one. Look at the competition. Governmental hostility has been emasculating public radio while Congress allowed a few corporations to buy out and debase private radio stations. Television has steadily lowered its standards of what is entertaining until most programs are either brain-numbing or actively nasty. Hollywood remakes remakes and tries to gross out, with an occasional breakthrough that reminds us what a movie can be when undertaken as art. And the internet offers everything to everybody: but perhaps because of that all-inclusiveness there is curiously little *aesthetic* satisfaction to be got from web surfing. You can look at pictures or listen to music or read a poem or a book on your computer, but these artifacts are made accessible by the web, not created by it and not intrinsic to it. Perhaps blogging is an effort to bring creativity to networking, and perhaps blogs will develop aesthetic form, but they certainly haven't done it yet.

Besides, readers aren't viewers; they recognize their pleasure as different from that of being entertained. Once you've pressed the on button, the TV goes on, and on, and on, and all you have to do is sit and stare. But reading is active, an act of attention, of absorbed alertness—not all that different from hunting, in fact, or from gathering. In its silence, a book is a challenge: it can't lull you with surging music or deafen you with screeching laugh tracks or fire gunshots in your living room; you have to listen to it in your head. A book won't move your eyes for you the way images on a screen do. It won't move your mind unless you give it your mind, or your heart unless you put your heart in it. It won't do the work for you. To read a story well is to follow it, to act it, to feel it, to become it—everything short of writing it, in fact. Reading is not "interactive" with a set of rules or options, as games are: reading is actual collaboration with the writer's mind. No wonder not everybody is up to it.

The book itself is a curious artifact, not showy in its technology but complex and extremely efficient: a really neat little device, compact, often very pleasant to look at and handle, that can last decades, even centuries. It doesn't have to be plugged in, activated, or performed by a machine; all it needs is light, a human eye, and a human mind. It is not one of a kind, and it is not ephemeral. It lasts. It is reliable. If a book told you something when you were fifteen, it will tell it to you again when you're fifty, though you may understand it so differently that it seems you're reading a whole new book.

This is crucial, the fact that a book is a thing, physically there, durable, indefinitely reusable, an object of value.

I am far from dismissing the vast usefulness of electronic publication, but my guess is that print-on-demand will become and remain essential. Electrons are as evanescent as thoughts. History begins with the written word. Much of civilization now relies on the durability of the bound book—its capacity for keeping memory in solid, physical form. The continuous existence of books is a great part of our continuity as an intelligent species. We know it: we see their willed destruction as an ultimate barbarism. The burning of the Library of Alexandria has been mourned for two thousand years, as people may well remember and mourn the desecration and destruction of the great library in Baghdad.

To me, then, one of the most despicable things about corporate publishers and chain booksellers is their assumption that books are inherently worthless. If a title that was supposed to sell well doesn't "perform" within a few weeks, it gets its covers torn off—it is trashed. The corporate mentality recognizes no success that is not immediate. This week's blockbuster must eclipse last week's, as if there weren't room for more than one book at a time. Hence the crass stupidity of most publishers (and, again, chain booksellers) in handling backlists.

Over the years, books kept in print may earn hundreds of thousands of dollars for their publisher and author. A few steady earners, even though the annual earnings are in what is now dismissively called "the midlist," can keep publishers in business for years, and even allow them to take a risk or two on new authors. If I were a publisher, I'd rather own J. R. R. Tolkien than J. K. Rowling.

But capitalists count weeks, not years. To get big quick money, the publisher must risk a multimillion-dollar advance to a hot author who's supposed to provide this week's bestseller. These millions—often a dead loss—come out of funds that used to go to pay normal advances to reliable midlist authors and the royalties on older books that kept selling. Many midlist authors have been dropped, many reliably selling books remaindered, in order to feed Moloch. Is that any way to run a business?

I keep hoping the corporations will wake up and realize that publishing is not, in fact, a normal business with a nice healthy relationship to capitalism. Elements of publishing are, or can be forced to be, successfully capitalistic: the textbook industry is all too clear a proof of that. How-to books and the like have some market predictability. But inevitably some of what publishers publish is, or is partly, literature—art. And the relationship of art to capitalism is, to put it mildly, vexed. It has not been a happy marriage. Amused contempt is about the pleasantest emotion either partner feels for the other. Their definitions of what profiteth a man are too different.

So why don't the corporations drop the literary publishing houses, or at least the literary departments of the publishers they bought, with amused contempt, as unprofitable? Why don't they let them go back to muddling along making just enough, in a good year, to pay binders and editors and modest advances and crummy royalties, while plowing most profits back into taking chances on new writers? Since kids coming up through the schools are seldom taught to read for pleasure and anyhow are distracted by electrons, the relative number of book readers is unlikely to see any kind of useful increase and may well shrink further. What's in this dismal scene for you, Mr. Corporate Executive? Why don't you just get out of it, dump the ungrateful little pikers, and get on with the real business of business, ruling the world?

Is it because you think if you own publishing you can control what's printed, what's written, what's read? Well, lotsa luck, sir. It's a common delusion of tyrants. Writers and readers, even as they suffer from it, regard it with amused contempt.

Great Nature's Second Course

Written about 2009, not previously published.

When my brother was about twelve and I about nine, he told me he liked to dream as much as he could every night. I asked why, and he said, "Because I'm *doing* something instead of just lying there." I was impressed by this energetic attitude. I hadn't thought of dreams as activity. We talk about "having" dreams, not "doing" them. In fact, I still can't convince myself that I do my dreams. They seem to use me for their own purposes. Another brother, the psychologist, told me that in fact I'm responsible for them: I do dream my dream, nobody else does, and everybody in it is me. He's right, but I hate to admit it. I don't want to take on that responsibility, I want to escape it.

Dreams may not offer escape, but sleep does. Indeed it escapes us. It eludes description, it evades. It's what you don't know you're doing while you do it. Sleep is hard to talk about.

Scientists have been trying hard to talk about it for decades now. Wikipedia starts off bravely: "Sleep is the natural state of bodily rest observed throughout the animal kingdom. . . . In humans, other mammals, and a substantial majority of other animals . . . regular sleep is necessary for survival. . . . Its purposes are only partly clear and are the subject of intense research." That research is fascinating (as you can see in such books as William C. Dement's *Some Must Watch While Some Must Sleep*), but so far teasingly inconclusive. Here is something every human being, dog, cat, and mouse does for a third or more of their lifetime, an activity we humans assiduously practice, with a time set aside for it (night) and a special place to do it in (bed) and even special clothes to wear for it (sheep pajamas). The scientists can describe it, yet can't claim to understand it. We know sleep in our body, we recognise it as deeply familiar—but the mind cannot lay hold of it.

Sleep gets some really good PR from poets, who are used to talking clearly about things we don't understand.

> Care-charmer Sleep, son of the sable night,
> Brother to Death, in silent darkness born;
> Relieve my languish, and restore the light,
> With dark forgetting of my care return,
> And let the day be time enough to mourn . . .
>> Samuel Daniel

> Come, Sleep! O Sleep, the certain knot of peace,
> The baiting-place of wit, the balm of woe,
> The poor man's wealth, the prisoner's release,
> Th' indifferent judge between the high and low . . .
>> Philip Sidney

> O magic sleep! O comfortable bird
> That broodest o'er the troubled sea of the mind
> Till it is hushed and smooth . . .
>> John Keats

> Oh sleep! it is a gentle thing,
> Beloved from pole to pole,
> To Mary Queen the praise be given!
> She sent the gentle sleep from heaven
> That slid into my soul . . .
>> Samuel Coleridge

> The silence that is in the starry sky,
> The sleep that is among the lonely hills . . .
>> William Wordsworth

> Methought I heard a voice cry, 'Sleep no more!
> Macbeth does murder sleep,' the innocent sleep,

> *Sleep that knits up the ravell'd sleave of care,*
> *The death of each day's life, sore labour's bath,*
> *Balm of hurt minds, great nature's second course,*
> *Chief nourisher in life's feast . . .*

William Shakespeare

I picked those almost at random from about 180 index items for "sleep" in the *Oxford Dictionary of Quotations*. Poets appreciate sleep. In fiction, it seldom plays much of a role, except by not being there when a character wants it. He tosses, she turns, they thump the hot pillow, and so goes the insomniac routine we're all familiar with. When a character actually goes to sleep, the novelist tiptoes quietly out of the bedroom—unless, of course, the character has a dream, the only drama sleep provides. Once the author has said that somebody's breathing grew quiet and regular, that's it. We don't really want a record of each breath in and each breath out. So sleep eludes fiction, leaving only the footprints of dream.

Patrick O'Brian, that marvelous teller of sea stories, almost caught sleep in the net of prose. His character Stephen Maturin, an insomniac, sometimes dabbles a little too deep in his sedatives and sometimes is miserably wakeful, but there are times when, very tired, he falls asleep naturally, slipping with pleasure into an abyss deeper and darker than the sea his ship is sailing. In those passages the author catches by suggestion the actual experience of going to sleep, and it is magical. O'Brian, a supremely good action writer, makes you realise that to go to sleep is, in fact, an action—an act that changes everything.

An act; a change; a journey. "Go to sleep," we say to the baby in our arms. Go to that place, that other place, where everything is different, where you won't have to cry . . .

For young babies, of course sleep is the natural state. They return to it with angelic constancy, and when they're kept from it by hunger or discomfort they let us know their misery and rage. The infant's moments of awareness form a little archipelago of islets in a vast, soft sea. It's only unfortunate that the islets tend to cluster, clamorously, endlessly, right where the parent's need for sleep is deepest.

Growing up means being awake more and more often. The baby's islands of awakeness increase and join into the continent of daylight on which we adults move purposefully about, doing business, certain that we're aware, because we're awake.

As those who practice meditation testify, the two things aren't the same. You can be wide awake all day without a single moment of awareness. Multitasking is the newest and by far the most successful form of awareness avoidance. People who drive a car while drinking coffee and talking to their broker on a cellphone have mastered a form of narrowly localised consciousness completely impenetrable to awareness. Yet however well provided we are with instruments of electronic distraction, still the sea of sleep surrounds us, whether we're aware or merely awake, and calls us nightly for the journey back into mystery.

We can will ourselves to go to sleep, and have our will frustrated for what seems forever, but is in fact rarely as much as a whole night. Insomnia is an indescribable misery, but continued sleeplessness is so ruinous to mind and body that only the torment of pain can prolong it more than fifty hours or so.

We can will ourselves not to go to sleep—and eventually, inevitably, be defeated. No matter how we try to cling to consciousness, when the time has come for it to melt away, there's no holding on to it. It's just gone, quietly taking the universe with it.

Because our consciousness seems to be our self, our humanity, even our life, we may fear the loss of it. There are people who dread sleep because they dread any loss of control, or because their dreams are all nightmares. "Macbeth has murdered sleep," says sleepwalking Lady Macbeth, unconscious, yet hideously conscious of the one terrible thing. There are people who, like my brother at twelve, resent sleep as a waste of time and brain, envying those famous few who need only two or three hours of it. Think how much we could do, they say, if we didn't have to lie around snoring all night! I read a science-fiction novel about people who are genetically altered so as not to need sleep. They all become geniuses, immensely superior to the rest of us. I was sceptical. Having twenty-four hours a day to think and work and make mistakes instead of sixteen or eighteen would make a difference in the quantity of human thought, work, and judgment, but would it raise the quality? How? Why?

It's just six or eight hours more to do the same stuff in, including the mistakes. And at what cost?

In college, we used to boast about our sleepless nights—how many beers we'd drunk or, before finals, how much studying we'd got done. But the next day, the Sandman I'd fended off so successfully all night was right beside me, reminding me uncomfortably about the beer, making it hard for my gritty eyes to focus on the exam I'd studied for. He is gentle, but he is ineluctable and unpersuadable, that Sandman. He is one of those awful people who knows—who really knows—what's good for us.

Researchers have exhibited by experiment that if we're systematically deprived of sleep, we go crazy, and if it were possible to totally keep us from sleeping, we'd die. Torturers are well aware of this.

One of the strangest things about the strange traditional training of doctors in the United States was the custom of making medical students do their practical internship in extended shifts with few and brief recuperative breaks until they were incompetent with fatigue and lack of sleep. I know no rational justification for this torment, which obviously put patients in danger. But then, hospitals are generally hostile to sleep. No real darkness; no real silence; a rigid schedule that leaves rest out of account. Even though the healing qualities of natural sleep are thoroughly researched and acknowledged, still the nurse comes bustling in to wake you up to take your sleeping pill. And the intensive care unit, entirely lacking silence, darkness, privacy, peace, and rest, is as hostile, as toxic an environment for recovery as could be imagined.

Sleep gives us something we need, and we know it; but what it gives us is something we can't know, though we may feel it slip from us as we wake. Refreshment, is it? Solace, simplification, innocence?

People asleep look stupid. Knowing that, we hate to be seen asleep. We deny it fiercely. "I wasn't asleep, I was just thinking!" with my mouth hanging open, drooling slightly. . . . But people asleep often also look childish. They look innocent. They are innocent. The word innocent means "doing no harm." The coldest-hearted murderer, the cruelest dictator, the most dangerous maniac, is harmless so long as he sleeps.

There has been throughout human history a pretty strong feeling against killing a sleeping person or even animal. It was seen not only as unsporting, but as wicked. While asleep your enemy is not only helpless, but actually innocent. He has to be awake to be your enemy. Any such moral discrimination was lost when we started slaughtering at a safe distance and wholesale. In the target area being bombed there is only the Enemy, an abstract entity which is not considered human and therefore does not sleep and cannot be innocent. It cannot even provide statistics. How can bomber pilots keep a body count? What do drones care?

I wish war could cease with darkness, as it used to until less than two centuries ago, so the people under the bombing planes and the people who fly them could be allowed some hours of innocence out of every murderous day.

But now the drones are to do it all for us, so none of us can ever be innocent again.

I wish we had more respect for the great gift we are given, the silent hours, the interval of unknowing. Every night offers us a deep draft of the water of forgetfulness, the river Lethe, which we drink in remembrance of where we came from and in practice for our return. From it we rise renewed. Sleep is the strangest of initiations, the kindest of mysteries, a ceremony whose observance is blessing. I wish we held it in the honor and gratitude it deserves.

What Women Know

Revised from two talks given at the Winter Fishtrap Gathering in Joseph, Oregon,
in February, 2010. Each talk preceded open group discussion of the topic.

The First Evening

Our topic for tonight is: What do we learn from women?

Many of us find ourselves surprisingly defensive on the subject of how men's and women's roles differ, how gender is constructed and enacted. Since generalisations about human behavior are easy to derail by bringing up exceptions, I suggest that to keep our discussion profitable, we footnote the exceptions. We're entering the Forest of Gender, where it's awfully easy to get lost. If we keep foregrounding a tree here and a tree there, we'll lose sight of the very big, dark woods we're trying to find a way through.

So, in answer to the question What do we learn from women? my first huge generalisation is that we learn how to be human.

Over the millennia, in all societies, right up to now in Oregon, women have supplied most of the basic instructions on how to walk, talk, eat, sing, pray, play with other children, and which adults we should respect, and what to fear, what to love—the basic skills, the basic rules. The whole amazing, complicated business of staying alive and being a member of a society.

In most times and most places, babies and little children have been taught predominantly, often solely, by mothers, grandmothers, aunts, neighbors, village women, preschool and kindergarten teachers. And this continues in America now. Every time you see a young mother with her kids in the supermarket, you see a life-scholar, a teacher teaching an incredibly complex curriculum. Whether she does it well or not so well doesn't affect the rule: Most of the time, it's she who does it.

The basic skills she teaches are largely genderless. Boys and girls both learn them. As they become social skills, they may be colored blue or pink, as when a girl is taught to be quiet and civil among adults while a boy is taught to yell and pester, or when a girl is praised for dancing with flowers on her head while a boy is shamed for it. But over all, the elemental skills and manners taught by women obtain for both genders.

By contrast, what young children learn from men is often gendered. Men may be more interested than women in making sure the pink and the blue don't mix. Fathers often teach their children sex roles: the boys how to be manly, the girls how to be womanly. Men often take over the teaching of boys entirely as the boys grow up, while ignoring further education of girls. For thousands of years, the education of girls has been almost entirely domestic and female, and still is in many places. Men teaching girls who are not their own daughters are mostly a quite recent phenomenon. For thousands of years, male priests laid down the laws outside the house; the father of the family enforced them inside the house, teaching little or nothing to the daughters but obedience. The general rule has been that, after age six or so, boys learn from men and girls learn from women, and the more absolute the gender division and hierarchy, the purdah or sharia law, the truer that is.

By teaching only male knowledge only to boys over a certain age, men have left women the major role in teaching young children the manners and morals of their people—how to be human without reference to their sex. And here lies, perhaps, a fertile ground for change, even for subversion.

The teaching of the fathers tends to maintain hierarchy and uphold the status quo. Social and moral change may begin with women, who have less invested in the hierarchy, as they try to teach their kids how to adapt to new circumstances. I think of the covered wagons on the Oregon Trail; while the men filled the traditional role of aggressively defending their women from strangers assumed to be hostile and dangerous, the women, often surreptitiously, it appears, talked with Indian women, bartered a little with them, left the kids free to nose around one another. . . .

The rigid white male story excluded the strangers; the opportunistic white female story began to admit them.

A vast amount of what we learn, we learn as story. We hear and read and learn the myths and histories that tell us who we are and who we belong to—the fireside tales that tell us about our immediate people, our family—the official histories of our tribe or nation.

Who tells those stories, who do we learn them from?

Over the centuries, it's been the women of the family who kept alive the stories of who our family is and how members of the family, our immediate tribe, behave. Male priests, shamans, leaders, chiefs, and professors taught the stories of who we are and how we should behave as members of our larger tribe, our people, our nation. Women transmit the individual stories, men transmit the public history.

Again, the men's teaching is likely to support the status quo, while the women's teaching, being individualistic, is more likely to be subversive.

The two teachings can be contradictory.

For example, the public, male story I learned of How the West Was Won was about men exploring, leading wagon trains, leading cattle drives, hunting and killing animals, hunting and killing Indians. The stories my great-aunt Betsy told me of her early days in the West were different. I remember Betsy's story of driving away from their burning ranch house with everything they owned in a one-horse wagon. Or her story of how her older sister Phoebe, my grandmother, then twelve, looked after her little brothers in the cabin on Steens Mountain during the Indian troubles while their parents made the three-day trip to town for groceries. The Indians, displaced and harried by government troops, were hostile, and Phoebe was afraid of them, but in the version of the story I remember, nobody hunted or killed anybody.

The public, male teachings and the private, female teachings may differ, and the differences may be confusing: as when a single mother in the inner city teaches her children the story that society expects them to respect themselves and behave as honest citizens, but what they learn from the young men who are the leaders in the streets, and all too often from teachers and policemen, is that they are characters in a story that allows them only one role—to be addicts and criminals, useless or worse.

Or when a family brings up its sons in a story of living in peace and with mercy, but then a male institution, the army, puts them into a war story, where they are driven to kill and be cruel without remorse.

Or when a mother includes her daughters in a rich tradition of skills such as cooking and housekeeping, but then businessmen and politicians persuade them that in the story of capitalist society such work has no value at all. It is not even called work.

A very frequently repeated story tells us that women, innately unadventurous and conservative, are the great upholders of traditional values. Is that true? May it be a story men tell in order to be able to see themselves as the innovators, the movers and shakers, the ones who get to change society's ways, the teachers of what is new and important?

I don't know. I think it's worth thinking about.

The Second Evening

One of the props that has supported the dominance of men in our society and culture is the idea that great art is made by men, that great literature is by and about men.

When I was in school, women—teachers working, as teachers must, within the male hierarchy—taught me this; and then men taught it to me in college: the really important books are by men, and men are at the center of the important books.

However, my mother, who was not a feminist, and would disavow any subversive intentions, gave me lots of books by women, including *Little Women* and *Black Beauty*, and later on, *Pride and Prejudice* and *A Room of One's Own* . . .

When I began to write fantasy and science fiction, that genre of literature really was all about men; very few women wrote it, and its women characters consisted of a princess here and there, a pretty girl screaming in the tentacles of a purple alien, or a pretty girl batting her eyes—"Oh, Captain, please explain to me how the temporestial figilator works!"

So even though I'd given my heart to several great women writers as well as several great male ones, and welcomed the appearance of actual women characters in science fiction, for a long time I didn't question the idea that fiction was about men, what men did, what men thought. Because I didn't really think about it.

However, along in the 1960s and 1970s those fearsome feminists with their bonfires of bras were thinking and asking questions: Who gets to decide what's important? Why are war and adventure important while housekeeping and child-bearing and child-rearing are not?

By then I had not only written several novels, but kept house for years and had several children, all activities that struck me as fully as important as anything else people did. So I began to think: If I'm a woman, why am I writing books in which men are at the center and primary, and women are marginal and secondary—as if I were a man?

Because editors expect me to, reviewers expect me to. But what right have they to expect me to be a transvestite?

Have I ever even tried to write as who I am, in my own skin instead of a borrowed tuxedo or jockstrap? Do I know how to write in my own skin, my own clothes?

Well, no. I didn't know how. It took me a while to learn. And it was other women who taught me. The feminist writers of the sixties and seventies. The women authors of older generations, who'd been buried by the masculinist literary establishment and were rediscovered, celebrated, reborn in books like *The Norton Anthology of Women Writers*. And my fellow fiction writers, mostly younger than I, women writing as women, about women, in defiance of the literary old guard and the genre old guard too. I learned courage from them.

But I didn't and still don't like making a cult of women's knowledge, preening ourselves on knowing things men don't know, women's deep irrational wisdom, women's instinctive knowledge of Nature, and so on. All that all too often merely reinforces the masculinist idea of women as primitive and inferior—women's knowledge as elementary, primitive, always down below at the dark roots, while men get to cultivate and own the flowers and crops that come up into the light.

But why should women keep talking baby talk while men get to grow up? Why should women *feel* blindly while men get to *think*?

Here is a character in my novel *Tehanu* expressing her belief in gendered knowledge. The central character, Tenar, and her friend Moss, an old, poor, ignorant witch, are discussing male wizards and their power. Tenar asks, What about women's powers? And Moss says:

"Oh, well, dearie, a woman's a different thing altogether. Who knows where a woman begins and ends? Listen, mistress, I have roots, I have roots deeper than this island. Deeper than the sea, older than the raising of the lands. I go back into the dark." Moss's eyes shone with a weird brightness in their red rims and her voice sang like an instrument. "I go back into the dark! Before the moon I was. No one knows, no one knows, no one can say what I am, what a woman is, a woman of power, a woman's power, deeper than the roots of trees, deeper than the roots of islands, older than the Making, older than the moon. Who dares ask questions of the dark? Who'll ask the dark its name?"

Over and over, women are heard and read by both men and women as saying what is expected of them, even while saying just the opposite. That speech has been quoted a hundred times by people approving it, endorsing it. Never I have seen a reader or critic pay attention to what Tenar answers.

"Who'll ask the dark its name?" says Moss—a grand rhetorical question.

But Tenar answers it. She says, "I will." And she adds, "I lived long enough in the dark."

Moss is saying what a masculinist society wants to hear women say. She's proudly claiming the only territory men leave to women, the primitive, the mysterious, the dark. And Tenar is refusing to be limited to that. She lays claim to reason, knowledge, thought, she claims not only the dark but also the daylight as her own.

Tenar speaks for me in that passage. We've lived long enough in the dark. We have an equal right to daylight, an equal right to learn and teach reason, science, art, and all the rest. Women, come on up out of the basement and the kitchen and the kids' room; this whole house is our house. And men, it's time you learned to live in that dark basement that you seem to be so afraid of, and the kitchen and the kids' room too. And when you've done that, come on, let's talk, all of us, around the hearth, in the living room of our shared house. We have a lot to tell each other, a lot to learn.

Disappearing Grandmothers

Written in 2011, not previously published.

I, the High Priestess
I, Enheduanna

There I raised the ritual basket
There I sang the shout of joy

But that man cast me among the dead
—*Enheduanna, ca. 2300 BCE*
translated from the Sumerian by Betty De Shong Meador

What happens to the women?

I've been writing about it for decades now: the masculine orientation of discussion of books and authors in the press.

Literature is now taught at least as often by women as by men (though the percentage of women professors drops as the prestige of the position and the institution rises), and feminist theory has played a strong part in shaping recent literary thinking and curricula—but all that is, literally, academic. To the leaders of critical opinion, to the establishers of rank and value for the general public, to the canoneers, male value and male achievement remain both the standard and the norm. Which means that the canon of literature remains persistently, inflexibly, though now more subtly exclusive of women.

I'm aware of four common techniques or devices (often, though not always, employed quite unconsciously) for excluding women's fiction from the literary canon book by book, author by author. These devices are *denigration, omission, exception,* and *disappearance.* Their cumulative effect is the *continuing marginalisation* of women's writing.

Denigration

Once bald and forthright, denigration of women's writing now seldom comes right out as misogyny. Only imitators of the flaunting masculinist mystique of Hemingway and Mailer still treat all women's writing as second-rate, beneath notice. But assumptions can be made without being stated.

I don't know of a reviewer these days who would drag out Johnson's comparison of a woman writing (preaching, actually) with a dog walking on its hind legs, or shriek with Hawthorne at the thought of an army of scribbling women grimly advancing on him. The prejudice goes unspoken, the bias is shown by omission. Critics can dismiss whole genres unread if they are associated with women. If mysteries or war novels were brushed off as contemptuously as romance commonly is, or if a male-centered genre got a label as contemptuous as "chick lit," there would be indignant protest. Many women call certain types of macho writing "prick lit," but I haven't seen the term used in criticism yet.

A patronizingly jocular tone often serves to denigrate the woman author. Women's writing may be called charming, elegant, poignant, sensitive, but is very seldom called powerful or rugged or masterful. The fact of an author's gender seems to dominate the journalistic mind, gender being read as sexual attractiveness. It's rare to find any discussion of George Eliot that doesn't mention that she was "plain." The *New York Times* obituary of Colleen McCullough, author of *The Thorn Birds,* included the same tasteful and relevant information. Live or dead, male authors are discussed without mentioning that they are or were ugly or unattractive men, but the sin of not having a pretty face is held against women even when they're dead.

Comparing a book written by a woman to work by other women but not to work by men is a subtle and effective form of denigration. It allows the reviewer never to say a woman's book is better than a man's, and helps keep women's achievement safely out of the mainstream, off in the hen coop.

Omission

Periodicals almost universally review more books by men than by women, at more length.

Women's books are reviewed by either men or women, but men's books are reviewed very much more often by men.

Books by women are often grouped together in a joint review, while men's books are reviewed individually.

The most outstanding technique of omission is, as you might expect, in the most directly competitive field: literary prizes. Prize juries commonly short-list books by both men and women, but give the award to a man.

Except for a prize limited to women authors, I have never seen a short list for any literary prize consisting only of women. I was on a jury once which unanimously picked a short list of four women. Another juror, a woman, persuaded us that we had to bump one of the women and include a man, or we would be accused of prejudice and our prize would "lack credibility." I am very sorry that we let her persuade us.

Short lists consisting only of men used to be taken for granted, but are now rarer, since they too may be accused of prejudice. To prevent protest, some women are included on the list. The prize, however, will go to one of the men, from two times out of three to nine times out of ten, depending on the prize.

Anthologies tend to show the same gender imbalance. A science-fiction anthology recently published in England contained no stories by women. A fuss was made. The men responsible for the selection apologised by saying they had invited a woman to contribute but it didn't work out, and then they just somehow didn't notice that all the stories were by men. Ever so sorry about that.

"Somehow" one feels that if all the stories had been by women, they would have noticed.

Exception

A novel by a man is very seldom discussed with any reference to the author's gender. A novel by a woman is very frequently discussed with reference to her gender. The norm is male. The woman is an exception to the norm, from which she is excluded.

Exception and exclusion are practiced both in criticism and in reviewing. A critic forced to admit that, say, Virginia Woolf is a great English novelist may take pains to show her as an exception—a wonderful fluke. Techniques of exception and exclusion are manifold. The woman writer is found not to be in the "mainstream" of English novels; her writing is "unique" but has no influence on later writers; she is the object of a "cult"; she is a (charming, elegant, poignant, sensitive) fragile hothouse flower that should not be seen as competing with the (rugged, powerful, masterful) vigor of the male novelist.

Joyce was almost instantly canonized; Woolf was either excluded from the canon or admitted grudgingly and with reservations for decades. It is quite arguable that *To the Lighthouse*, with its subtle and effective narrative techniques and devices, has been far more influential on later novel-writing than *Ulysses*, which is a monumental dead end. Joyce, choosing "silence, exile, cunning," led a sheltered life, taking responsibility for nothing but his own writing and career. Woolf led a fully engaged life in her own country in an extraordinary circle of intellectually, sexually, and politically active people; and she knew, read, reviewed, and published other authors all her grown life. Joyce is the fragile person, Woolf the tough one; Joyce is the cult object and the fluke, Woolf the continuously fertile influence, central to the twentieth-century novel.

But centrality is the last thing accorded a woman by the canoneers. Women must be left on the margins.

Even when a woman novelist is admitted to be a first-rate artist, the techniques of exclusion still operate. Jane Austen is vastly admired, yet she is less often considered as an exemplar than as unique, inimitable—a wonderful fluke. She cannot be disappeared; but she is not fully included.

Denigration, omission, and exception during a writer's lifetime are preparations for her disappearance after her death.

Disappearance
I use the word in its active, Argentine sense and in full awareness of its connotations.

Of all the crass or subtle techniques used to diminish women's writing, disappearance is the most effective. Once she is silent and powerless, male solidarity quickly closes ranks against the outsider. Female solidarity or the instinct of justice is rarely strong enough to force the ranks back open, and if the effort succeeds, it must continue endlessly, for the male ranks keep effortlessly reclosing.

I have written before of instances of disappearance that particularly gall me: Elizabeth Gaskell and Margaret Oliphant. Both even now are often referred to only as "Mrs," the title indicating their gender and their social condition. (We do not refer to "Mr Dickens" or "Mr Trollope.") Gaskell and Oliphant were well known, popular, respected, and taken seriously while they lived. When they died, they were promptly disappeared. Gaskell's work was reduced to the "sweet" *Cranford*. Social historians of the Victorian era kept reading her novels as documentation, as they read Dickens, but this did not count among the literary canoneers. Oliphant's work was wholly forgotten but for one novel, *Miss Marjoribanks*, not her best, mentioned by historians of literature but not kept in print.

The injustice of these dismissals is as painful as their wastefulness. There really weren't so many excellent Victorian novelists that we can afford to throw out two of them simply because they weren't men. Yet what other reason can be given for the disappearance of their novels? Gaskell is now fairly well reinstated, thanks to feminists and film; Oliphant is not. Why? She and Trollope have a good many similarities; their limitations are obvious, but not fatal; both wrote solidly entertaining novels, psychologically canny and perceptive, which are also fascinating social documents. But only hers vanished. Changing styles put Trollope out of fashion, but he had a great revival during the Second World War when Britons homesick for the old imaginary certainties found them in his books. Nobody remembered or revived Oliphant until the 1970s, when female solidarity in the form of feminist criticism and publishers rescued some of her books at least temporarily.

The rawest case I know of actively disappearing a woman writer is Wallace Stegner's treatment of Mary Hallock Foote. He took the setting, characters, and story of his novel *Angle of Repose* from her autobiography, which was published as *A Victorian Gentlewoman in the Far West*. Even his title is taken from a sentence in her book.

Stegner degraded the character of the author he stole from, making her into an adulterous wife whose carelessness kills her child—a cruel travesty of the actual relationships recounted in the autobiography, the manner of the daughter's death, the depth of the mother's grief. Throughout, Stegner coarsened and cheapened Foote's perceptions of people and landscapes.

Nowhere did he mention Foote or her book's title, deliberately hiding the fact that she was a published author. The only hint he gave of his source was a sentence in the acknowledgments thanking some friends of his, descendants of Foote, "for the loan of their grandmother."

Grandmothers are much easier to handle than women who write. Grandmothers don't even have names.

Of course artists borrow constantly from one another, but what Stegner did was not borrowing, it was expropriation. I would call it plagiarism. It is clear that to him Foote's book simply did not exist in its own right. It was mere raw material for him, the man, the admired novelist, the Stanford professor, to use as he chose. To him, Foote herself did not exist. She was an object for his use.

Rob the grave, just don't say who you left buried in it.

Many who have read Mary Foote's book think it better than Stegner's. Her story was based, selectively, on events of her own life, recounted with emotional control and accuracy. She drew her pioneers and engineers and the Western landscape from life, not secondhand. Stegner sensationalised and conventionalised the setting, the emotions, and the characters. But he was a famous male writer playing the part of famous male writer to the hilt. It worked. He got a Pulitzer for it. His book continues to be printed, praised, and studied.

Mary Foote was a woman writer with a moderate popular reputation and no pretension to fame. Her book disappeared. Was disappeared. Though women's solidarity during the second wave of feminism was enough to get it reprinted after a century of neglect, who knows about it? Who reads it? Who teaches it?

Who will think it matters?

———

I'm thinking now of a woman writer who died not long ago, one who is, I fear, particularly vulnerable to being disappeared: a singularly original and powerful storyteller and poet, Grace Paley. The problem with Paley is that she *was*—truly and genuinely—unique. Not a "fluke," certainly, but like so many women writers, she was not part of any major recognised school or trend in fiction or poetry acknowledged by the male-centered literary establishment.

And unlike so many men writers, she was not much interested in the advancement of her ego. She was ambitious, all right, fiercely so, but her ambition was to further social justice in her time.

I fear that if women critics, feminist writers, fair-minded scholars and teachers and lovers of literature, do not make a conscious and consistent effort to keep Paley's work visible, studied, taught, read, and reprinted, it will be quietly brushed aside within the next few years. It will lapse out of print. It will be forgotten, while the work of lesser writers will be kept alive simply because they were men.

It won't do. We really can't go on letting good writers be disappeared and buried because they weren't men, while writers who should be left to rot in peace are endlessly resurrected, the zombies of criticism and curriculum, because they weren't women.

I'm no beauty, but don't give me a headstone that says She Was Plain. I am a grandmother, but don't give me a headstone that says Somebody's Grandmother. If I have a headstone, I want my name on it. But far more than that, I want my name on books that are judged not by the gender of the writer but by the quality of the writing and the value of the work.

Learning to Write Science Fiction from Virginia Woolf

Published in the Manchester Guardian, April 2011.

You can't write science fiction well if you haven't read it, though not all who try to write it know this. But nor can you write it well if you haven't read anything else. Genre is a rich dialect, in which you can say certain things in a particularly satisfying way, but if it gives up connection with the general literary language, it becomes a jargon meaningful only to an in-group. Useful models may be found quite outside the genre. I learned a lot from reading the ever-subversive Virginia Woolf.

I was seventeen when I read *Orlando*. It was half revelation, half confusion to me at that age, but one thing was clear: that she imagined a society vastly different from our own, an exotic world, and brought it dramatically alive. I'm thinking of the Elizabethan scenes, the winter when the Thames froze over. Reading, I was there, saw the bonfires blazing in the ice, felt the marvelous strangeness of that moment five hundred years ago—the authentic thrill of being taken *absolutely elsewhere*.

How did she do it? By precise, specific descriptive details, not heaped up and not explained: a vivid, telling imagery, highly selected, encouraging the reader's imagination to fill out the picture and see it luminous, complete.

In her novel *Flush*, Woolf gets inside a dog's mind, that is, a nonhuman brain, an alien mentality—very science-fictional if you look at it that way. Again what I learned was the power of accurate, vivid, highly selected detail. I imagine Woolf looking down at her dog asleep beside the ratty armchair she wrote in and thinking *what are your dreams?*

and listening . . . sniffing the wind . . . after the rabbit, out on the hills, in the dog's timeless world.

Useful stuff, for those who like to see through eyes other than our own.

The Death of the Book

This piece began as a blog post in 2012, was revised in 2014 for publication in Technology: A Reader for Writers *(ed. J. Rodgers, Oxford University Press, 2014), and again revised slightly for this book.*

People love to talk about the death of whatever—the book, or history, or Nature, or God, or authentic Cajun cuisine. Eschatologically minded people do, anyhow.

After I wrote that, I felt pleased with myself, but uneasy. I went and looked up "eschatological." I knew it didn't mean what scatological means even though they sound very much alike, but I thought it had to do only with death. I didn't realise it concerns not one thing but the Four Last Things: Death, Judgment, Heaven, and Hell. If it included scatology it would be practically the whole ball of wax.

Anyhow, the eschatologists' judgment is that the book is going to die and go to heaven or hell, leaving us to the mercy of Hollywood and our computer screens.

There certainly is something sick about the book industry, but it seems closely related to the sickness affecting every industry that, under pressure from a corporate owner, dumps product standards and long-range planning in favor of high, predictable sales and short-term profits.

As for books themselves, the changes in book technology are cataclysmic. Yet it seems to me that rather than dying, "the book" is growing—taking on a second form and shape, the e-book.

This has been a vast, unplanned change, as confusing, uncomfortable, and destructive as most unplanned changes. Certainly it's put huge strain on all the familiar channels of book publication and acquisition, from the publishers, distributors, bookstores, and libraries to readers afraid that the latest bestseller, or perhaps all literature, will suddenly pass them by if they don't rush out and buy it as an e-book and an electronic device to read it on.

But that's it, isn't it? That's what books are about—reading?

Is reading obsolete, is the reader dead?

Dear reader: How are you doing? I am fairly obsolete, but by no means, at the moment, dead.

Dear reader: Are you reading at this moment? I am, because I'm writing this, and it's very hard to write without reading, as you know if you ever tried it in the dark.

Dear reader: What are you reading on? I'm writing and reading on my computer, as I imagine you are. (At least, I hope you're reading what I'm writing, and aren't writing "What Tosh!" in the margin. Though I've always wanted to write "What Tosh!" in a margin ever since I read it years ago in the margin of a library book. It was such a good description of the book.)

Reading is undeniably one of the things people do on the computer. On the various electronic devices that are capable of and may be looked upon as "for" telephoning, taking photographs, playing music and games, etc., people may spend a good while texting Sweetie Pie, or looking up recipes for authentic Cajun gumbo, or checking out the stock report—all of which involve reading. People use computers to play games or wander through picture galleries or watch movies, and to do computations and make spreadsheets and pie charts, and a few lucky ones get to draw pictures or compose music, but mostly, am I wrong? isn't an awful lot of what people do with computers either word processing (writing) or processing words (reading)?

How much of anything can you do in the e-world *without* reading? The use of any computer above the toddler-entertainment level is dependent on at least some literacy in the user. Operations can be learned mechanically, but still, the main element of a keyboard is letters; icons take you only so far. Texting may have replaced all other forms of verbality for some people, but texting is just a primitive form of writing: you can't do it unless you no u frm i, lol.

It looks to me as if people are in fact reading and writing more than they ever did. People who used to work and talk together now work each alone in a cubicle, writing and reading all day long on screen. Communication that used to be oral, face to face or on the telephone, is now often written, e-mailed, and read. None of that has much to do with book reading, true; yet it's hard for me to see how the death of the book is to result from the overwhelming prevalence of a technology that makes reading a more valuable skill than it ever was.

Ah, say the eschatologists, but it's competition from the wondrous, endless everything-else-you-can-do-on-your-iPad—competition is murdering the book!

Could be. Or it might just make readers more discriminating. A recent article in the *New York Times* ("Finding Your Book Interrupted . . . By the Tablet You Read It On," by Julie Bosman and Matt Richtel, March 4, 2012) quoted a woman in Los Angeles: "With so many distractions, my taste in books has really leveled up. . . . Recently, I gravitate to books that make me forget I have a world of entertainment at my fingertips. If the book's not good enough to do that, I guess my time is better spent." Her sentence ends oddly, but I think it means that she prefers reading an entertaining book to activating the world of entertainment with her fingertips. Why does she not consider books part of this world of entertainment? Maybe because the book, even when activated by her fingertips, entertains her without the moving, flickering, twitching, jumping, glittering, shouting, thumping, bellowing, screaming, blood-spattering, ear-splitting, etc., that we've been led to identify as entertainment. In any case, her point is clear: if a book's not as entertaining on some level, not necessarily the same level, as the jumping, thumping, bleeding, etc., then why read it? Either activate the etc., or find a better book. As she puts it, level up.

When discussing the death of the book, it might be a good idea to ask what "the book" is. Are we talking about people ceasing to read books, or about what they read the books on—paper or a screen?

Reading on a screen is certainly different from reading a page. I don't think we yet understand what the differences are. They may be considerable, but I doubt that they're so great as to justify giving the two kinds of reading different names, or saying that an e-book isn't a book at all.

If "the book" means only the book as physical object, then to some devotees of the internet its death may be a matter for rejoicing—hurray! we're rid of another nasty heavy bodily Thing with a copyright on it! But mostly the death of the book is an occasion of lament and gloom. People to whom the physicality of the book printed on paper is important, sometimes more important than the contents—those who value books for their binding, paper, and typography, buy them in fine editions, collect them—and the many who simply take pleasure in holding and handling the book they're reading, are naturally distressed by the idea that the book on paper will be totally replaced by the immaterial text in a machine.

I can only suggest, Don't agonize—organize! No matter how the corporations bluster and bully and bury us in advertising, the consumer always has the option of resistance. We don't get steamrollered by a new technology unless we lie down in front of the steamroller.

The steamroller is certainly on the move. Some kinds of printed book such as manuals and DIY are being replaced by e-books. The low-cost e-book edition threatens the mass market paperback. Good news for those who like to read on a screen, bad news for those who don't, or who like to buy from AbeBooks and Alibris or pounce on 75-cent beat-up mysteries at the rare surviving secondhand bookstore. But if the lovers of the material book are serious about valuing good binding and paper and design as essential to their reading pleasure, they will provide a visible, steady demand for well-made hardcover and paperback editions, which the book industry, if it has the market sense of a sowbug, will meet. The question is whether the book industry does have the sense of a sowbug. Some of its behavior lately leads one to doubt. But let us hope. And there's always the "small press," the corporation-free independent publisher, many of which are as classy and as canny as can be.

Other outcries about the death of the book have more to do with the direct competition offered on the web. "The world of entertainment at our fingertips" makes reading obsolete.

Here "the book" usually refers to literature. At the moment, DIY manuals, cookbooks, and guides to this or that are the kinds of book most often replaced by information on a screen. *Encyclopedia Britannica* just died, a victim, as it were, of Google. I don't think I'll bury our Eleventh Edition just yet, though. The information in it, being a product of its time (a hundred years ago), can be valuably different from that furnished by the search engine, which is also a product of its time. The annual encyclopedias of films/directors/actors were killed a few years ago by information sites on the Net—very good sites, though not as much fun to get lost in as the books were. We keep a 2003 film guide because, being ourselves ancient, we use it more efficiently than we do any site, and it's still useful and entertaining even if dead. That is more than you can say of the corpse of almost anything but a book.

I'm not sure why anyone, no matter how much they like to think the sky is falling, believes that the *Iliad* or *Jane Eyre* or the *Bhagavad Gita* is dead or about to die. The great works of literature have far more competition than they used to, yes; people may see the movie and think they know what the book is; the books can be *dis*placed by the world of entertainment at our fingertips; but nothing can *re*place them. So long as people are taught to read (which may or may not happen in our underfunded schools), particularly if people are taught what there is to read and how to read it intelligently (extensions of the basic skill now often omitted in our underfunded schools), some of those people will prefer reading to all the titillations accessible to their fingertips.

They will read books, on paper or on a screen, as literature, for the pleasure and the augmentation of existence literature gives.

And they will try to ensure that the books continue to exist, because continuity is an essential aspect of literature and knowledge. Books occupy time in a different way than most art and entertainment. In longevity perhaps only architecture and sculpture in stone outdo the book.

And here the issue of electronic versus paper has to reenter the discussion. Much of the transmission of human culture still relies on the relative permanence of what is *written*. This has been true for over four thousand years. It's possible that the highest and most urgent value of a book may be its mere, solid, stolid, physical existence.

I'll be talking now not about "the book" in America in 2012 so much as about how things are all over the world in the many places where electricity may be intermittent, or nonexistent, or available only to the rich; and how things may be in fifty or a hundred years if we continue to degrade and destroy our habitat at the present rate.

The ease of reproducing an e-book and sending it all over the place can certainly secure its permanence for so long as the machine to read it on can be made and turned on. It's well to remember, though, that electric power is not to be counted on in the same way sunlight is.

Easy and infinite reproducibility also involves a certain risk. The text of the book on paper can't be altered without separately and individually altering every copy in existence, and alteration leaves unmistakable traces. With e-texts that have been altered, deliberately or by corruption (pirated texts are often incredibly corrupt), it may be impossible to establish an original, authentic, correct text if no paper copy exists. And the more piracies, errors, abridgments, omissions, additions, and mash-ups are tolerated, the less people will understand what textual integrity is.

People to whom texts matter, such as readers of poetry or scientific monographs, know that the integrity of a text may be essential. Our nonliterate ancestors knew it. *Speak the words of the poem exactly as you learned them or it will lose its power.* The three-year-old being read to demands it. *Daddy! You read it wrong! The chipmunk says "I did not do that," not "I didn't do that!"*

The physical book may last for centuries. Even a cheap paperback on pulp paper takes decades to degrade into unreadability. At this stage of e-publication, continuous changes of technology, upgrades, deliberate obsolescence, and corporate takeovers have left behind them a debris of texts unreadable on any available machine. Moreover, e-texts have to be periodically recopied to keep them from degrading. People who archive them are reluctant to say how frequently this must be done, because it varies a great deal; but as anyone with e-mail files over a few years old knows, the progress into entropy can be rapid. A university librarian told me that as things are now, they expect to recopy every electronic text the library owns every eight to ten years, indefinitely.

Imagine if we had to do that with printed books!

If at this stage of the technology we decided to replace the content of our libraries entirely with electronic archives, a worst-case scenario would have informational and literary texts being altered without our consent or knowledge, reproduced or destroyed without our permission, rendered unreadable by the technology that printed them, and fated within a few years or decades, unless regularly recopied and redistributed, to turn inexorably into garble or simply blink out of existence.

But that's assuming the technology won't improve and stabilize. Let us hope it does. Even so, why should we go into either/or mode? It's seldom necessary and often destructive. Computers may be binary, but we aren't.

Maybe the e-book and the electricity to run it will become available to everyone everywhere forever. That would be grand. But as things are or are likely to be, having books available in two different forms can only be a good thing, now and in the long run. Redundancy is the key to species longevity.

Despite all the temptations at our fingertips, I believe there will continue to be, as there has long been, an obstinate, durable minority of people who, having learned to read books, will go on reading them—however and wherever they can find them, on pages or screens. And because people who read books mostly want to share them, and feel however obscurely that sharing them is important, they'll see to it that, however and wherever, the books are there for the next generations.

Human generations, that is, not technological generations. At the moment, the technological generation has shortened to about the life span of the gerbil, and might yet rival that of the fruit fly.

The life span of a book is more like that of the horse or the human being, sometimes the oak, even the redwood. Which is why it seems a good idea, rather than mourning their death, to rejoice that books now have not one but two ways of staying alive, getting passed on, enduring.

Le Guin's Hypothesis

*Rewritten from a blog post on my website and at Book View Café,
June 14, 2012, this piece was given as a talk at the
Sigma Tau Delta Conference in Seattle, March 2013.*

In a *New Yorker* article last year about literature and genre, Arthur Krystal called reading genre novels "a guilty pleasure." I responded in my blog, saying that the phrase "succeeds in being simultaneously self-deprecating, self-congratulatory, and collusive. When I speak of my guilty pleasure, I confess that I know I sin, but I know you sin too, nudge nudge, aren't we sinners cute?"

So. Literature is the serious stuff you have to read in college, and genre is what you read for pleasure, which is guilty.

But what about the non-guilty pleasure, the true pleasure, that we may get from any novel, whatever its category?

The trouble with opposing Litfic to Genrefic is that what looks like a reasonable distinction of varieties of fiction hides an unreasoned value judgment: Lit superior, Genre inferior. This is mere prejudice. We must have a more intelligent discussion of what literature is. Many English departments have largely ceased trying to defend their ivied ivory towers by shooting down every space ship that approaches; many critics are aware that a lot of literature is happening outside the sacred groves of modernist realism: but still the opposition of literature and genre is maintained, and as long as it is, false categorical value judgment will cling to it.

To get out of this boring bind, I propose an hypothesis:

Literature is the extant body of written art.

All novels belong to it.

———

The value judgment concealed in distinguishing one novel as literature and another as genre vanishes with the distinction. The elitist snobbery that conflates the popular with the commercial, the Puritan snobbery of virtuous "higher" pleasure and guilty "lower" pleasure, become irrelevant, and very hard to defend.

Though no genre is inherently, categorically superior or inferior, genres exist, forms and types and kinds of fiction exist and need to be understood.

The many genres that go to make up the literature of fiction include mystery, science fiction, fantasy, naturalism, realism, magical realism, graphic, erotic, experimental, psychological, social, political, historical, bildungsroman, romance, Western, war, Gothic, young adult, horror, thriller . . . along with the proliferating cross-species and subgenres such as dysfunctional-suburban-family-semifactual-confessional, noir police procedural, and parallel history with zombies.

Some of these categories are descriptive, some are maintained largely as marketing devices. Some limit invention narrowly, others encourage it. Some are old, some new, some ephemeral.

Each reader will prefer certain genres and be bored or repelled by others. But anybody who claims that one genre is categorically superior to all others must be ready and able to defend their prejudice. And that involves knowing what the "inferior" genres actually consist of, their nature and their forms of excellence. It involves reading them.

If we approached all fictional genres as literature, we'd be done with the time-wasting, ill-natured diatribes and sneers against popular novelists who don't write by the rules of realism, the banning of imaginative writing from MFA courses, the failure of so many English teachers to teach what people actually read, and the endless, silly apologising for actually reading it.

If critics and teachers gave up insisting that one kind of literature is the only one worth reading, it would free up more time for them to think about the different things novels do and how they do it, and above all, to consider why certain *individual books* in every genre are, have been for centuries, and will continue to be more worth reading than most of the others.

Because there is the real mystery. Why is one book entertaining, another disappointing, another a revelation and a lasting joy? What is quality? What makes a good book good and a bad book bad?

Not its subject. Not its genre. What, then? That's what good criticism, good book talk, has always been about.

We won't be allowed to knock down the Litfic/Fixfic walls, though, as long as the publishers and booksellers think their business depends on them—capitalizing on the guilty pleasure principle.

But then, how long will the publishers and booksellers last against the massive aggression of the enormous corporations that are now taking over every form of publication in absolute indifference to its content and quality so long as they can sell it as a commodity?

Making Up Stories

A talk given at the Terroir Festival of Writing and Literature in McMinnville, Oregon, in 2013, slightly revised for publication.

Thank you for having me to the first of what I hope will be many successful Terroirs, especially when we all learn how to pronounce it. My problem is I used to know French and so I know it isn't actually pronounced terwha. Terwha is probably an Eastern Oregon county in one of Molly Gloss's novels. But if I try calling it *terrrroirrr* in French all day, I will get a sore throat, and anyhow, who cares? This is Orrregon. And we are having a festival of writing and literature, which is a wonderful thing to do.

I promised to talk about making up stories, which is how I have spent the best part of my life. Then I hope we can converse for a while about anything you want to talk about. But please don't ask me where I get my ideas from. I have managed to keep the address of the company where I buy my ideas a secret all these years, and I'm not about to let people in on it now.

All right. There are two major kinds of story: the kind where you tell what happened, and the kind where you tell what didn't.

The first kind is history, journalism, biography, autobiography, and memoir. The second kind is fiction—stories you make up.

We Americans tend to be more comfortable with the first kind. We distrust people who make things up. We're comfortable with stories about "real things" and "real life." We want stories that tell us about "reality." We want them so bad that when we stage completely fake situations and film them, we call it "reality TV."

The problem with all this is that your real is not my real. We don't all perceive reality the same way. Some of us in fact do not perceive reality at all. You can definitely see that if you watch Fox News.

These differences in how we define reality are probably why we have fiction.

It seems common sense that fact should be our common ground. But in fact, fact is so hard to come by, so dependent on point of view, so debatable, that we may be more likely to meet a shared reality in fiction. By telling—or by reading—a story of what didn't in fact happen, but could have happened or could yet happen, to somebody who isn't an actual person but who might have been or could be, we open the door to the imagination. And imagination is the best, maybe the only way we have to know anything about each other's minds and hearts.

In workshops on story writing, I've met many writers who want to work only with memoir, tell only their own story, their experience. Often they say, "I can't make up stuff, that's too hard, but I can tell what happened." It seems easier to them to take material directly from their experience than to use their experience as material for making up a story. They assume that they can just write what happened.

That appears reasonable, but actually, reproducing experience is a very tricky business requiring both artfulness and practice. You may find you don't know certain important facts or elements of the story you want to tell. Or the private experience so important to you may not be very interesting to others, requires skill to make it meaningful, moving, to the reader. Or, being about yourself, it gets all tangled up with ego, or begins to be falsified by wishful thinking. If you're honestly trying to tell what happened, you find facts are very obstinate things to deal with. But if you begin to fake them, to pretend things happened in a way that makes a nice neat story, you're misusing imagination. You're passing invention off as fact: which is, among children at least, called lying.

Fiction is invention, but it is not lies. It moves on a different level of reality from either fact-finding or lying.

I want to talk here about the difference between imagination and wishful thinking, because it's important both in writing and in living. Wishful thinking is thinking cut loose from reality, a self-indulgence that is often merely childish, but may be dangerous. Imagination, even in its wildest flights, is not detached from reality: imagination acknowledges reality, starts from it, and returns to it to enrich it. Don Quixote indulges his longing to be a knight till he loses touch with reality and makes an awful mess of his life. That's wishful thinking. Miguel Cervantes, by working out and telling the invented story of a man who wishes he were a knight, vastly increased our store of laughter and of human understanding. That's imagination. Wishful thinking is Hitler's Thousand-Year Reich. Imagination is the Constitution of the United States.

A failure to see this difference is in itself dangerous. If we assume that imagination has no connection with reality but is mere escapism, and therefore distrust it and suppress it, it will be crippled, perverted, it will fall silent or speak untruth. The imagination, like any basic human capacity, needs exercise, discipline, training, in childhood and lifelong.

One of the best exercises for the imagination, maybe the very best, is hearing, reading, and telling or writing made-up stories. Good inventions, however fanciful, have both congruity with reality and inner coherence. A story that's mere wish-fulfilling babble, or coercive preaching concealed in a narrative, lacks intellectual coherence and integrity: it isn't a whole thing, it can't stand up, it isn't true to itself.

Learning to read or tell a story that is true to itself is about the best education a mind can have. Even in America many of us give our children imaginative books to read—*Alice in Wonderland, Charlotte's Web.* In high school, science fiction and fantasy are at last recognised in the English curriculum. If only kids were seriously required to write not only What I Did on My Vacation, but also What I Didn't Do on My Vacation! Once they got past childish wish-fulfillment (I shot down forty enemy planes! I got to be the Queen of Mars and ride a unicorn! I hit that dumb Jackie Beeson in the eye!), they'd get some training in following their imagination farther, using it wisely, using it well. They'd learn it is a way into the truth. An indispensable tool for being human.

If as a writer you get over the peculiar puritanical terror of making things up—if you realise that you don't have to tell episodes from your life experience directly, but can use your life experience as the substance to make stories from, as the material of your imagination—you may find yourself suddenly free. Your story isn't "your" story any more. It isn't about you. It's just *a story*—and you're free to go with it, go where the story wants to go, let it find its true shape.

Gary Snyder gave us the image of experience as compost. Compost is stuff, junk, garbage, anything, that's turned into dirt by sitting around a while. It involves silence, darkness, time, and patience. From compost, whole gardens grow.

It can be useful to think of writing as gardening. You plant the seeds, but each plant will take its own way and shape. The gardener's in control, yes; but plants are living, willful things. Every story has to find its own way to the light. Your great tool as gardener is your imagination.

Young writers often think—are taught to think—that a story starts with a message. That is not my experience. What's important when you start is simply this: you have a story you want to tell. A seedling that wants to grow. Something in your inner experience is forcing itself up towards the light. Attentively and carefully and patiently, you can encourage that, let it happen. Don't force it; trust it. Watch it, water it, let it grow.

As you write a story, if you can let it become itself, tell itself fully and truly, you may discover what it's really about, what it says, why you wanted to tell it. It may be a surprise to you. You may have thought you planted a dahlia, and look what came up, an eggplant! Fiction is not information transmission; it is not message-sending. The writing of fiction is endlessly surprising to the writer.

Like a poem, a story says what it has to say in the only way it can be said, and that is the exact words of the story itself. Which is why the words are so important, why it takes so long to learn how to get the words right. Why you need silence, darkness, time, patience, and a real, solid knowledge of English vocabulary and grammar.

Truthful imagining from experience is recognisable, shared by its readers. The great stories of imagination have meanings beyond any message and are meaningful to all kinds of people over hundreds of years. The *Odyssey, Don Quixote, Pride and Prejudice, A Christmas Carol, The Lord of the Rings, Honey in the Horn, The Jump-Off Creek*: none of those stories is factual. All are pure fiction. And they are about all of us, they're our story. They include us in a greater story, the human story, the reality of being human.

That's why I love fiction and encourage people to make up stories. And to take the time to learn how to get the words right. It takes a while to learn how to use words. It takes practice. It takes work, years of work. And then what you write may never get published. Even if it does it almost certainly won't ever make you enough to live off of. But if it's what you want to do, nothing, nothing in the world, can give you a sweeter reward than doing it, doing the work itself—and then knowing you did it, you got the words right, you made a story up and told it truly. Truth-telling is a great thing, and a rare one. Enjoy it!

A few words more about reading in the brave new world of the internet. Here we all are talking about writing, and everybody is telling us that nobody is reading. Pundits wail that the book is dead. Johnny not only can't read, he won't read. Americans read a quarter of a book apiece every ten years, or some such statistic. How can Homer compete with the iPad? Nobody wants *Don Quixote*; it can't be tweeted. So what are we doing here at our festival of writing?

The same thing writers have always done. We write for people who read, and they've always been a minority. I don't say an elite, simply a minority. The majority of people in this world have never read for pleasure and never will. Some can't; some won't.

This is nothing to tear hair about. It takes all kinds to make a world. Watching men hit balls with bats for hours on end is not a pleasure to me, nor to many other people in the world. That doesn't mean baseball—or even cricket—is dead.

We've gone into an unnecessary panic about reading, when what's changed is not reading, but publishing. There, some panic is warranted. Our technology has got so far ahead of our brains that we're in danger of throwing out perfectly reliable methods of keeping readers freely supplied with reading matter and writers adequately supplied with peanut butter. The big publishers, who for all their faults were pretty good at both those jobs, are now controlled by huge corporations that demand they publish only what will sell fast and die fast—profiteers who have no interest in books or authors other than profit-making control of the market and the commodities sold in it. Copyright, the only guarantee writers and publishers have that they can make a living, is in imminent danger of being abandoned with nothing to replace it. Growth capitalism is by nature inimical to the craftsman and the artist. Copyright was a kind of loophole that allowed us to live within capitalism, but by using reactionary elements in the government, the corporations are actively seeking ways to wreck copyright, exploit us, and control what we write.

How can we use e-publication and the internet to our advantage so we can write what we want and get paid for it? I am too old to have any idea. You here are going to have to figure that out. And you will. People do want to read. Sometimes it seems that everybody wants write, but believe me, even more of them want to read. And somewhere in the loopholes and crannies of the huge machinery of capitalist technology, writers and readers will find each other, as we always have done. If you're aware that it's up to you to make that happen, you'll find out how to do it. I wish you courage, and the best luck in the world.

Freedom

A speech in acceptance of the National Book Foundation Medal for Distinguished Contribution to American Letters, November 2014.

To the givers of this beautiful reward, my thanks, from the heart. My family, my agents, my editors, know that my being here is their doing as well as my own, and that the beautiful reward is theirs as much as mine. And I rejoice in accepting it for, and sharing it with, all the writers who've been excluded from literature for so long—my fellow authors of fantasy and science fiction, writers of the imagination, who for fifty years have watched the beautiful rewards go to the so-called realists.

Hard times are coming, when we'll be wanting the voices of writers who can see alternatives to how we live now, can see through our fear-stricken society and its obsessive technologies to other ways of being, and even imagine real grounds for hope. We'll need writers who can remember freedom—poets, visionaries—realists of a larger reality.

Right now, we need writers who know the difference between production of a market commodity and the practice of an art. Developing written material to suit sales strategies in order to maximise corporate profit and advertising revenue is not the same thing as responsible book publishing or authorship.

Yet I see sales departments given control over editorial. I see my own publishers, in a silly panic of ignorance and greed, charging public libraries for an e-book six or seven times more than they charge customers. We just saw a profiteer try to punish a publisher for disobedience, and writers threatened by corporate fatwa. And I see a lot of us, the producers, who write the books and make the books, accepting this—letting commodity profiteers sell us like deodorant, and tell us what to publish, what to write.

Books aren't just commodities; the profit motive is often in conflict with the aims of art. We live in capitalism, its power seems inescapable— but then, so did the divine right of kings. Any human power can be resisted and changed by human beings. Resistance and change often begin in art. Very often in our art, the art of words.

I've had a long career as a writer, and a good one, in good company. Here at the end of it, I don't want to watch American literature get sold down the river. We who live by writing and publishing want and should demand our fair share of the proceeds; but the name of our beautiful reward isn't profit. Its name is freedom.

Thank you.

Book Introductions
and Notes on Writers

Most of these pieces about various authors were written as introductions to a new edition of a book, a few as freestanding essays. They are arranged alphabetically by the author's last name.

The essay on José Saramago, "Examples of Dignity," is the only piece in this book that differs substantially from its form(s) as originally published. Joy Johannessen, who licked this book into shape, combined two essays and two book reviews from different years into a single, very much less repetitive essay. Again, the earlier versions can be found in the periodicals where they were published, or on my website; and reviews of two Saramago novels, not incorporated into this piece, can be found in the next section, Book Reviews.

I wouldn't agree to write an introduction for a book I didn't admire, or write at length about an author who didn't interest me intensely, so these pieces give a glimpse of the kind of fiction I like. But they're totally useless as an indication of what I read, or as a list of favorite writers. People think of me as a science-fiction writer, and so I'm asked to write about science fiction, and that's fine, but still—three pieces on H. G. Wells and none on Virginia Woolf?

The two subjects I picked freely for myself were H. L. Davis's great Western novel Honey in the Horn, *at the generous invitation from* Tin House *magazine to write about any book I liked, and Charles McNichols's* Crazy Weather, *an introduction written for Harry Kirchner of Pharos Books. He invites writers to pick an out-of-print book and tell us why it should be back in print, and then he publishes it. A notable venture, resulting in an extraordinary publication list.*

A Very Good American Novel: H. L. Davis's *Honey in the Horn*

First published in Tin House, 2013.

Writers west of the Mississippi are up against the Eastern notion that everything west of the Mississippi, except maybe Stanford, is cactus. Many Easterners also hold that "regional" fiction is inferior and that a "region" is anywhere that isn't the East. You can't beat logic like that. It's amazing that H. L. Davis of Oregon won a Pulitzer, even in 1936. Lately, however, he's been so neglected, so lost to literature, that readers may be startled to recognise in his style and tone a model for Ken Kesey in *Sometimes a Great Notion*, Don Berry in *Trask*, and most other serious novelists of the West, including even the high-toned Wallace Stegner. Molly Gloss, in *The Jump-Off Creek* and *The Hearts of Horses*, is his true heir, the one I think he might have acknowledged as getting it pretty near all the way right.

Davis's prize-winning masterpiece was *Honey in the Horn*. Its protagonist, Clay, is a likable, mule-headed, mixed-up boy of eighteen or so who has already been through a good deal, but hasn't yet shut down in self-defense. His instincts are decent, but he falls in with an unlawful posse and takes enthusiastic part in hunting down and lynching his own worthless father, who might only be his uncle. His girl, Luce, the most vivid character in the book, is a wonderful mixture of forthright honesty and wary elusiveness. It's a good love story, always balanced on the high wire between possibility and tragedy. Clay and Luce are both quite capable of murder, which keeps the tension up. Both are ignorant, intelligent, young but already damaged, haunted by bad mistakes, pursued by past darkness, yet struggling to find a moral sense in the huge complexity of life. Of the wildly various people they meet or travel with, some have sunk contentedly into crime, many into futility, some are merely restless, and some, like Clay and Luce, keep groping vaguely toward a clearer standard, a better way to live, maybe just over those mountains there . . .

Clay takes a lively interest in the world, and through him, in a deceptively easygoing style, Davis gives us his own stunningly vivid perceptions of people and places. Here we're riding with Clay across a hardpan desert:

> In the big stretches the alkali reflected the exact dark blue of the sky, and that parted to right and left as he rode into it, so that he rode with the sky rubbing either elbow and washing softly back from the mare's feet as she advanced. There were places where spots in the clear air expanded with heat and magnified distant sections of scenery so they seemed only a few feet away, and then they would go on expanding till they got gigantic, until a couple of sage rats cutting grass would look as big as colts; and then they would vanish as if they had been dissolved in water.

Davis was a generous, cross-grained man who drank too much, as journalists and male novelists were expected to do. He wrote several fine novels and stories, including the unforgettable "Open Winter," all of them about the Oregon country and the people who worked in it. He said he wanted *Honey in the Horn* to contain an example of every job people did in Oregon in 1912. That statement itself takes us back to a faraway world of hard, skilled, physical, and infinitely various work, such as cowboying, or blacksmithing, or cooking for ranch hands, or fishing for salmon by dangling off a rope in a waterfall with a gaff in hand, or sewing grain sacks shut. The novel was written during the Great Depression, when work was something very much on people's minds. The time it describes is now a century ago. Given the rate of technological change, it's been the longest hundred years in human history. To some, Davis's picture will be meaningless, to others fascinating. In any case, it's worth considering that from the beginning of human culture until a generation or two ago, everybody lived in the work world he describes; and it won't take much to put us back into it.

For all its vivid, vigorous language, its dry, teasing humor, its grand scenery indicated by a few easy strokes, and its crowd of cantankerous characters noisily causing trouble for themselves and everybody else clear across two mountain ranges, the essential feeling the book leaves me with is loneliness. Or what I think of as the American version of the word: *lonesomeness.* Lonesome people. That could be a strike against it. We may adulate the lone hero, but we don't want to be him. Lonesomeness is what the ever-present TV and cellphone and social media save us from. All the same, it's what a lot of people in the West came looking for— room, space, silence. We're social animals, but we crave solitude to make our souls. Americans cherish their opinions at least as much as their souls, and opinions allowed to take root where nobody's around to crowd them grow great and very strange. Davis takes a good deal of pleasure describing them.

He had some strong opinions of his own, including a low one of "developers," the people who turned the West into desirable real estate, filled alkali flats with little white stakes marking out unbuilt avenues and opera houses, and fooled the hopeful with talk of ten-foot topsoil, railroads certain to come, fortunes to be made, orange orchards in the sagebrush. Developers are loyal, active servants of capitalism, of course; possibly that explains his opinion of them.

The kind of super-respectful language used today when speaking of non-white peoples, language that white racists label "political correctness," was as unknown to Davis as it was to Shakespeare. He treats everybody exactly alike. Nobody gets any respect from him who hasn't individually earned it. He speaks of Native Americans not across a gulf of wishful thinking, but from a personal knowledge of difference so rare in fiction that it will shock people these days (and may be part of the reason why *Honey in the Horn* has been dropped from the canon). The many Indian groups are clearly, vividly differentiated. In a sketch of a coastal village, he describes a tiny isolated group of Athabascans:

There was a kind of hopelessness about that lost tag-end of a great people, stuck off in such a place without anything to use their brains on if any of them ever developed any, with nothing that they could ever amount to except to become chief of a shack town containing maybe six dozen human beings, with strange people and strange languages all around them so that there could be no chance of ever getting away. Not that there was anything mournful about it. They didn't want to get away, and they had stayed where they were for pretty close to a thousand years without the slightest suspicion that any place in the world could be finer or more interesting than their own twenty acres of it.

Davis omits the probability that this village, like many on the Oregon Coast, had recently lost eighty or ninety percent of its people to white diseases; and he was a desert man, who couldn't imagine liking the rainy coast. Otherwise, he mocks these people only as he mocks everybody— his picture of white settlers near this Indian village is just as unsparing. Disrespectful of conventional pieties but fascinated by and respectful of cultural difference, Davis can feel sympathy with the Indians without feeling obliged to share their view of life. What's more, he knows that his judgment of it is immaterial. Such fair-minded plain speaking is too easily silenced by the emotional rant of racism/antiracism. When *Huckleberry Finn* is banned, calumniated, and bowdlerized for using the word nigger, despite the fact that "Nigger" Jim is the moral hero of the book, how can any lesser book survive?

For all their failure to attain any goal or even do anything that makes much sense, the book's characters are fiery with life—absurdly tragic, painfully funny, ornery as all get-out. Through the grand indifference of the Oregon landscape Davis sends a cavalcade of mavericks and loners, a crazy symphony of dissenting voices, a pilgrimage of obdurate souls. In them, with some reluctance, with some relief and even delight, I see my countrymen as they can be seen only from the farthest West, the farthest stretch of the extraordinary American experiment in how to be human.

Philip K. Dick:
The Man in the High Castle

An introduction to the Folio Society edition of 2015.

The Man in the High Castle was published at the end of 1962, before what we think of as the sixties was under way, and long before science fiction was considered as having anything to do with American literature. When the book came out, there was a smell of gunpowder in it, the whiff of revolution. And indeed it played a part both in the deconstruction of conventional thinking that led to the social upheavals of the sixties and seventies, and in the dilapidation of the wall that critics had set up between realistic fiction and the larger realities of fiction.

Since few reviewers of the time ever crossed that wall, only the science-fiction community took much notice of the novel. It found readers outside the genre, but could always be marginalized as a "cult" book (one of those handy dismissive adjectives dear to critics). The 1982 film *Blade Runner,* nominally based on Dick's 1968 novel *Do Androids Dream of Electric Sheep?,* sacrificed most of the intelligence and ethical complexity of the story to sensational effects and violent action, but its success brought Dick's name into some prominence. By the nineties, a more informed and generous criticism was beginning to appreciate the unsettling energy and disquieting power of *The Man in the High Castle.*

Sometimes awkward, sometimes obscure, thoroughly unpredictable —literally plotted by the chance fall of coins or yarrow sticks, yet ultimately controlled and driven by rational, moral purpose—this novel continues to fascinate both the critical interpreter and the common reader. It may be the first big, lasting contribution science fiction made to American literature.

Its form, alternate history, rearranges actual, familiar events on earth without introducing new technologies or alien worlds, thus reassuring people who are afraid of science fiction that the book can be read as safely as an ordinary historical novel; in this case, a snare and a delusion: the author was a master of both. His rearrangements of the outcome of World War II are not altogether historically probable, but fictively they are horribly convincing. To read the book is to be drawn into the perceptual vividness of a vision, the disorienting and lasting conviction of nightmare. Since 1963, I've been unable to forget that the Nazis might? did? control the East Coast of the United States and the Japanese the West. And I have been haunted by the awful shadow-memory of Africa as a silent graveyard.

A year older than I, Philip Kindred Dick spent his adolescence in the city I grew up in, Berkeley. We both graduated from Berkeley High School in 1947. That there were over three thousand students at the school may explain why I never even knew his name, yet it seems a little odd. Absolutely no one I've spoken to from our Berkeley High years remembers him. Was he a total loner, was he out sick a great deal, did he take "shop" courses rather than the more academic ones? His name is in the yearbook but there is no picture of him. In Dick's life as in his fiction, reality seems to slither from the grasp, and ascertainable facts end up as debatable assertions or mere labels.

Much later in our lives, he and I corresponded for a couple of years, always about writing; he knew how much I admired his work. We talked on the phone two or three times, but never met.

American male writers of our generation—just too young to fight in the war—often went to considerable trouble to prove their manly credentials, taking jobs as loggers, on freighters, hunting, hitchhiking, living ostentatiously rough, and so on. Phil Dick didn't. After a very brief try at college he clerked for a couple of years in a music shop on Telegraph Avenue. He married five different women. Otherwise it's hard to find out anything he did besides write. Writing was his vocation from the start. He worked very hard to make a living from it, with little encouragement from the publishing world. Like many Western authors he lacked personal contacts in the eastern-centered literary establishment and could count only on persistence and luck to find him an editor. The Scott Meredith Literary Agency took on his first novels (written in the fifties to the standards of the realist canon), but they sent all five of them back to him as unsalable in 1963, the year after he published *The Man in the High Castle*. Only one of those early novels was published during his lifetime, though they are all available now, and have their admirers. My opinion is that his failure to get them published forced him, harshly but fortunately, away from the glum realism of the fifties into broader regions of the imagination where he could find his own way.

He was born a twin. His sister died when they were six weeks old. He wrote and spoke of this connection and this loss as if they were retrievable memories, sometimes implying that his sister lived on in him. Twins, doubles, simulacra populate his stories. Certainly he was a man who contained disparate and perhaps incompatible elements, to the point of being both uncertain and overassertive of his own identity. He laid himself open to charges of unreliability, of an uncalculating, profitless, but real duplicity. In his writing life, the persona he hoped would dominate—the conventionally respectable, successful literary novelist—became the sterile shadow. The reality appeared to be the author of pulp fiction, the science-fiction writer turning out stuff as fast as he could for money.

Well-known authors like Hemingway who boast that they write only for money are one thing, obscure writers who do it because it's their job are another. My respect is reserved for them. Writing fiction for a living is a hard trade, highly skilled work done almost always for low or uncertain gain. For a writer of unconventional gifts it can be slavery. Yet like any craft or art it rewards the serious practitioner with the knowledge of doing something as well as you can do it; and there may be the bonus of an inward conviction that you're doing something as well as it can be done. A structural element in much of Dick's best work, including this novel, is his deep respect for the honest, modest craftsman. For a long time that is what he was himself. I don't know if, in the hard years of the fifties, he was fully aware of the high quality of some of his pulp-magazine fiction. Certainly he struggled with the market's demand for low standards and incessant production; but he kept on seeking his own vein, finding it, mining it deeper, till he hit the mother lode with *The Man in the High Castle.*

The book won the Hugo Award, nominated and voted for by the members of the major annual science-fiction meeting of readers, writers, editors, publishers, and agents in the field. Yet most of the sf community accepted him simply as a workhorse and were slow to recognize him as a star. Perhaps it was because of his lack of clout with publishers and editors; perhaps it was because he wrote so differently from the established, successful writers of the so-called Golden Age of Science Fiction, authors like Robert Heinlein and Isaac Asimov, who set the tone and dominated the thinking of the field for years. Unlike them, Dick could be accused of committing literature. The Old Boys and the Young Engineers of science fiction were as bigoted as any English professor; genre prejudice, genre defensiveness, cut both ways.

But many science-fiction writers of Dick's generation and younger were busy creating what was called the New Wave. It was in fact one wave after another, gathering at last into a tide that would overflow the artificial limits of the genre, rejoining it inevitably to the "sea of story," the entirety of literary fiction, from which both critical theory and genre parochialism had kept it segregated for decades. I don't know to what extent Phil Dick saw himself as a part of this wave-making group. My guess is that he didn't see himself as belonging to any group or fellowship. His need was to pursue a solitary vision, to surrender himself to an angel who spoke to him alone.

In the seventies, as the use of "recreational" drugs became commonplace and, for some, socially obligatory, and the mysticisms of the time sought to obviate practical discipline via chemical shortcuts, slightly unstable personalities could be and were seriously unbalanced by indiscriminate self-induced hallucination. My memory of one of our telephone conversations, forty-odd years ago, is of Phil telling me about the discussions he had been having with John the Evangelist in Greek, a language he didn't know. His earnest pleasure in receiving wisdom directly from the saint and his conviction of its immense importance were disarming.

After 1969, occult revelations of this kind increasingly dominated Dick's thinking and his fiction. They have been taken as seriously as he took them, but I have seen no successful attempt—including his own *Exegesis*—to make a coherent whole of them. To some of his admirers the increasing influence of his mystic insights and visitations on his work is positive, or even transcendent, on the order of Blake's Prophetic Books. To others his insights appear too disconnected, his visions too disordered to enter successfully into his art. I myself see them as drawing him into a brilliant, manic solipsism, farther and farther away from the extraordinary sensitivity to ordinary people and their ordinary moral anguish that I value most highly in his novels.

Such sensitivity must have been a very heavy burden to bear. I wonder if the figure of Mr. Tagomi in *The Man in the High Castle* reflects that element of the author's complex personality. Mr. Tagomi is a commonplace, conventional, limited, moderately decent middle-aged businessman who is forced to perceive, and tries to face up to, unmitigated human evil. In his terror, his courage, and his humiliation, he is as far from heroes with ray guns in Outer Space as he is from antiheroes with sex problems in Upper Manhattan. Perhaps the word hero, like the word lady, has run its course. We need another word, a deeper, less showy, less performative one, for people like Mr. Tagomi.

Phil Dick's prose is transparent, plain, often rather flat. It avoids complex syntax and uses no fancy vocabulary except now and then a heavy slug of Jungian or other specialized lingo. The code of science fiction in the fifties and sixties decreed that style was for snobs. Real sf writers just wrote it like it was (never mind the fact that they were making it all up). This stance may have influenced Dick, but his apparently direct, unmusical, seemingly reportorial language also serves to camouflage a subtle, tricky art. The French got on to Dick long before anglophone critics did, and were writing thoughtful articles about him while, over here, he was still trying to live off what the pulp magazines paid. The French were crazy about Edgar Allan Poe, too; I've wondered if this was because a French ear can't hear that Poe's poetry is often delivered by sledgehammer. Maybe they can't hear how clunky Dick's prose sometimes is. But maybe that leaves them free to feel the risky, effective tension between the manner of his style and its matter.

In any case, in this one novel, Dick uses a strange, telegraphic mannerism. The novel is told from the point of view of one character at a time (limited third person narration, the mode that has dominated fiction since the time of Henry James): we get the story through what people in the story are thinking. And they frequently think without articles—"a" and "the"—and sometimes without pronouns. Since most of them live on the West Coast of North America under Japanese dominion or are Japanese by birth or ancestry, this could be a rather crude attempt at suggesting the influence of the Japanese language. But when reader finds character from German-dominated East Coast also thinking same kind of thought, minus articles and pronouns, must pause to wonder.

A similar but deeper puzzle is why these transplanted Japanese and their North American subjects all run their lives according to the dictates of the Chinese Book of Changes, the *I Ching*, which was never culturally very important in Japan. And the mystery deepens if the report is true that in writing *The Man in the High Castle* the author left every plot decision, every choice as to where the story should go next, to this ancient oracle.

The singular indifference to plausibility, the multiplicity of random possibilities, and the growing interpenetration of what appears to be reality with what appears not to be reality bring us to the brink of the Dickian abyss—the disconnect between probability and improbability, between the authentic and the imitation, between history and invention, the no-man's-lands of what happened, what might have happened, what didn't happen, what might happen, a place that is no place, where there is no solid footing and nothing can be counted on—a mental vortex with which Dick's imagination was desperately familiar, and which he could represent to the reader in a straightforward, perfectly plausible way, in an ordinary tone of voice.

He dismantles the world as we know it as calmly as other novelists describe a walk or a dinner party. He is appallingly subversive.

The meditations throughout the novel on historicity, on forgery, on what makes a real thing real and a fake thing fake, profoundly motivate the plot and the characters' thoughts and choices. These thoughts and the acts that follow from them arrive at no final insight or solution, but are left unresolved, vital, active. Mr. Tagomi is given a brief, frightening vision of the San Francisco of "our" reality, the reality in which Germany and Japan lost the war; the agent of his vision is an unpretentious bit of metal jewelry, the work of a Jewish craftsman who previously made his living by forging artifacts for Japanese collectors. The eponymous man in the high castle doesn't live in a high castle, but in a suburban house in Wyoming. He is the author of a science-fiction novel, an alternate-history novel, in which Germany and Japan lost the war. Its title, *The Grasshopper Lies Heavy*, confidently stated to be from the Bible, vaguely resembles a phrase in Ecclesiastes. Its author appears only very near the end of the novel after a long, suspenseful buildup, clearly leading to a final dramatic scene—but the drama happens almost casually, and the final scene is quietly, masterfully anticlimactic.

Full of fearful tensions, erupting more than once into unplanned murder, this novel never seeks its justification in thrills or its solution in violence. Fearfully aware of the power of human evil and familiar with various forms of at least incipient insanity, Philip Dick was tempted both by the vertigo of infinite instability and by the possibility of the existence of one solid thing: the goodwill, the goodness, in the most banal sense, of ordinary people. Whether our hard-won good intentions are all we have to trust or only pave our way to hell, his evasive artistry forbade him to say. But I think it legitimate to read his characters' inadequate, blundering attempts at doing right as the central events of this extraordinary novel.

Huxley's Bad Trip

An introduction to the Folio Society edition of
Aldous Huxley's Brave New World, *2013.*

When *Brave New World* came out in 1931 it wasn't called science fiction, because the term was scarcely used then; and it has seldom been called science fiction since, because such a description might be taken as implying that it has no literary value. Now that the critics are at last giving up such generic prejudice, we can call the book what it obviously is: a dazzling work of early science fiction.

Aldous Huxley intended his novel to be a warning about the future, but it did more: it lived into the future itself, remaining immensely influential in literature for decades after its publication. Its success in providing a model of "futuristic" writing for lesser writers may indeed make it seem, to a postmillennial reader, rather over-explanatory and predictable. What was new and daringly original to readers in 1931 has become cliché. Fiction and film have made us more or less familiar with vast laboratories, fetuses ripening in bottles, programmed children, ever-nubile women, hordes of indistinguishable clones, the vision of a materialistic paradise where nothing is lacking except imagination, spontaneity, and freedom. Occasionally we even catch glimpses on the daily TV news of the programmed, uniformed children, the smiling clones exercising in unison.

Both in reality and in fiction, the rational utopia and the rational dystopia modeled on it run much to the same pattern. And they are quite small places, with remarkably little variety. Huxley was brilliant in his paradoxical depiction of a perfect heaven which is a perfect hell; but neither heaven nor hell, conceived rationally, conceived politically, can offer much to the imagination. Only the poets, a Dante or a Milton, can find the grandeur of heaven and hell, infusing them with passion.

Does *Brave New World* ever surpass its rational, dystopic limits and hint at that greater poetic vision? I am not sure it does, not sure it doesn't.

The cautionary novel does what many people assume all science fiction does: it predicts the future. However much they may exaggerate dramatically or satirically, predictive writers extrapolate immediately from fact. And, believing that they know what's going to happen in the future, for good or for evil, they want the reader to believe it too. A great deal of science fiction, however, has nothing to do with the future, but is a playful or serious thought experiment, such as H. G. Wells's *War of the Worlds* or Ray Bradbury's *Martian Chronicles*. Thought experimenters use fiction to recombine aspects of reality into forms not meant to be taken literally, only to open the mind to possibility. They don't deal with belief at all.

This distinction enforced itself on me when I realised that Huxley himself appears to have believed quite literally in his prediction.

In 1921, early in the Soviet social experiment, Yevgeny Zamyatin's great dystopic novel *We* drew a powerful picture of an over-rationalised society under total governmental control. Far earlier than that, in 1909, E. M. Forster had written the amazing visionary story "The Machine Stops," which Huxley surely knew. *Brave New World*, then, had worthy ancestors in a specific tradition of anti-totalitarian dystopias. And by 1931, when most of Asia and much of Europe was being run by or taken over by dictatorships, it was perfectly realistic to see totalitarian government as the most immediate and appalling threat to any kind of freedom.

But in 1949, Huxley was still speaking of his novel not only as a cautionary tale, but as describing nascent reality. He wrote to George Orwell when *Nineteen Eighty-Four* was published, generously praising it as "fine and profoundly important," but adding, in defense of his own vision against Orwell's subtler yet more brutal dystopia, "Within the next generation I believe that the world's leaders will discover that infant conditioning and narco-hypnosis are more efficient, as instruments of government, than clubs and prisons, and that the lust for power can be just as completely satisfied by suggesting people into loving their servitude as by flogging them and kicking them into obedience."

Evidently he still believed that "hypnopaedia," the essential technique of the mental programming of the citizens of the World State, was a proven, effective method, only waiting to be used. Psychological theories of the time, such as B. F. Skinner's "operant conditioning," could be taken to support this belief, and most of the experiments disproving the effectiveness of "sleep-learning" were yet to come. On the other hand, no experiment had ever been accepted as proving it. Hypnopaedia was to Huxley not so much a fictional invention or scientific hypothesis as an article of faith.

Why did he invest so much in a shaky theory and call it science? What was his fundamental attitude to science?

His grandfather, Thomas Henry Huxley, "Darwin's bulldog," and his brothers Andrew and Julian were all biologists of extraordinary distinction and humanity. Thomas Henry Huxley invented the word "agnostic" to name, and so create, an open space for the spirit equivalent to the open space for the mind offered by science. Ideally, the scientist, while always seeking to know and to know more, forgoes any claim to final knowledge. A sound hypothesis supported and modified by endless testing (such as Harvey's theory of the circulation of the blood, or Darwin's theory of evolution) is as far as science goes towards certainty. Scientists don't deal in belief.

Aldous Huxley of course knew this. He also knew that few scientists attain the ideal openness of mind of agnosticism, and that many of them talk as if they alone know anything worth knowing. Here in the real world the smug conviction of incontestable rightness displayed by the technicians of the World State is at least as common in laboratories as it is in seminaries.

Huxley's novels were mostly cynical, but the hideous scientism of his dystopia reveals something fiercer than cynicism. To some temperaments the open mind, the acceptance of final uncertainty, is not only insufficient but frightening and hateful. He knew enough science to make the inventions of his novel plausible, but whatever made him dislike and distrust it, the role he gives scientific technology in his novel is domineeering and sinister. It appears that, seeing science as heartless, emotionless rationalism, he thought that the pursuit of science could never attain true meaning or do true good, but was inevitably at the service of evil. The scion of a great humanistic scientific tradition portrayed science as the enemy of humanity.

And the young author of cold, scathing satires of British intellectual and social mores became in middle age a member of the mystical Vedanta Society of Los Angeles and a guru of the drug movement that was gathering strength when he died in 1963, his suffering eased by a hundred-milligram dose of LSD.

California is what you make of it, and what it makes of you. *Brave New World* was written in the Old World, a long time before the Summer of Love. Yet rereading it now, I was impressed by the importance in it of soma, the wonder drug on which everybody in the World State, and the World State itself, is dependent. It's partly a plot gimmick, to be sure, but surely also significant of the author's preoccupations. Soma enhances all pleasures, sex above all, of course. It never causes bad trips, but induces bliss, invariably—even eternally, if you keep taking it. If it has any adverse effects on health they aren't mentioned. Whether it's addictive is a moot point. If you had unlimited access to a drug that would give you a perfect high for hours or days at a time, at any time, without doing you any bodily harm, and with the enthusiastic approval of your entire society, would you be likely to abstain from it?

You're not allowed to. You must consume your daily dose of soma because it's what holds everything together in happy inertia. Consumption is the basis of the World State, the state of delusion.

And in this, Huxley's science fiction was undeniably and radically visionary, leaping decades beyond the society of his day into the post-millennial world of obligatory consumerism and instant gratification.

Here, too, he introduces an element of the book that greatly augments its emotional, vital power. Into the delusional world where everybody is made and kept perfectly, vapidly happy, he brings a character who isn't.

Bernard Marx, dwarfed, meanspirited, and frustrated, at first seems to be this misfit or rebel, but turns out to be only the lead-up to him. The stranger to bliss, the tragic outsider, is John. He is called the Savage, but might more accurately be called the Puritan. Despite the miseries of his childhood among the "primitives" outside the World State, John has seen enough actual love and happiness to be sure that a chemical can deliver only imitations of them, that there are no shortcuts to the experience of the real. Trapped in the hell he thought would be heaven, he tries to opt out of delusion, to regain reality, to abstain from the drug that maintains the World State.

The word soma is Greek for "body." Today we see it mostly in the word psychosomatic, but Huxley could assume that a great many of his readers had enough classical education to recognise it directly.

A Puritan is one who abjures the body and the pleasures of the body to save his soul. To what extent is *Brave New World* a study of body-hating, world-renouncing, self-castigating mysticism, concealed within a novel about politics and power?

The Savage has a long conversation, the most conventionally utopic passage of the novel, with the local World Controller, whose splendidly villainous name is Mustapha Mond. It's hard not to see the Controller as a conscious competitor with the Grand Inquisitor of Dostoyevsky's *Brothers Karamazov*. "There used to be something called God," he begins airily, "before the Nine Years' War." The Savage knows a good deal about God, having grown up in a violent stew of Catholicism and Native religions, and can hold up his end of the conversation. In their discussion of the nature of God, he asks, "How does he manifest himself now?" and Mustapha Mond replies, "Well, he manifests himself as an absence." They go on to argue about human spiritual need, John insisting that we need God to guarantee the value of virtue and self-denial, the Controller brushing aside such notions as "symptoms of political inefficiency." "You can't have a lasting civilization without plenty of pleasant vices," he says, and, triumphantly, "You can carry at least half your morality about in a bottle. Christianity without tears—that's what soma is."

John's final refutation of a tearless existence, his claim to have God, poetry, danger, freedom, goodness, and sin, his declaration of his right to be unhappy, are the high point of the novel; but a high point that can only be followed by a fall. The poor Savage will indeed find his unhappiness.

And thus he is the only character in the novel likely to remain in the reader's mind as a person rather than an allegorical figure or intellectual construct. When I came to reread the book, I had forgotten Mustapha Mond and Bernard Marx and the pneumatic Lenina. I was glad to rediscover them. But I had remembered the Savage for fifty years.

Huxley's later experiments with drug-taking seem almost a search for real-life soma, religion in a bottle. Did he think that mescaline and LSD and the other psychedelic drugs he consumed and endorsed falsified his perceptions and endangered his soul, or that they were a high road to enlightenment, shortcuts to a greater truth? Perhaps he thought both. The Savage and the Controller were, after all, both creations of his own mind, where their conflict might, perhaps must, continue unresolved.

Written with the aplomb of his class and culture, yet with a searing urgency; concealing obscure or unexamined motivations behind a fireworks of invention; showing pleasure as inevitably disgusting and degrading and freedom as mindless license, yet offering no escape from the sordid world where these are the only options, Brave New World is a troubled, troubling book, a masterpiece of the Age of Anxiety, a vivid record of the anguish of the twentieth century. It may also be a valid and very early warning of the risk of keeping civilisation on the course Aldous Huxley saw it beginning to follow more than eighty years ago.

Stanislaw Lem: *Solaris*

An introduction written in 2002 for a German-language edition of Solaris *from Heyne Verlag in Munich, in which it appeared in translation.*

First published in 1961, *Solaris* appeared in an English translation in 1970. It was a revelation to us in America, not only of a brilliant book, but of a science-fiction writer who we now learned was immensely popular in his native land and well known throughout Europe, but of whom most of us knew nothing. Stanislaw Lem? We knew the acronym LEM, the Lunar Excursion Module—a wonderfully apt name for a writer of science fiction. And *Solaris* was clearly the work of a master of his art.

Several other Lem novels were soon translated into English, among them the marvelous *Eden*, and were well received critically. In 1973, Lem was made an honorary member of the Science Fiction Writers of America, but this was in the clammy depths of the Cold War, and many members of the association disapproved strongly of admitting a citizen of a Communist nation. Apparently it made no difference to them that Lem was a Pole, not a Russian, and that his books could be read as containing a cogent and subversive critique of Stalinist aims. The whole thing became a tiny *cause célèbre*. A magazine poll of science-fiction authors on the question of the Vietnam war showed them split half and half into hawks and doves, and the division over Lem followed much the same lines. There was great fulmination on both sides, to which I contributed. Finally the officers of the SFWA, citing a technicality, withdrew Lem's honorary membership. Having assumed a lofty moral stance, I was trapped in it and felt I must refuse the Nebula Award voted me by the members of the SFWA for a story which was—all too ironically—about intellectual and political oppression. That the award therefore went to the runner-up, Isaac Asimov, a vociferous Cold Warrior, perfected the irony to an almost Lemian degree.

For many Americans, Tarkovsky's film *Solaris*, released in 1972, unfortunately eclipsed the book itself. It is a thoughtful and beautiful film, but I do not think it equals the intellectual breadth and moral complexity of the novel. And indeed, though Lem enjoys giving us dramatic descriptions of the strange shapes and constructs created by the planetary ocean of Solaris, suggesting the unearthly galleries of Piranesi and the Borgesian perspectives of Escher, the book resists filmic interpretation, since in essence it is not conceived visually or even sensually. It is above all a work of the mind, about the work of the mind.

Rereading the novel, I saw again how immediately one perceives it as a genuinely serious work of science fiction in the tradition of the older masters of the form. Lem resembles Jules Verne in the audacity of his invention and in a certain stateliness or aloofness of style even when narrating in the first person. He is like H. G. Wells in his alertness to where the cutting edge of science lies at the moment, and to the social implications of his fable. Like both Verne and Wells, he is a shamelessly good storyteller, using all the tricks of withholding and revealing information to keep the reader in suspense. His ambition to produce a literally universal parable is reminiscent of Olaf Stapledon.

In his perceptive afterword to the 1970 American edition of *Solaris*, Darko Suvin—one of the very few critics writing in English who were capable of appreciating Lem at the time—makes perhaps the most revealing literary parallel, calling the novel a variation on the eighteenth-century *conte philosophique*. The term is precisely descriptive and offers a useful approach to the book.

Yet the clear, amused gaze of a Voltaire is not how Lem sees his universe. His narrative promptly establishes an atmosphere of confusion, mystery, tension, suspense. The opening chapter, the arrival on the planet Solaris, is full of shocks, hints, glimpses, apparent hallucinations, unexplained events, enigmatic behaviors. The gradual, eventual development of the implications of these riddles throughout the book will offer the reader, just as a detective novel does, the profound and simple satisfaction of understanding, of solving the puzzle. But all such solutions remain, as it were, held *in* solution: for the explanations serve only to offer hints and glimpses of further mysteries on a deeper plane. The novel is an exhibition of the inability of human understanding to achieve a final stage of knowledge; perhaps it implies also that human understanding at best can understand itself, but nothing outside itself.

An early adept of cybernetics and information theory, Lem created in *Solaris* an extremely sophisticated narrative structure for exemplifying the frustration of the desire to understand. Dense, vivid, explicit, packed with implications, the words of his story lead us through tumultuous, suggestive, successive images to theory after theory, question after question, only to arrive at last at a word-constructed but wordless silence.

One element of this pursuit will delight anyone who has had to read much of what is called "academic research." To such a reader the hitherto unknown field of Solaristics will be all too familiar. Lem's sarcastic wit is at its sharpest as he goes through the library of Solaristics: the claims of the experts, the quarrels of the scholars, explanations that replace explanations ad infinitum, theories that jostle one another into oblivion—he has it all in a few brilliant pages.

Satire in the mode of Jonathan Swift, philosophical fiction in the mode of Voltaire, and science fiction in its parable mode are all likely to offer us more light than warmth. Seeking general truths about humanity, they must forgo the irreducible recalcitrance of human individualities from which other fictions draw their vitality. These narrative modes also tend to gender themselves strongly as male. They may denigrate women; they may include them as stereotypes, perceived as existing only in relation to the male characters; they may omit them altogether. All this was nothing unusual in literature (with the exception of the novel) in the eighteenth century and all the centuries before it. And all too often, by creating a "future" for only half of humanity, science fiction narrowed the intellectual and moral potential of the genre till it could be dismissed as a set of naïve adventure stories for boys.

The scientists and scholars of Solaristics in the library seem all to have been men; the present crew of scientists stationed on Solaris consists of men; so, evidently, did all previous crews. In a serious fiction written in the late twentieth century, to establish an intellectual realm that includes no women at all is to imply a statement by omission, intentional or not. The reader may legitimately wonder if the intellectual realm is somehow established *by* the exclusion of women. Will it collapse if women are admitted? Is that the implication?

There is nothing naïve about Lem. *Solaris* provides a unique and peculiarly interesting example of the womanless universe. For there is a woman at the center of the book. She is absolutely a key figure, and though she is essentially passive, her action proves decisive. Yet she does not exist.

Not only was she the wife of the protagonist, Kelvin, but she is far more indissolubly part of him, more absolutely his, than a wife can be, even a dead wife. A creation of the enigmatic Solaris-ocean, Rheya is a figment, a simulacrum, constituted from Kelvin's memories. She is capable of thought and choice, up to a point, yet her seeming existence is altogether dependent on his existence: and she is literally, appallingly, unable to exist apart from him. What kind of love is it, then, that grows in him for her? We learn that he allowed her to kill herself once in real life; now, if she tries to kill herself again, and again . . . ? What is the function of these powerful, moving scenes, this pattern, in the narrative? What has this relationship (or is it an autism?) to do with Solaristics, or with the quest for final meaning? Has Rheya's sacrifice any necessary connection to the ultimate glimpse of fragile, tentative redemption Kelvin attains at the end of the book, or can he attain it only once the disruptive feminine element is out of the way and the universe can be reduced once more to the play of pure, "genderless"—that is, masculine—mind?

To some readers, this may be the most fascinating problem of the book, even more fascinating than the paradoxical questions it poses openly, teasing us with its dense and marvelous imagery, goading us to distrust all information, leading us through hallucination to vision which may itself be delusion. To ask questions which must be asked yet cannot be answered, to create images which can be neither forgotten nor explained—this is the privilege of the most courageous artists.

George MacDonald:
The Princess and the Goblin

An introduction written for the Puffin Classics edition of 2011.

George MacDonald, born in 1824, grew up in a world where people did as everybody had always done—traveled on foot or on horseback, warmed the house with fire and lighted it with candles, wrote with goosefeather pens. They knew their neighbors, but nobody else; towns fifty miles apart might be utterly strange to each other. Compared to ours, that world seemed timeless, changeless, and yet, far more than ours, it was filled with mystery, danger, dark places, the unknown.

It's still the world of our folk and fairy tales and most of our fantasy stories. Our imagination is still at home there. Many of us are willing to erase all the automobiles and airplanes and electricity and electronics, escape from the machines we made that now control us, and let a story take us straight into the timeless green kingdoms of legend and fantasy.

We learn about those kingdoms early. Our guides are the authors who began writing stories for children just about the time the timeless green world began to vanish, to become the world of the past—outside time—the country of "There was once a little princess . . ."

George MacDonald was one of the first of those authors. *The Princess and the Goblin* is an old book now, but it was written for young readers. The heroine is eight and the hero twelve, and the language is mostly quite plain and straightforward. But MacDonald also uses words like "excogitation." Some of his sentences are complicated. Some of the meanings of his sentences are very complicated. He wrote for children, not down to them. He didn't confuse being young with being simpleminded. I think he expected that a reader could either figure out "excogitation" or look it up in the dictionary, and that the deeper meanings that underlie his exciting story would gradually come clear to any thoughtful child.

He is often stern; he can be tender, but he's never soft. And his green kingdom isn't very green: it's more like the north of Scotland where he grew up, a great, stony, stormy landscape of high hills and poor farms, a lonesome, lofty land, beautiful in the play of cloud and mist and rainbows. A perfect place for magic shining in the air and goblins under the ground.

MacDonald is also stern and clear about what nobility is. It has nothing to do with money or social status. A princess is a girl who behaves nobly: a girl who behaves nobly is a princess. Curdy the miner, being brave and kind, and behaving (or anyhow trying to behave) nobly and wisely, is a prince. The king is king because he's a good man. No other definition is allowed. This is radically moral democracy. It's very different from the lazy-minded stories that call some characters good and others bad although they all behave exactly the same way, only the Goods win the battles and the Bads lose them, besides being ugly. MacDonald's goblins are ugly only because they behave badly. Treated unjustly, instead of standing up for their rights they went underground to sulk revengefully down in the dark, and so they got all twisted, with weird feet and no toes . . .

This is a great story, and I love it all, but I love the goblins best.

The Wild Winds
of Possibility:
Vonda McIntyre's
Dreamsnake

A piece e-published on Book View Café, June 2011.

Dreamsnake is in some ways a strange book, unlike any other in science fiction, which may explain the even stranger fact that it's not currently in print.

When people ask me what sf books influenced me or what are my favorites, I always mention *Dreamsnake*. Invariably I get a warm, immediate response—Oh yes!—and people tell me how much the book meant to them when they first read it and ever since. But these days, many younger readers don't know it exists.

The short story the book was based on won the 1973 Nebula; the book was an immediate success; it became and still is beloved. Its moral urgency and rousing adventure story are not at all dated. It should have gone from one paperback reprint to another.

Why didn't it?

I have some theories.

Theory #1: Ophidiophobia. The phobia is common and extends to pictures, even the mention, of snakes; and the book features them even in the title. A heroine who lets snakes *crawl* on her, and she's *named* Snake? Oh, icky . . .

Theory #2: Sex. It's an adult book. Snake, though, is barely more than a kid, setting out on her first trial of prowess, so that young women can and do identify with her, happily or longingly, as they do with

Ayla in Jean Auel's Earth's Children books, though Snake's taste in men is far better than Ayla's. But could the book be approved in schools? The sexual mores are as various as the societies, including some very unorthodox customs, and Snake's sexual behavior is both highly ethical and quite uninhibited. She can afford to be fearless because her people know how to control their fertility through biofeedback, how to prevent insemination through a simple, learned technique. But alas we don't. Given the relentless fundamentalist vendettas against "witchcraft" and "pornography" (read *imaginative literature* and *sexual realism*) in the schools, few teachers in the 1980s could invite the firestorm that might be started by a right-wing parent who got a hint of how young Snake was carrying on. Sexless hard sf or Heinleinian fantasies of girlish docility were much safer. I think this killed the book's chance of being read widely as a text in junior high or high school, and even now may prevent its being marketed to the YA audience.

Theory #3. The hypothesis of gendered reprinting. It appears that as a general rule books written by men get reprinted more frequently and over more years than books written by women. If this is so, Heinlein has always been given a handicap over McIntyre and will always have one.

On the other hand, good writing tends to outlive mediocre writing, real moral questioning to outlast rant and wishful thinking. *Dreamsnake* is written in a clear, quick-moving prose, with brief, lyrically intense landscape passages that take the reader straight into its half-familiar, half-strange desert world, and fine descriptions of the characters' emotional states and moods and changes. And its generosity to those characters is quite unusual, particularly in science fiction with its tendency to competitive elitism.

Take the birth-control-via-biofeedback idea—certainly one of the great technological-imaginative inventions, and appreciated as such by many of McIntyre's readers, although male critics have tended to ignore it because it's not hard tech and is subversive of gender dominance. McIntyre doesn't make it a subject of celebration, excitement, or question; it's taken for granted, it's how things are. Meeting a young man whose education has been so cruelly mismanaged that he doesn't know how to control his fertility, Snake is appalled, but sympathetic. She knows how bitterly humiliated he is by what he can see only as a personal failure, like impotence, but worse, because for him to have a heterosexual relation might involve damage to the *other* person.

They do manage to solve his problem.

Yes, there is some wishful thinking in McIntyre's book, but it is so thoroughly, thoughtfully worked out in terms of social and personal behavior that its demonstration of a permanent streak of kindness in human nature is convincing—and as far from sentimentality as it is from cynicism.

The writer Moe Bowstern gave me a slogan I cherish: "Subversion Through Friendliness." It looks silly till you think about it. It bears considerable thinking about. Subversion through terror, shock, pain is easy—instant gratification, as it were. Subversion through friendliness is paradoxical, slow-acting, and durable. And sneaky. A moral revolutionary, rewriting rules the rest of us were still following, McIntyre subverted us so skillfully and with such lack of self-promoting hoo-ha that we scarcely noticed. And thus she has seldom if ever received the feminist honors she is due, the credit owed her by writers to whom she showed the way.

What I mean by sneaky: Take the character called Merideth. When I first read *Dreamsnake* I thought the odd spelling of the name Meredith was significant and tried so hard to figure out why this enigmatic, powerful person was called "merry death" that I totally missed what's really odd about Merideth. Three-cornered marriages being usual in this society, Merideth is married to a man and a woman—sure, fine—but we don't know whether as husband or as wife. We don't know Merideth's gender. We never do.

And I never noticed it till, in conversation about the book, I realised that I'd seen Merideth as a man—only because I knew Meredith as a Welsh male name. There is no other evidence one way or the other, and McIntyre avoids the gender pronoun unerringly, with easy grace.

June Arnold's *The Cook and the Carpenter* came out in 1973 to much acclaim by feminists and was read mostly by feminists. *Dreamsnake* was published five years later as science fiction and read by everybody who read science fiction. How many of them even noticed that the gender of a character had been left up to them to decide, or refuse to decide? I still remember the shock of realising that I'd been well and truly subverted. All the stuff we were saying about gender as social construct, as expectation, was revealed to me as built solidly into my own mind. And by that revelation my mind was opened.

I wish this beautiful, powerful, and highly entertaining book were back in print for the generation of sf readers who missed it, and all the young readers ready to have their mind blown open by the wild winds of possibility. *Dreamsnake* is a classic, and should be cherished as such.

Getting It Right:
Charles L. McNichols's
Crazy Weather

An introduction to the Pharos Edition of 2013.

I don't know a novel like Charles L. McNichols' *Crazy Weather*. I don't think there could be one. It's a book written out of a unique knowledge and life experience in a place way off the beaten track.

Its singularity is both its virtue and its bane. The book that's unlike any other has no ready-made niche in the shelves of the store, the library, or the mind of the literary critic. But such a book often has a unique place in the hearts of readers fortunate enough to find it.

An author writing about a group of people he doesn't belong to runs two risks. One is of misunderstanding, misrepresentation—getting it wrong. The other is of exploiting, expropriation—*doing* wrong. Writers of a dominant group who assume the right to speak for members of a less powerful one take these risks in complacent ignorance of their existence. Such ignorance, however good the intentions, dooms the result.

Columbus brought to the New World the White man's conviction of being by nature and God's will controller, owner, and rightful exploiter of everything and everyone else. The Indians have been up against that enormous sense of entitlement ever since.

To speak for those who have been silenced is one thing; to co-opt their voice or drown it out with yours is another. This wrong was done for so long that maybe no amount of honest goodwill and good work can ever entirely clear the White novelist (or memoirist, or anthropologist)

143

writing about Indians of the suspicion of expropriation. Guilt is there in the whole history of Indian-White relations, unavoidable.

Guilt is useless unless by acknowledging it you can move away from it to a better place. Over the last century, thanks principally to tireless consciousness-raising by Indian writers and activists, we've been slowly heading towards that better place. White writers gradually realised that enthusiastic identification can be a gross transgression, that idealization can be as much an insult as demonization. By now, few undertake naïvely to write fiction from "the Indian point of view."

Natachee Scott Momaday's 1994 introduction to *Crazy Weather* is an act of the greatest and most gracious generosity, not only in her affectionate presentation of McNichols's book, but in her approving mention of older fiction by White authors about Southwestern Indians. I discovered some fine novels I hadn't known of by looking up those she mentions. I'd like to take the liberty of adding to her list the children's book *Waterless Mountain*, by Laura Adams Armer, with its tender picture of a young soul at home and at peace in the world of the Navajo.

But this book, *Crazy Weather*, is about a soul not at home and not at peace: South Boy, who on the verge of manhood is living in and between two worlds, without a clear way to go in either.

I haven't been able to find out much about the author of *Crazy Weather*. He flew for the navy in the First World War, was a journalist, wrote for the movies, but published only the one novel. He knew a great deal about the Mojave Indians and all their neighbors in that wild corner of the Southwest, but he was not Indian.

And his young hero isn't either. South Boy hasn't really found out yet who and what he is, and Momaday's introduction speaks of him as a "mixed-blood," but his parents are both White. In the novel we hear the voices of many kinds of people, Indians, Mexicans, Whites, we hear what they say and sing and shout and tell us, but we only know what one person thinks. Everything and everyone is seen through South Boy's eyes.

He was nursed by an Indian foster mother, and as his Mojave friend Havek says, "Milk becomes flesh and blood. In so much, then, you are a

Proper Person. So as you dream, thus you are." Living on a remote cattle ranch deep in Mojave country, South Boy has grown up with and among Indians, has learned most of what he knows from Indians, and does a very large part of his thinking like an Indian. But he isn't an Indian. He isn't of mixed blood but of mixed culture, mind, heart. He has two souls. And at the age of fifteen, he sees that he's going to have to choose one and leave the other, forever.

Maybe coming of age is always a matter both of finding your own people and of going into exile.

My father, an anthropologist, liked and admired *Crazy Weather*. He said something I don't remember his saying about any other novel about Indians: "I think McNichols got it right." My father meant the understanding of Mojave life and thought and religion that comes to us through the words and behavior of the characters. Having lived some time in Mojave country and worked with people there recording the kind of dream-journey-myths that are retold in the novel, he had strong affection and respect for both the tellers and the tales.

His praise of the book spurred me to read it, a year or two after it first came out in 1944. I was fifteen or so. I liked it a lot, and understood parts of it. This being the case with most books I read at that age, it's of no significance except to say that I never forgot the book, and, rereading it some seventy years later, liked it even better, and understood more of it.

There's a lot to understand. This is not a simplistic pitting of Native wisdom against White blindness, or wise young innocence against stupid adult villainy. The author's view of all the characters is ironic, compassionate, and complicated. And while the author is unfolding the coming-of-age story through a rapid and exciting series of events and characters, he's also guiding us through a way of life and thought most of us know nothing of, profoundly different from any White cultural tradition, yet just as profoundly and immediately human.

I can't say how much I admire the offhanded skill, the ease, with which McNichols takes us deep into a complex society and the complex minds and hearts of its people. His retelling of Mojave myth is light-handed, accurate, sympathetic, and irreverent. He is never disrespectful of Mojave ways, yet is as unsentimental as a coyote. And his humor is dry and understated, like an Indian's. That's probably one reason a good deal of the book was over my head in 1945.

These days, *Crazy Weather* might have been published as a "young adult" novel, a marketing category that tacitly excludes older adults, assuming that stories about teenagers are for teenagers. Like *Huckleberry Finn* and *Romeo and Juliet?* . . . After all, every reader older than fifteen has been fifteen. We can be grateful to an author like McNichols who can bring to us the brilliant intensity of perception and the muddle-headed confusion, the knowledge of dawning power with no idea how to use it, the fearlessness and vulnerability, the morbid lows and glorious highs and wrenching passions that a fifteen-year-old, spendthrift of life, can run through in a few days or hours.

South Boy's dramatic rite of passage takes place in four days of terrible desert heat building to apocalyptic thunderstorm—a dangerous, beautiful, crazy journey in crazy weather.

The world of the story is a world coming, in some ways, to an end. To the timeless landscape and long-kept customs of the Southwest, the Christian twentieth century is bringing rapid, cataclysmic change. South Boy and his friend Havek set off happily to do brave deeds in a war with the Piute, which turns out to be a disorganized hunt for one miserable psychopath. The glory days are over. "Thus we come to imitate coyotes when the days of our greatness are ended," groans the great old warrior Yellow Road. "World's end! World's end!" shouts the Mormonhater, who may have been a White man once. Trapped in hurricane-force rain and wind on a crumbling cliff trail, Mojave boys sing aloud, "throwing away their dreams," and South Boy tries to fight his own fear of death with their belief—but his mother's hellfire teachings of damnation rise up and overwhelm him:

> He had sinned—and long hair, the sign and symbol of the
> heathen world, was whipping his face. Over all the other

noise he heard his own voice cry, "O God, I'll cut my hair—
I'll cut my hair!" And the wind died, then, as though it had
never been.

The clash of superstition with superstition at the moment of death,
the collision of shame with glory, the great deed which is a ridiculous
mistake, the mixed-up friendship and enmity of White and Indian or
Indian and Indian, the sublime inextricably involved with the utterly
absurd—the whole story consists in a marvelous interweaving of such
stark contrasts. It's as dramatic as a Shakespeare tragedy, and as fiercely
unromantic as the *Iliad*.

And its ending is as fortuitous yet inevitable as everything else that
happens. During the strange, wild funeral for the old warrior, during the
storm and in the aftermath of the storm, South Boy begins to see what
he has to do. Doing it will take him where he has to go and make him
what he has to be. It is a revelation, a way out of his confusion, a road to
manhood. But to choose such a way into the future means to abandon all
other ways. As he's about to part with Havek, he thinks:

> Last year, at the Great Cry—the annual celebration for the
> year's distinguished dead—they had sat together with the
> other boys, holding the feathered wands for the young-
> men-who-run. Next summer, when the celebration would
> be for the great Yellow Road, with singing and running and
> "preaching" and a drama of great deeds, Havek would be
> a young-man-who-runs. South Boy would be sitting on his
> horse among the white men, just watching.

The last pages of the story move quickly to a satisfactory conclusion, a
happy ending. South Boy has made his choice, found his people. It was
quite a while after finishing the book that I thought suddenly, But what
is his name among his people?

We never know it.

———

Natachee Scott Momaday tells us to read *Crazy Weather* slowly, savoring it, and she's right—but it may be a hard thing to do the first time you read it. Once the two boys ride off into the fantastic landscape of myth and adventure, dream and danger, things happen fast, and the suspense grows fast. You have to ride and run with them into the storm and through it.

Then after a while, maybe, come back and read it again. Now you can do as the Grandmother says: take it slow. Realise the richness, think about the strangeness, and wonder how it is that so many mistakes, misunderstandings, follies, and griefs can add up to a story of such force and beauty.

On Pasternak's *Doctor Zhivago*

First written for the National Public Radio segment
You Must Read This, May 2008.

Fifty years ago this September, Boris Pasternak's novel *Doctor Zhivago* came out here in English. He couldn't publish it in his own country.

It was my birthday present that October—I was twenty-eight. It bowled me over. The Cold War muddied our thinking in the fifties, and I didn't really understand the complex political stance of the book—but it's a book you understand emotionally: it is fiercely intelligent, but it must be understood with the heart.

Pasternak was a mystical realist, equipped to tell us about a strange time in human history—what living through the great Revolution of 1917 was like, day by day, for ordinary Russians: a huge chaos of ideas and ideals, everything changed, the familiar in ruins, a new order brutally established and suddenly knocked apart again, endless factional war and destruction—and the spiritual resilience of common people somehow getting through it, day by day.

What a joy to come back to the great passages, like Yury Zhivago's long train trip with his wife and child, crammed with other refugees in a freight car, from Moscow to the Urals. The book's full of unforgettable images, like the long, empty trains standing on the tracks in the snow in Siberia, black, dead; and the quiet, terrifying sentences that tell of ripe grainfields heaving and rustling, not with wind, but with mice—the villagers are dead, the grain uncut, mice breeding in it by millions—as Yury makes his way on foot, alone, all the way back from the Urals to Moscow.

It's all journeys, partings, and meetings—dozens of characters disappear and reappear, they bond together in passionate love but can't hold on to each other, passionate hatred unites them as closely as love, they meet and part and weep, meet again and don't know it. It's not disorder, but a wild complexity of interconnection, like the tracks in a great train station—all these crisscrossing destinies, all these souls full of earnest intention, all of them helpless as dust blown on the great wind of the Revolution.

I realise now how much I learned about how to write a novel from Pasternak: how you can leap across miles and years so long as you land in the right place; how accuracy of detail embodies emotion; how by leaving more out you can get more in . . .

It's a huge book. Five hundred pages isn't long to contain all Russia, forty years of history, a man's life and dreams. But it is vast, like a human soul. It holds immensities of pain, betrayal, and love. I love it, this maybe last of the great Russian novels, this beautiful, noble testimony from a terrible century.

Examples of Dignity: Thoughts on the Work of José Saramago

A composite of "Examples of Dignity" (Guardian, 2008) and my introduction to the electronic edition of Saramago's novels (Houghton Mifflin Harcourt, 2010), along with reviews of Seeing *(Guardian, March 2006), and* The Elephant's Journey *(Guardian, July 2010).*

My friend the poet Naomi Replansky wrote me that she was reading a great novel, *Blindness*, by José Saramago. I knew he had been awarded the 1998 Nobel Prize, but it was Naomi's judgment that moved me to trot out and buy a copy.

I was a bit put off by the first page when I saw the eccentric punctuation. Saramago likes run-on sentences, eschews quotation marks, and is loath to paragraph. Punctuation seems to me one of the few human inventions without bad side-effects, and I am so fond of all the little dots and curls that I once taught a whole writing course devoted to them. So a Saramago page, one dense thicket from top to bottom with only commas to indicate the path, was hard going for me, and I was inclined to resent it.

And soon, as I pushed on through the thicket, I began to get scared. The story was, to put it mildly, a nightmare. Tough-minded thrillers I'd read were custard sauce to this. The idea of everybody in a city suddenly going blind, not all at once but at random over several days, is fairly horrible in itself; Saramago's even, quiet narrative tone brings the horror home as he describes it through the eyes (all too literally) of one ordinary person after another. Despite or because of governmental efforts at control, the city soon begins to break down—cars driven by blind drivers, fires in homes, panicky soldiers faced with panicky citizens.

A disused mental hospital where the early blind are locked away very soon becomes a hellish concentration of the worst that terror and weakness can bring out in people—bullying, enslavement, gratuitous cruelty, rape. . . . At this point I stopped reading the book. I couldn't handle it.

To read on, to be willing to read about terrible cruelty, I had to trust the author unquestioningly, the way one trusts Primo Levi. I had to know that Saramago was not merely putting on a horror show, exploiting his power over his readers. I was quite ready to admit the power, his Dostoyevskian gift for communicating suffering, but I needed to trust him enough to let him tell me this fearful story in the confidence that he'd make it worth enduring. The only way to find out if he deserved such trust was to read his other books. So I did.

That is, I read all of them I could get in English. Saramago writes in Portuguese, his native language. Exploring his novels, I found out a little about the man himself; he tells us as much as he feels we need to know in his fine, honest, eloquent, reticent Nobel lecture. Born in 1922 to a peasant family, he went barefoot till he was fourteen. His maternal grandparents kept six pigs, their livelihood; on cold nights they brought the weaker piglets into their bed. Poverty forced him out of college-track schooling into trade school, and he worked some years as a mechanic before he could begin to follow his literary vocation. He writes in the Nobel lecture of "[c]ommon people I knew, deceived by a Church both accomplice and beneficiary of the power of the State and of the landlords, people permanently watched by the police, people so many times innocent victims of the arbitrariness of a false justice. . . . I haven't lost, not yet at least, the hope of meriting a little more the greatness of those examples of dignity proposed to me in the vast immensity of the plains of Alentejo."

He became, and is, a communist. When he was forty-four he published his first book of poetry; he wrote for various papers and published editorials and essays, and also worked for years as a translator, putting writers as various as Colette and Tolstoy into Portuguese. In the 1980s, in his sixties, he was able to turn his full energy to writing novels; the first of these, *Baltasar and Blimunda*, was an international success, and he hasn't had to look back since then. He has paid a price among some critics for his outspoken criticism of Israel's U.S.-backed policies, though critics often seem to ignore his politics, shrugging off the notion that anybody now could seriously hold to socialist principles. Indeed it takes a man of intransigent character to do so. But he is not really a political novelist, and anything but preachy. His themes are complex, both earthy and elusive.

My course of reading—*The Late Ricardo Reyes* (also published as *The Year of the Death of Ricardo Reis*), *The Stone Raft*, *The Cave*, and several other books (of which more later)—was entirely successful. I returned to *Blindness* and began it again from the beginning, by now used to the thickets and confident that wherever Saramago took me, however hard the going, it would be worth it.

Others may not find the book as frightening as I did. Too many novelists, like too many filmmakers, cram their stories with ruthless violence gloatingly described, seeking to violate a shock threshold that grows ever higher, using cruelty to sell their books, to "thrill" readers who have been trained to think that nothing is interesting but "action," or to keep their own demons at bay by loosing them on other people. And too many realists, following the principle that if it isn't ugly it can't be true, are as alert as fire wardens to make sure any glimpse of decency or gleam of hope is promptly extinguished. Siding more with Keats on this point, I generally avoid such fictions—hence both my liking for nonrealist writers and my initial reluctance to trust Saramago's painfully ugly story. Those inured to fictional brutality and blood-spattered film screens will lack my squeamishness about horrors they take for granted. That is a pity, because they will not have the experience I had in finally reading *Blindness* straight through, which was of a genuinely miraculous rising up out of awful darkness into a clear, truthful light.

I say miraculous not intending to suggest any supernatural intervention; that's scarcely Saramago's line. He is generally polite about God, and his novel about Jesus is affectionate towards Jesus, though he judges Jehovah as a hanging judge should be judged. He looks for no help from Heaven. In the dark story of *Blindness*, the thin glimmer of light is that of a solitary human soul trying to do the right thing. She can do right, protect her husband, only by doing wrong, by lying. She pretends to be blind like everybody else, but she is not, so she must witness unbearable horrors. Behind her dilemma stands the old, cynical adage "In the country of the blind the one-eyed man is king." H. G. Wells wrote one of his best and strangest tales to disprove it. Saramago develops the disproof yet further, and makes of it as powerful a moral novel as has been written in the past fifty years. To me it is almost unbearably moving, and the truest parable of the twentieth century. It completely changed my idea of what literature, at this strange time of paralysis in crisis, can be and do.

Saramago died in the summer of 2010, at eighty-seven. That fall, Houghton Mifflin Harcourt published an electronic edition of his novels, and it's fitting that they should have such an edition, a virtual presence, for it was Saramago who in one of his blog posts first spoke of virtual literature—a fiction that "seems to have detached itself from reality in order better to reveal its invisible mysteries." He credits Jorge Luis Borges with the invention of this genre, but he himself brought to it the one quality of greatness that Borges's fictions lack: a passionate and compassionate interest in ordinary people and everyday human life.

We probably don't really need any more categories, but virtual literature might be a useful one, differing from science fiction and speculative fiction with their extrapolative bent, fantasy with its wholly imagined realities, satire with its meliorative indignation, magic realism which is indigenous to South America, and modernist realism with its fixation on the banal. I see virtual literature sharing ground with all these genres, as indeed they all overlap, yet differing from them insofar as its aim is, as Saramago put it, the revelation of mystery.

In his books, this is revelation of the most secular and unpretentious kind—no grand epiphanies, only a gathering and slow arrival of light, as in the hour before sunrise. The mystery revealed is that of daylight, of seeing the world clearly, the mystery that happens literally every day.

Saramago wrote his first major novel when he was over sixty, and finished his last, *Cain*, a little before he died. I have to go on speaking of him in the present tense, he lives so vividly in his writings, these works of a "senior citizen," our patronizing euphemism for the dreaded words "old man." His extraordinary gifts of invention and narration, his radical intelligence, wit, humor, good sense, and goodness of heart, will shine out to anyone who values such qualities in an artist, but his age gives his art a singular edge. He has news for us all, including old readers tired of hearing the young or the wannabe young telling us the stuff we used to tell everybody when we were young. Saramago has left all the heavy breathing decades behind him. He has grown up. Heresy as it may seem to the cultists of youth, he is more than he was when he was young, more of a man, a person, an artist. He's been farther and learned more. He has seen most of the twentieth century, and has had time to think about it, decide what matters, and learn how to say it. The energy and mastery with which he says it is a marvel. He is the only novelist of my generation who tells me what I didn't know, or rather, what I didn't know I knew: the only one I still learn from. He had the time and the courage to earn that subtle and unpretentious kind of understanding we call, inadequately, wisdom. But it's not the glib reassurance often labeled wisdom. He's anything but reassuring. Though he doesn't parrot the counsels of despair, he has little confidence in that kindly trickster, hope.

Radical means "of the root," and Saramago was a deeply rooted man. Accepting the Nobel Prize in a king's court, he spoke with passion and simplicity of his grandparents in the plains of the Alentejo, peasants, very poor people, to him a lifelong, beloved presence and moral example. His love for his native country is the motive force of his *Journey to Portugal*, the only nonfiction work in the electronic anthology. A detailed guidebook of travel through the land from north to south, it is also a voyage of discovery, of rediscovery, a journey (back) to the country from which he was self-exiled for years in protest against the religious bigotry of its government. He was radically conservative in the true meaning of the word, which has nothing to do with the reactionary quacking of the neocons, whom he despised. An atheist and socialist, he spoke out, and suffered for, not mere beliefs or opinions, but rational convictions, formed on a clear ethical framework which could be reduced almost to a sentence, but a sentence of immensely complex political, social, and spiritual implication: it is wrong to hurt people weaker than you are.

His international reputation has suffered most from his steadfast opposition to Israeli aggression against Palestine. His demand that Israel, remembering the suffering of the Jews, cease to inflict the same kind of suffering on their neighbors has cost him the approval of those who conflate opposition to Israel's aggressive policy with anti-Semitism. To him religion doesn't enter into it, while Jewish history simply supports his argument: it is a matter of the powerful hurting those weaker than they are.

Saramago famously said, "God is the silence of the universe, and man is the cry that gives meaning to that silence." He isn't often so dramatically epigrammatic. I would describe his usual attitude to God as inquisitive, incredulous, humorous, and patient—about as far from the ranting professional atheist as you can get. Yet he is an atheist, anticlerical and distrustful of religion, and the potentates of piety of course detest him, a dislike he cordially returns. In his fascinating *Notebook* (blog posts from 2008 and 2009) he castigates the Mufti of Saudi Arabia, who, as he says, legalized pederasty by legalizing marriage for girls of ten, and the Pope of Rome, so reluctant to condemn pederasty among his priests—again, a matter of the powerful hurting the defenseless. Saramago's atheism is of a piece with his feminism, his fierce outrage at the mistreatment, underpayment, and devaluing of women, the way men misuse the power over women given them by every society. And this is all of a piece with his socialism. He is on the side of the underdog.

He is without sentimentality. In his understanding of people, Saramago brings us something very rare—a disillusion that allows affection and admiration, a clear-sighted forgiveness. He doesn't expect too much of us. He is perhaps closer in spirit and in humor to our first great European novelist, Cervantes, than any novelist since. When the dream of reason and the hope of justice are endlessly disappointed, cynicism is the easy out; but Saramago the stubborn peasant will not take the easy out.

Of course he was no peasant. He worked his way up from ancestral poverty and a job as a garage mechanic to become a cultivated intellectual and man of letters, an editor and journalist. For years a city dweller, he loved Lisbon, and he deals as an insider with the issues of urban and industrial life. Yet often in his novels he also looks on that life from a place outside the city, a place where people make their own living with their own hands. He offers no idyllic pastoral regression, but a realistic sense of where and how common people genuinely connect with what is left of our common world.

The most visibly radical thing about his novels is the aforementioned punctuation. Like me, readers may be put off by his use of commas instead of periods and his refusal to paragraph, which makes the page a forbidding block of print, and the dialogue frequently a puzzle as to who is speaking. This is a radical *regression*, on the way back to the medieval manuscript with no spaces between the words. I don't know his reason for these idiosyncrasies. I learned to accept them, but without enthusiasm. His use of what teachers call "comma fault" or "run-on sentences" induces me to read too fast, so that I lose the shape of the sentences and the speech-and-pause rhythm of conversation. When I read him aloud I have little difficulty, probably because it slows me down.

Grant him that quirk, and his prose (which I know through his splendid translator Margaret Jull Costa) is clear, cogent, lively, robust, perfectly suited to narrative. He wastes no words. He is a great storyteller (again: try reading him aloud), and the stories he has to tell are not like any others.

Here are some brief notes about them, reflections on my own process of learning how to read Saramago, an education by no means completed. *Baltasar and Blimunda*, published in Portugal in 1982, earned prompt acclaim in Europe. A wild historical fantasy full of such unexpected and unpredictable elements as Domenico Scarlatti, plague, the Inquisition, a witch, and flying men, it is odd, charming, funny, teasing, and tells an endearing love story. To me it seems a warmup for the greater novels to come, but it made his reputation, and many hold it to be among his best.

Of all his books, I have the most difficulty with *The Year of the Death of Ricardo Reis*. This is Saramago at his most intellectually Borgesian, and perhaps at his most Portuguese. It asks of the reader, if not some knowledge of its subjects (the writer Fernando Pessoa, Portuguese literary culture, the city of Lisbon), at least a fascination with masks, doubles, and assumed identities, a fascination Saramago certainly had and I almost entirely lack. A reader who shares that fascination will find this (and later *The Double*) a treasure.

Of his next book, in his Nobel speech he says simply, "In consequence of the Portuguese government censorship of *The Gospel According to Jesus Christ* (1991), vetoing its presentation for the European Literary Prize under the pretext that the book was offensive to Catholics, my wife and I transferred our residence to the island of Lanzarote in the Canaries." Most men who leave their homeland in protest against tyrannical bigotry go off shouting, pointing their fingers, shaking their fists. He just transferred his residence. I confess that the subject of the book is not of the highest interest to me, but it is a subtle, kind, and quietly unsettling work, an outstanding addition to the long list of Jesus novels (which may begin, as the title of this one implies, with the Gospels themselves).

The Stone Raft is science fiction, a lovely novel that had the very rare fortune of being turned into a lovely movie, made in Spain. Europe cracks apart at the Pyrenees, and the Iberian peninsula drifts wonderfully, cataclysmically off past the Canary Islands towards America. Saramago takes full advantage of this opportunity to make fun of the impatient and impotent pomposity of governments and the media when faced with events beyond the scope of bureaucrats and pundits, and also to explore the responses of some obscure citizens, "ordinary people," as we call them, to the same mysterious events. This one of his funniest books. And here also we find the first important Saramago dog.

There is a dog in *Blindness* too. Nobody in the book has a name, and the dog is known only as the dog of tears. He is an unforgettable dog. There is, I believe, a dog in all of Saramago's best books. His dogs embody a deep, essential element of his stories. They do not tell us what it is since they cannot speak; their silence is part of their importance. I'm not sure why I tend to rank his novels with a dog in them higher than the ones without, but it may have something to do with his refusal to consider Man as central in the scheme of things. The more people fixate on humanity, it sometimes seems, the less humane they are. I have learned, whenever I begin a new Saramago, to hope for the arrival of the dog.

Next—he was in his seventies now, and writing a novel every year or two—comes *The History of the Siege of Lisbon*. The first time I read it, I liked it but felt stupid and inadequate, because it is or appears to be about the founding event of Portuguese history, and I know no Portuguese history. I was reading too carelessly to realise that my ignorance made no difference at all. Rereading it, I found that of course everything you need to know is in the novel—the "real" history of what happened in the twelfth century when the Christians besieged the Moors in Lisbon, and the "virtual" history that comes to be interwoven with it, through the change of a single word, a no to a yes, a deliberate mistake introduced into a new *History of the Siege of Lisbon* by a proofreader in Lisbon in the twentieth century, one Raimundo Silva, who wants to subvert the authority of "historical truth." Raimundo is "a simple, common man, distinguished from the crowd only by believing that all things have their visible sides and their invisible ones and that we will know nothing about them until we manage to see both." Raimundo the proofreader is the hero of the story (and the love story), and that alone was enough to win my heart.

Immediately after this mellow and meditative tale came *Blindness* (its Portuguese title is *An Essay on Blindness*); soon after came "The Tale of the Unknown Island," an endearing and witty fable, and soon after that, *All the Names*, perhaps the most Kafkaesque of his novels, with its satire of a monstrous bureaucracy. Comparing Saramago with Kafka is a tricky business, though; he is dryer and gentler than Kafka, his anger deep and temperate. I can't imagine Saramago writing "Metamorphosis" any more than I can imagine Kafka writing a love story. And *All the Names*, with its unforgettable Registry leading back into impenetrable darkness, and its protagonist, Senhor José, a clerk driven to seek the person behind one of the innumerable names in the files of the Registry, if not exactly a love story, is a story about love.

After the *Journey to Portugal*, mentioned above, Saramago wrote *The Cave*, which in some ways I like the best of all because I like the people in it so much. Saramago will tell us what the book is about—though when he wrote this in *The Notebook* he wasn't talking about his novel, but about the world he saw in May 2009.

Every day species of plants and animals are disappearing, along with languages and professions. The rich always get richer and the poor always get poorer. . . . Ignorance is expanding in a truly terrifying manner. Nowadays we have an acute crisis in the distribution of wealth. Mineral exploitation has reached diabolical proportions. Multinationals dominate the world. I don't know whether shadows or images are screening reality from us. Perhaps we could discuss the subject indefinitely; what is already clear is that we have lost our critical capacity to analyze what is happening in the world. We seem to be locked inside Plato's cave. We have jettisoned our responsibility for thought and action. We have turned ourselves into inert beings incapable of the sense of outrage, the refusal to conform, the capacity to protest, that were such strong features of our recent past. We are reaching the end of a civilization and I don't welcome its final trumpet. In my opinion, neoliberalism is a new form of totalitarianism disguised as democracy, of which it retains almost nothing but a semblance. The shopping mall is the symbol of our times. But there is still another miniature and fast-disappearing world, that of small industries and artisanry. . . .

This is the framework of *The Cave*, an extraordinarily rich dystopia that uses science-fictional extrapolation with great skill in the service of a subtle and complex philosophical meditation that is at the same time, and above all, a powerful novel of character. One of the principal characters is a dog.

In 2004 came *Seeing*, which picks up the setting and some of the characters of *Blindness*, but uses them in an entirely different way (nobody could accuse Saramago of writing the same book over, or anything like the same book). It is a heavy-hitting political satire, very dark—far darker, paradoxically, in its end and implications than *Blindness*.

In his Nobel speech, the author, calling himself "the apprentice," said this:

The apprentice thought, "we are blind," and he sat down and wrote *Blindness* to remind those who might read it that we pervert reason when we humiliate life, that human dignity is insulted every day by the powerful of our world, that the universal lie has replaced the plural truths, that man stopped respecting himself when he lost the respect due to his fellow-creatures.

It is, on the face of it, an odd description of *Blindness*, for in that book it is powerless people who insult human dignity, ordinary people terrified at finding themselves and everyone else blind and out of control. Some behave with stupid, selfish brutality, *sauve qui peut*, indeed abandoning self-respect and human decency, like the men who take over the asylum and abuse its inmates. They are a microcosm of the corruption of power. But the truly powerful of our world don't even appear in *Blindness*, while *Seeing* is all about them, the perverters of reason, the universal liars.

Very evidently Saramago's novels are not simple parables. It would be rash to "explain" what all the people (but one) in the first book were blind to, or what the citizens of *Seeing* see. What's clear is that they're the same people in the same city a few years later: one book illuminates the other in ways I can only begin to glimpse.

The story begins with those ordinary citizens, who not so long ago regained their sight and their tranquil day-to-day life, doing something that seems quite unconnected with vision or lack of it. It's voting day, and 83% of them, after not going to the polls in the morning, go in the late afternoon and cast a blank ballot. We see the dismay of bureaucrats, the excitement of journalists, the hysteria of the government. The satire is at first quite funny, and I thought I was in for a light Voltairean tale. I was missing signals.

Turning in a blank ballot is a signal unfamiliar to most Britons and Americans, who aren't yet used to living under a government that has made voting totally meaningless. In a functioning democracy, one can consider not voting a lazy protest liable to play into the hands of the party in power (as when low Labour turnout allowed Margaret Thatcher's reelections, and Democratic apathy both elections of George W. Bush). It comes hard to me to admit that a vote is not in itself an act of power. I was at first quite blind to the point Saramago's nonvoting voters are making, but I began to see it at last, when the minister of defense announces that what the country is facing is terrorism.

Other ministers oppose him, but he gets what he wants, a state of emergency. A bomb is exploded (by terrorists of course, as the media report), killing quite a few people. An attempted evacuation of the 17% of voters who marked their ballots ends in failure because the government forgets to tell the troops blocking the roads to let the refugees through. The nonvoters, the so-called terrorists, help the refugees carry home all they tried to take with them, the tea service, the silver platter, the painting, grandpa . . .

The humor is still tender, but the tone darkens, tension rises. Characters, individuals, begin to come to the fore, all nameless except for Constant, the "dog of tears" from *Blindness*. A superintendent of police is sent into the city to find the woman who did not go blind when everyone else did four years ago, the suspected link between the "plague of white blindness and the plague of blank ballots." The superintendent becomes our viewpoint and mediator; we begin to see as he begins to see. He brings us to the woman who did not go blind, the gentle light-bearer of the first book, but where that story began with an awful darkness slowly opening into light, this one goes right down into the dark. *Seeing* says more about the days we are living in than any novel I have read.

By now Saramago was well into his eighties, and not surprisingly chose to write a book about death—a subject an old man understands with an intimacy no young writer, no matter how many bulls he fights or airplanes he jumps from, can quite equal. The premise of *Death with Interruptions* (also published as *Death at Intervals*) is irresistible. Death (who isn't one person, but many, each with a locality she's responsible for—bureaucracy, after all, is everywhere) gets sick of her job and takes a vacation from it. This is a major theme in Saramago, the humble employee who decides to do something just a little out of line, just this once . . . So in the region for which this particular Death is responsible, nobody dies. For a time it seemed that the genially morbid tale was going to bog down in recounting the paralytic idiocy of governmental rivalries and bureaucratic infighting, all too reminiscent of the American Congress. Then the dog showed up, and I knew everything was all right.

With the dog would come people, real people, who would do brave, stupid, and unpredictable things. They would fall in love, have sex, play the cello, make mistakes, they would be Saramago characters, they would be foolishly, painfully, nobly, simply human. Even if one of them—the only one with a name—was Death.

In 2010, very shortly after Saramago's death, *The Elephant's Journey* was published in English. It may be his most perfect work of art, as pure and true and indestructible as a Mozart aria or a folk song.

History attests that in 1551 an elephant made the journey from Lisbon to Vienna, a present from King João III of Portugal to Archduke Maximilian of Austria. In the novel, Solomon the elephant and his mahout, Subhro (whom the archduke renames, with true Habsburg infelicity, Fritz), proceed through various landscapes at an unhurried pace, attended by various functionaries and military men, and meeting along the way with villagers and townsfolk who variously interpret the sudden enigma of an elephant entering their lives. And that's the story.

It is extremely funny. Old Saramago writes with a masterfully light hand, and the humor is tender, a mockery so tempered by patience and pity that the sting is gone though the wit remains vital.

The passage that begins with the mahout discussing religion with the Portuguese captain is particularly endearing. Having explained that he is a Christian, more or less, Subhro undertakes to tell the soldiers about Ganesh. You obviously know a good deal about Hinduism, says the captain. More or less, sir, more or less, says the mahout, and goes on to describe how the god Shiva cut off his son Ganesh's head and replaced it with an elephant's head. "Fairy tales," says a soldier, and the mahout says, "Like the one about the man who, having died, rose on the third day." Peasants from the nearby village are listening with interest. They have agreed, "There's not much to an elephant, really, when you've walked round him once, you've seen all there is to see." But the religious discussion arouses them and they go wake up their priest to inform him of the important news: "God is an elephant, father." The priest protests and promises to exorcise the elephant: "Together," he tells them, "we will fight for our holy religion, and just remember, the people united will never be defeated." The whole episode is a series of contained miracles of absurdity, quiet laughter rising out of a profound, resigned, affectionate wisdom.

In his Nobel talk, Saramago said, "As I could not and did not aspire to venture beyond my little plot of cultivated land, all I had left was the possibility of digging down, underneath, towards the roots. My own but also the world's, if I can be allowed such an immoderate ambition." That hard, patient digging is what gives so light and delightful a book as this its depth and weight. It is no mere fable, as the story of an elephant's journey through the follies and superstitions of sixteenth-century Europe might well be. It has no moral. There is no happy ending. Solomon will get to Vienna, yes; and then two years later he will die. But his footprints may remain across the reader's mind, deep, round impressions in the dirt, not leading to the Austrian Imperial Court or anywhere else yet known, but indicating, perhaps, a more permanently rewarding direction to be followed.

Those tracks are now imprinted on electrons as well as in the dirt, on the page, in the mind; they are now in the vibrations in our computers, the symbols on our screens, as real and intangible as light itself, for all who will to see and read and follow. Saramago writes with wit, heartbreaking dignity, and the simplicity of a great artist in full control of his art. Let us listen to a true elder of our people, a man of tears, a man of wisdom.

Arkady and Boris Strugatsky: *Roadside Picnic*

An introduction to the Chicago Review Press edition of 2011.

Part of this introduction is taken from a review of *Roadside Picnic* I wrote in 1977, the year the book first came out in English. I wanted to keep some record of a reader's response at a time when the worst days of Soviet censorship were fresh in memory, so that intellectually and morally interesting novels from Russia still had the glamor of risk-taking courage about them. A time, also, when a positive review of a work of Soviet science fiction was a small but real political statement in the United States, since part of our science-fiction community had undertaken to fight the Cold War by assuming every writer who lived behind the Iron Curtain was an enemy ideologue. The moral purity of these reactionaries was preserved (as it so often is) by not reading, so they didn't have to see that many Soviet writers had been using science fiction for years to write with at least relative freedom from Party ideology about politics, society, and the future of mankind.

Science fiction lends itself readily to imaginative subversion of any status quo. Bureaucrats and politicians, who can't afford to cultivate their imagination, tend to assume it's all ray guns and nonsense, good for children. A writer may have to be as blatantly critical of utopia as Zamyatin in *We* to bring the censor down upon him. The Strugatsky brothers were not blatant, and never (to my limited knowledge) directly critical of their government's policies. What they did, which I found most admirable then and still do now, was to write as if they were indifferent to ideology—something many of us writers in the Western democracies had a hard time doing. They wrote as free men write.

Roadside Picnic is a "first contact" story with a difference. Aliens—the Visitors—have visited the earth and gone away again, leaving behind them several landing areas (now called The Zones) littered with their refuse. The picknickers have gone; the pack rats, wary but curious, approach the crumpled bits of cellophane, the glittering flip-tops from beer cans, and try to carry them home to their holes.

Most of the mystifying debris is extremely dangerous. Some proves useful—eternal batteries which power automobiles—but the scientists never know if they are using the devices for their proper purpose or employing (as it were) Geiger counters as hand axes and electronic components as nose rings. They cannot figure out the principles of the artifacts, the science behind them. An international Foundation sponsors research. A black market flourishes; "stalkers" enter the forbidden Zones and, at risk of various kinds of ghastly disfigurement and death, steal bits of alien litter, bring the stuff out, and sell it, sometimes to the Foundation.

In the traditional first contact story, communication is achieved by courageous and dedicated spacemen, and an exchange of knowledge, or a military triumph, or a big-business deal ensues. Here, the visitors from space, if they noticed our existence at all, were evidently uninterested in communication; perhaps to them we were savages, or perhaps pack rats. There was no communication, there can be no understanding.

Yet understanding is needed. The Zones are affecting everyone who has to do with them. Corruption and crime attend their exploration; fugitives from them are literally pursued by disaster; the children of the stalkers are genetically altered until they seem scarcely human.

The story set on this dark foundation is lively, racy, unpredictable. The setting appears to be North America, perhaps Canada, but the characters have no particular national characteristics. They are, however, individually vivid and likable; the slimiest old stalker-profiteer has a revolting and endearing vitality. Human relations ring true. There are no super-brilliant intellects; people are commonplace. Red, the central figure, is ordinary to the point of being ornery, a hard-bitten man. Most of the characters are tough people leading degrading, discouraging lives, presented without sentimentality and without cynicism. Humanity is not flattered, but it's not cheapened. The authors' touch is tender, aware of vulnerability.

This use of ordinary people as the principal characters was fairly rare in science fiction when the book came out, and even now the genre slips easily into elitism—super-brilliant minds, extraordinary talents, officers not crew, the corridors of power not the working-class kitchen. Those who want the genre to remain specialised—"hard"—tend to prefer the elitist style. Those who see science fiction simply as a way of writing novels welcome the more Tolstoyan approach, where a war is described not only from the generals' point of view, but through the eyes of housewives, prisoners, and boys of sixteen, or an alien visitation is described not only by knowledgeable scientists, but by its effects on commonplace people.

The question whether human beings are or will be able to understand any and all information we receive from the universe is one which most science fiction, riding on the heady tide of scientism, used to answer with an unquestioning yes. The Polish novelist Stanislaw Lem called it "the myth of our cognitive universalism." *Solaris* is the best-known of his books on this theme, in which the human characters are defeated, humbled by their failure to comprehend alien messages or artifacts. They have failed the test.

The idea that the human race might be of absolutely no interest to a "more advanced" species could easily lend itself to overt sarcasm, but the authors' tone remains ironic, humorous, compassionate. Their ethical and intellectual sophistication becomes clear in a brilliant discussion, late in the novel, between a scientist and a disillusioned employee of the Foundation about the implications, the meaning, of the alien visit. Yet the heart of the story is an individual destiny. The protagonists of idea stories are marionettes, but Red is a mensch. We care about him, and both his survival and his salvation are at stake. This is, after all, a Russian novel.

And the Strugatskys raise the ante on Lem's question concerning human understanding. If the way humanity handles what the aliens left behind them is a test, or if Red, in the final, terrible scenes, undergoes trial by fire, what in fact is being tested? And how do we know whether we have passed or failed? What is "understanding"?

The final promise of "HAPPINESS! FREE! FOR EVERYONE!" rings with unmistakably bitter political meaning. Yet the novel can't possibly be reduced to a mere fable of Soviet failure, or even the failure of science's dream of universal cognition. The last thing Red says in the book, speaking to God, or to us, is "I've never sold my soul to anyone! It's mine, it's human! Figure out yourself what I want—because I know it can't be bad!"

Jack Vance:
The Languages of Pao

An introduction to the 2008 reprint of the novel by Subterranean Press.

Jack Vance loved to invent elaborate, gorgeous pageantries of costumes and manners, castes and classes, and to recount histories of powerful men scheming and striving for more power, set in countries with remarkable geographies and exotic names, on distant worlds, in a far future. On returning to those Vancean worlds after many years, the first thing I noticed, with surprise and affection, was how familiar they are. Despite the science-fictional apparatus of space flight and super-hi-technology, they aren't alien worlds or future worlds. They are our own lost world. They are Earth before the airplane, Earth in all the centuries when it was boundless, endlessly rich in mystery and strangeness—when there were blanks on the map, when Samarkand or Timbuctoo or California were names of legend, when Marco Polo was a stranger in Cathay, when Baghdad was where the Thief lived . . .

About the time we started to destroy that world, industriously shrinking it to the size of a theme park or a shopping mall, we started writing about worlds out in space and their alien beings and ways. When the *National Geographic* ran short of exoticism, science fiction took over. Jack Vance seems to have enjoyed that compensatory invention immensely for its own sake; and he did it with the true Thousand and One Nights flair, the deadpan realism of the best traveler's tales.

The Languages of Pao was my favorite of the many Vance novels I bought in the sixties, because I liked its subject. Vance was always aware that language is an interesting and tricky business—unlike many science-fiction writers who still routinely present a whole planet or even galaxy of people(s) all speaking the same tongue. It is easier to explain airily that everybody speaks Ing-Lish ever since Urth installed the Galactic Empire than it is to cope realistically with Babel. But the trouble with a monolinguistic universe is that it's shrunken, artificial—we're back in the theme park, the shopping mall. Vance didn't share the imperial, reductionist mind-set, common to his generation of sf writers, that dismisses variety as unimportant. Rather, he revels in it; his various peoples speak variously, and their names reflect the different phonologies of their languages.

Vance's writing style is certainly that of one to whom words, both the meaning and the sound, are important. He has—and it was a rare thing in science fiction in 1958—a real and personal literary style. His dialogue is often dignified and formal to the point of being stilted; people say things like, "This credence which you deprecate may be no more than fact." This is a mannerism, but, if you accept it, a rather endearing one. The rhythm of his narrative is calm, sedate, musical; his descriptive passages are direct and exact. He gives you a sense of what the weather is, what the colors of things are, he places you in a setting: "Above reared the rock slope, far up to the gray sky, where the wild little white sun swerved like a tin disc on the wind. Beran retraced his steps."

This little passage is typical, the first sentence for its vivid description, poetic, exact, restrained; the second for its slightly old-fashioned phrasing and its simplicity. Vance did not waste words. He is as far as possible from the grab-'em-by-the balls school of action writing, yet he was an action writer: his plots move forward, not rapidly but steadily, with an impetus that carries the reader right along. He was in full charge of his story. The characters, the plot, the scenes, descriptions, actions, all are under control. And control is, perhaps, one of his great subjects.

The Languages of Pao concerns a struggle for the control of a people: a political conflict, a moral debate. As in others of his books, it involves a vast population, but is acted out by a very few characters. One is a boy, Beran, inheritor of a world empire but reduced to dependence on a man of enormous power, Palafox. The plot is in fact the classic duel of father and son, complicated wonderfully by the fact that the father has literally hundreds of other sons. Pitting the father's pitiless megalomania against the boy's struggling sense of justice, Vance sets up his conflict cannily.

Palafox, for all his power, is utterly controlled by the perverse society that formed him, and even the language which gives him his power; while Beran, because he is not committed to any one alternative, has a hope of freedom.

The element of speculative science informing the plot is known as the Sapir-Whorf Hypothesis, which says (stated crudely) that our mental outlook is formed by our language: what one can think depends, to a large extent, on the words one has to think with. Because linguistics is a "soft" or social science, diehards of "hard" SF must dismiss this book as fantasy; but such quibbles grow ever quainter. Meeting the reasonable requirement of using a durable if much-questioned scientific hypothesis as a major element of the plot, *Pao* is excellent, solid science fiction. Vance understands Sapir-Whorf and, while applying it with due caution, elaborates it convincingly and spins a lively yarn out of it.

I feel a certain old-fashioned quality to *Pao*. Perhaps it was always there, inherent in Vance's dignified language, his unhurried pacing, and his avoidance of ubiquitous, gratuitous violence. But it may also have something to do, now, with Vance's inescapable masculinism—an almost universal failing of the genre at that time. Women are perceived, if at all, as contingent on men—appurtenances. A shadowy girl, Gitan, plays a brief, passive role. Some nameless victims of Palafox's lust are glimpsed. Beran has a father but no mother. He neither seeks nor finds a wife. Male interests are the only concern, men perform all actions except domestic service, men fill every leading position; even madness is gendered, for Palafox's psychotic plan to populate the world with his sons is merely a hideous exaggeration of the male sex drive, the selfish gene embodied. What women want, feel, think, or are plays no part whatever in the book. This is of course true of many novels, even now, even those with nominally female characters. Vance's lack of interest in half the population of the world was, at least, undisguised by hypocritical pieties.

Respecting his writing as I do, I tried to see the story as a critique of male dominance, and it can be read so, but the reading is unconvincing in the complete absence of active women characters. So this fine novel may seem, to a modern eye, maimed. It is benign and thoughtful, yet its omission of half of humankind from agency cripples an otherwise just, subtle, and generous moral stance.

Jack Vance made no pretense to literary greatness, I think, but he held himself to a far higher literary standard than most pulp-fiction and genre writers of his time, and he was true to his own vision. For that he deserves lasting honor. May a new generation of readers discover the joys of traveling far beyond the shopping mall and the theme park, to the eight continents of Pao, and the bleak heights of Breakness.

H. G. Wells:
The First Men in the Moon

An introduction to the Modern Library edition of 2002.

Since "genre" and "literature" are often supposed to be exclusive categories, many critics, publishers, and even authors, driven by commercialism or snobbery, deny that a work of literary science fiction is science fiction at all, and invent fancy names for it. H. G. Wells was not indulging in such squeamishness when he called his early stories "scientific romances." Writing science fiction years before the genre had a name, he was, like a good biologist, simply giving an accurate label to a non-descript, a newly discovered creature.

"Scientific romance" is a proper Linnaean double-barrel, genus and species. The word romance, alluding to the tradition of Lucian and Ariosto and Cyrano de Bergerac, links the older, imaginative and purely fantastical element of his stories with their speculative and intellectual element, which was without precedent.

For Wells was the first writer of real note to write fiction as a scientist, from within science, rather than as an outsider looking on with excitement or complacency or horror at the revelations and implications of the scientific revolution of the nineteenth century. Percy Shelley saw the beauty science revealed; Mary Shelley saw the moral ambiguity of it; Jules Verne saw it as an endless technological spree; but Wells saw through its eyes. He was the first literary writer to form his mind in the passionate study of science under a great scientist. His year in Thomas Henry Huxley's class in the Normal School of Science, in 1884, when modern biology was defining itself and redefining the world, gave him, as he said, his vision of the world.

And much of the ambiguity of that vision throughout his writing life is a faithful reflection of the troubled ethic of the discipline. In an 1891 essay, "The Rediscovery of the Unique," Wells wrote:

> Science is a match that man has just got alight. He thought he was in a room—in moments of devotion, a temple— and that his light would be reflected from and display walls inscribed with wonderful secrets and pillars carved with philosophical systems wrought into harmony. It is a curious sensation, now that the preliminary sputter is over and the flame burns up clear, to see his hands and just a glimpse of himself and the patch he stands on visible, and around him, in place of all that human comfort and beauty he anticipated—darkness still.

When he wrote that, the physicists, still happy in Newton's serenely illuminated universe, had not yet discovered their darkness; but the biologists had. It lay all round the match that Darwin struck. All Wells's scientific romances may be read as investigations into the dark immensity revealed by the brilliance of the hypothesis of evolution.

He has been scolded for the glaring impossibilities of his stories, their element of irresponsible romance. In *The First Men in the Moon*, published in 1901, the anti-gravity material, cavorite, is no more realistic than the dreams, gryphons, wings, and balloons that transported earlier moon voyagers—it might as well be a flying carpet. With typical self-deprecation (taken literally by too many critics trained only in the Jamesian forms of subtlety), he said in his preface to *Seven Famous Novels* that his method was "to trick his reader into an unwary concession to some plausible assumption and get on with his story while the illusion holds." Such prestidigitation is a characteristic ploy of science fiction: to make a nonexistent entity or impossible premise acceptable (often by scientific-sounding terms such as telepathy, extraterrestrial, cavorite, FTL speed) and then follow through with a genuinely realistic, logically coherent description of the effects and implications.

Of course the accurate narrative description of the nonexistent is a basic device of all fiction. The extension to the impossible is proper to fantasy, but since we seldom know with certainty what is or is not possible, it is a legitimate element of science fiction too. *What if?* is a question asked by both science fiction and experimental science, and they share their method of answering it: make a postulate and then carefully observe its consequences.

What if we had a device for getting to the moon (within some sixty years we would, though it wouldn't be cavorite), what if the moon had an atmosphere (Wells knew that it didn't), what if its inhabitants were a highly intelligent species that had taken their social evolution into their own rather clammy hands—what then?

The last of these *What ifs* is the big one. Wells's enterprise is considerably larger and riskier than extrapolation from a current technology to a possible future one, Verne's principal tactic. While Verne marvels happily at future mechanical wonders, Wells wonders where the amoral force of evolution may lead us, and, still more presciently, at what the social and moral implications of deliberate, rational control of evolution might turn out to be. This is a question that we, a hundred years later, watching corporate science blithely alter genetic codes in plants, animals, and human beings, are just beginning to ask.

In an 1896 article, "Human Evolution, an Artificial Process," Wells was one of the first to envisage Darwinian process as becoming no longer the work of blind chance, but of human management: unnatural selection. A year earlier, in *The Time Machine*, in the same year in *The Island of Doctor Moreau*, and five years later in *The First Men in the Moon*, he explored this vision through fiction.

In *The Time Machine*, if the separation of humankind into grim Morlocks and effete Eloi is a deliberate coding of the hierarchy of social class into human genetics, it backfires rather dreadfully, since the aristocrats have ended up as long pork for the working class. The result of the thought experiment in *Doctor Moreau* is no happier. In the shorthand terms of a pre-Mendelian fiction, the manipulation of evolution by an obsessed scientist is a hideous failure, engendering only monsters.

In *The First Men in the Moon*, the terms of the experiment are different and the outcome is ambiguous. It is not men who are selecting and breeding themselves for various uses and excellences, but alien beings, moon people. There is no doubt at all that the Selenites are rational and practical. As social insects have been shaped by millennia of random selection to fit their tasks perfectly, so the Selenites, through genetic management and by manipulation of fetuses or infants, have deliberately bred and molded themselves to form an efficient, peaceful, harmonious society, without poverty or violence. That their highly specialised individual bodies are to human eyes grotesque and frightful reflects more on our prejudices than on their morality. Aesthetically they are, to us, appalling; but ethically are they perhaps our superiors?

By leaving judgment on this interesting question to two narrators singularly ill equipped to make any ethical judgment on anything, Wells leaves it ultimately up to the reader.

The principal narrator, Bedford, is a venal, self-complacent bungler, ready for anything but good for nothing. Though his brutality, when it breaks out, is disgusting, he is acceptable as a comic hero rather than a villain because he is mostly so incompetent and so unconscious of his incompetence. Alone on the return voyage, he has one moment of cosmic understanding and piercing self-perception—"an ass . . . the son of many generations of asses"—but that soon evaporates. Back on earth he is quite himself again.

The scientist Cavor is good at only one thing, but very good at that. He is almost as specialised as the Selenites. He is as selfless as Bedford is selfish. "He simply wanted to know. . . ." When he is left alone on the moon, his messages back to earth are admirable in their intellectual courage; he will observe and record to the bitter end. But he has made a religion of knowledge, setting it above moral values, community responsibility, and practical consequences, and it is this blind faith that finally betrays and destroys him.

Earth's first emissaries to the strange beings who live in the moon are thus themselves deformed, one by ruthless capitalism, the other by ruthless scientism. This is a very dark comedy, harking back to Swift in its indignation, but with a satiric double edge that reaches straight forward from Wells's time to ours.

Told in Bedford's breezy, cheerful, bloodyminded style, it is also a thoroughly entertaining story, fast moving, often funny. It is lifted above mere adventure by intellectual riskiness and complexity, and also by its aesthetic power, which is uneven but in certain scenes unequaled—moments of the most dazzling descriptive intensity. The chapter "A Lunar Morning" might in itself provide an answer to the question, whether asked patronisingly or seriously, Why do people read science fiction? My paraphrase of that answer is: In hopes of receiving such writing as this—a ravishingly accurate vision of things unseen, an utterly unexpected yet necessary beauty: revelation as the scientist knows it.

The passage is also an answer to mandarin critics who try to dismiss Wells as ignorant of literary technique and indifferent to aesthetic value. A more careful reader, Darko Suvin, in his essay "Wells as the Turning Point of the Science Fiction Tradition," pointed to the poetic quality of Wells's writing: "This poetry is based on a shocking transmutation of scientific into aesthetic cognition, and poets from Eliot to Borges have paid tribute to it." The word shocking is well used. Such a transmutation remains rare enough to take the breath away.

Another memorable scene is given us, late in the story, in Cavor's drier voice. His Selenite guide has been showing him babies,

confined in jars, from which only the fore-limbs protruded, who were being compressed to become machine-minders of a special sort. The extended 'hand' in this highly developed system of technical education is stimulated by irritants and nourished by injection, while the rest of the body is starved. . . . It is quite unreasonable, I know, but such glimpses of the educational methods of these beings affect me disagreeably. I hope, however, that may pass off, and I may be able to see more of this aspect of their wonderful social order. That wretched-looking hand-tentacle sticking out of its jar seemed to have a sort of limp appeal for lost possibilities; it haunts me still, although, of course, it is really in the end a far more humane proceeding than our earthly method of leaving children to grow into human beings, and then making machines of them.

This fiercely ironic passage puts in question the whole issue of what is so euphemistically called "the division of labor," by showing how it can most economically be achieved. Anyone who has read Aldous Huxley's *Brave New World* will see what the grandson learned from his grandfather's student. I find Wells's satire both keener and more compassionate than Huxley's.

And then there is the Grand Lunar, with his enormous brain, "many yards in diameter," looming like a vast inflated bladder out of the blue-lit darkness of the deepest caves of the moon, the image of all-but-disembodied intellect, the ultimate dream of pure Mind. "It was great. It was pitiful," Cavor says, prevented by his own prized objectivity from realising that he is seeing an image of himself: mind isolated, without body, without love, trapped in darkness and the ugliness of hypertrophy.

The sleep of Reason engenders monsters. . . .

H. G. Wells:
The Time Machine

An introduction to the Modern Library edition of 2002.

The Time Machine was published in 1895, and has never been out of print. It was the first major work by a young man who would become one of the best-known writers of the early twentieth century. It was, in fact, the story that brought him his first fame.

Why, then, is the tone of Wells's own preface to the 1931 Random House edition, here reproduced, so diffident? "It is obviously the work of an inexperienced writer," he says, barely admitting that "there are still publishers and perhaps even readers to be found for it." He goes on for two pages in the third person before he breaks down and says "my story," and then calls it "an undergraduate performance." Modesty is a fine, rare trait, but this goes too far: he's behaving as in his own disarming description of his first paper for the Fabian Society, which, he says, he read to his necktie through his moustache. Only at the end of the preface, having thoroughly bashed the story, does he loosen up and call it "his dear old *Time Machine*."

H. G. Wells was an odd man, oddly mixed. Looking at the 1920 portrait of him on the cover of a biography, I see two faces in his face: one likable, warm, and genial, the other tense, keen, and curiously fugitive. His clear gaze seems direct and yet it does not meet you. One should not characterise so very accomplished and complex a life in a word, yet the word that keeps coming to my mind, reading about him and rereading his work, is *elusive*. Wells is quicksilver: substantial, heavy, brilliant, yet you can't pin him down. Oh, this is what he is, this is what he's saying, you think, and then you realise he isn't.

Probably he was disposed to be hard on this story, to distance himself from it, because he hoped his reputation would rest on his realistic novels and the social and political thinking embodied in the later, more ideological fictions he called "fantasies of possibility." And a writer can be pursued by a successful story till he's sick of hearing about it. Feeling with justification that he had thought hard and worked hard for thirty years to perfect his ideas and his art, he didn't wish all that to be overshadowed in the eyes of future readers by a story he wrote in a hurry at the age of twenty-eight.

And yet it seems that his living influence is concentrated increasingly in the early scientific romances, now all a century or more old: *The Time Machine, The War of the Worlds, The First Men in the Moon,* and *The Island of Doctor Moreau.* Imagery from these stories, particularly the first two, is so deep in our minds, so common to us, as to be genuinely archetypal, not only as scenes from films but as the far more deeply suggestive and resonant verbal images of the stories themselves. Nobody can write science fiction, or discuss science fiction as literature, without having read them; they are fundamental in a way even Verne is not, though Mary Shelley is. They established certain mythical tendencies in our fiction that we have explored ever since. I do not use the word myth lightly, to mean fantasizing or falsification, but in its proper sense: myth as a necessary story, concerning realities important to a people, and leading to moral perception and interpretation.

What those moral perceptions consist of can of course be fully stated only in the terms of the myth itself. The story is not a fortune cookie from which a message may be extracted. The perception *is* the story. The interpretation will vary with the reader and the age.

So people continue to argue about whether Wells was an optimist or a pessimist, a question which evidently puzzled him too. He loved science, which he met in its most promising and exciting season, the hopeful youth of modern physics, chemistry, astronomy, biology. He wanted to believe that science—reason—would lead mankind to a bright utopia; he worked hard at believing it. But as he said in 1933, "Now and then, though I rarely admit it, the universe projects itself towards me in a hideous grimace." It is courageous of him to admit that he did not want to admit it. He was far too honest an artist to hide it. He faced the hideous grimace, and it is that horror of darkness, the vision of "the aimless torture in creation," that gives the scientific romances their gravity.

He wrote tales of a hopeful future, such as *In the Days of the Comet* and *A Modern Utopia*, the one quite dull, the other falling, as rational utopias do, into intolerable elitism. He also wrote what may be the first genuine dystopia, *When the Sleeper Wakes*, showing how two centuries of social and technological "progress" lead to the dead end of a totalitarian corporate state. Even such a realistic novel of commonplace contemporary life as *Tono-Bungay* includes a haunting, terribly prescient vision of radioactivity as an uncontrollable cancer.

He loved the English countryside that was being built over and despoiled throughout his lifetime, and wrote of it vividly, with a nostalgia that undermined all visions of a rational technocracy. He dreaded the future when he saw it as utterly unmanageable; sometimes he struggled to find political ideologies to manage it, sometimes retreated to the scientist's stoical acceptance of what must be. He investigated and imagined all kinds of possibilities in his fiction and settled on none. He faced, evaded, repositioned, turned again to face what he feared.

His impulse, in his life as in his fiction, seemed always to be to disentangle himself, though he tried hard neither to deny nor to betray. This inability or refusal to settle is most striking, perhaps, in his attitude towards time itself. Many of his generation saw themselves, with good cause, as living at the end of one age and the beginning of another. Wells's fictions exhibit an intense temporal anguish, that of a man who feels he exists "between two times," pulled both back and forward, at home in neither. The idea of living in two times, of moving back and forth between them, is an almost obsessive theme in his work throughout his whole long career.

And here it is, in its pure essence, in his first novel.

I have no idea how old I was the first time I opened the fat dull-green volume called *Seven Scientific Romances*, or how many times during my childhood and adolescence I reread *The Time Machine*. The lawn among the rhododendrons under the White Sphinx is as familiar to me as the garden of the house I grew up in. The direct, clear, self-assured cadence of the language (so unlike the pasticheurs' notion of "Victorian prose") is still exemplary. Wells's narrator says of the Time Traveller's tale, "The story was so fantastic and incredible, the telling so credible and sober," and that is a good description not only of the piece itself, but of the characteristic narrative ploy of science fiction: to be sober in imagining and to tell the incredible credibly.

Along with the vastly, impossibly paradoxical notion of "travelling" through time as through space, there are quite a lot of lesser incredibilities, among them the Time Traveller's amazing improvidence. Reading as a child, I didn't notice, but I find it strange now that he sets off into the future without a notebook, without provisions of any kind, without even putting on outdoor shoes. He has matches in his pocket because he's a pipe smoker, but I'm not sure he took his pipe (Bilbo certainly would have). "Why didn't I bring a Kodak?" he asks himself eight hundred thousand years later. Why indeed? And why eight hundred thousand years? Wouldn't most time travellers be inclined to try a hop of a century to start with, or at most a millennium? The entire history of mankind goes back only about five millennia. He goes forward eight hundred. What ever made him do it?

There is no answer to that except an aesthetic one, and for me it is complete and satisfactory. He goes so far because the journey itself is so irresistible.

It is splendidly imagined, that account of the first great time-voyage, when night begins to follow day "like the flapping of a black wing" and the sun starts "hopping across the sky," and then the Traveller sees "trees growing and changing like puffs of vapour, now brown, now green; they grew, spread, shivered, and passed away." And the hills melt and flow, and the sun sways up and down from solstice to solstice . . . No wonder he "flung himself into futurity" with such abandon.

Again, at the end of his tale, for no rational reason at all he travels yet farther and farther into the future "in great strides of a thousand years or more," until he arrives at the "remote and awful twilight" of the beach at the end of earthly time. That scene, in its desolate grandeur and inhumanity, is surely the most wonderful passage of pure science-fictional imagination ever written.

Science fiction is almost the only kind of story that ever really admits of a world not dominated by human beings (or gods, animals, or aliens who act just like human beings). To raise one's eyes, once in a while, to the realms in which human action does not count and human concerns are simply negligible, the limitless universe, Lucretius's "coasts of light," may be to glimpse, for a moment, a freedom that exceeds consolation.

The Time Traveller's behavior as a human being among the morbid remnants of the species in the year 802,701 is neither wise nor admirable; he not only doesn't take notes or samples, he mislays his Time Machine, gets his one friend killed, and murders a lot of people more or less unintentionally but with enthusiasm—as if foreseeing the movies he'd soon star in. On the other hand, his gradual understanding via misunderstandings of the flower-children Eloi and then of their ghoulish guardians, and his efforts to understand how humanity came to be so divided and so fallen, are sympathetic and convincing, largely because they remain tentative. His tale leaves us with a great many unsettled and unsettling questions.

Except for a passage or two of melodramatic violence, it is all done with a light, quick, sure hand. There are many elegantly deft touches, such as the two flowers "not unlike very large white mallows" that are all the Traveller brings home with him, or the sentences describing exactly where the Time Machine is when it comes to rest again in the laboratory and why it is exactly there. Again, such details are of the purest essence of the science-fictional imagination. They are solid, impeccable. The whole garden is imaginary, but the toads in it are real.

The Time Machine was well named: it has seen three centuries so far without the least sign of aging, its bars of ivory and nickel and rods of rock-crystal intact, its brass rails unbent, its language and vision as fresh as when it set off one hundred and seven years ago. I would envy all who are about to ride it for the first time, if I didn't know that it's a journey one can take over and over and always discover something new.

Wells's Worlds

An introduction to my selection of H. G. Wells
short stories, Modern Library, 2003.

Herbert George Wells was born in 1866, in the heyday of Queen Victoria's reign, and died at eighty, just after the end of the Second World War. Like most of us, he experienced what is often dismissed as a science-fictional invention: existence in incompatibly different worlds, time travel to an unknown planet.

For the last couple of centuries, people who live more than thirty years or so have been likely to realise, suddenly or gradually, that they are strangers in a changed, incomprehensible world: lands of exile for refugees, cities of ruin for those whose nation suffers war, a labyrinth of high technology in which the untrained mind strays bewildered, a world of huge wealth which the poor stare at through the impenetrable glass of a shopwindow or a TV set. From the early nineteenth century on, the whole and single universes of preindustrial societies changed to a multiverse, and the pace of change increased continually.

Caught in those transformations, H. G. Wells wrote about them all his life.

He was no passive observer. He worked long and hard to change his world—in the first place, to get himself into a better situation in it. He was born into the servant class in a rigidly hierarchical society, his father a gardener, his mother a personal maid at Uppark, a country house of the gentry. The bright, ambitious boy got himself out of that (but always to look back with love at the lovely rural England of his childhood). He got himself out of apprenticeship to a cloth seller (where he learned a great deal about the lower middle class), and back into school—education, the road up. He won himself a scholarship to the Normal School of

Science, where he studied biology under Thomas Huxley and others, and the new universe of science opened out to him along with the social and intellectual realms of professional status. Injury and illness led him from teaching to writing. By his mid-thirties he was an increasingly successful and respected author, building himself a fine new house a world away from the servants' quarters at Uppark.

He was ambitious also to improve the world for other people. He became a socialist and briefly a member of the Fabian Society, which wasn't activist enough for him; he was variously a utopian futurist, a feminist (up to a point), a critic of society, of injustice, of capitalist commercialism, an unsuccessful Labour candidate, a tireless prophet both of cataclysm and of social betterment. In his late seventies, writing *Mind at the End of Its Tether*, after all the struggles and both the wars, after sticking it out in London through the Blitz, he was still looking for hope for mankind, though he could find it only in the idea of a new humanity, a changed, improved species: "Adapt or perish, now as ever, is Nature's inexorable imperative."

Trained as a biologist under a very great teacher, he never wavered in his acceptance of Darwin's dynamic view of existence: life understood not as a Social Darwinist struggle for mere domination, not as a Christian Darwinist ascent to humanity as a final goal, but life as evolution: necessary and unceasing change. What stays fixed dies. What adapts goes on. The more flexibly it adapts, the farther it goes. Openness is all. Change can be brainless and brutal or intelligent and constructive. Morality enters the system only with the thinking, choosing mind. Wells imagined both dark and bright futures because his creed allowed both while promising neither, and because the eighty years of his life were years of immense intellectual and technological accomplishment and appalling violence and destruction.

In his lifetime, and in his own eyes, Wells's important fictional work lay in his realistic novels. Idea-centered, observant of social class and stress, topical, provocative, often satirical, sometimes passionately indignant, books such as *Ann Veronica* and *Tono-Bungay* are comparable to Bernard

Shaw's plays, though they haven't worn quite as well. Wells was a quirky, sometimes heavy-handed novelist, and most of his novels, though entertaining and in flashes brilliant, have dated. What has lasted, beyond any expectation of his own and in defiance of all the snobberies of the critics, are his "scientific romances"—novellas and short stories of fantasy and science fiction.

They were written before the realistic works, most of them before he was forty. His early reputation was founded on them. Later on he was rather dismissive of them, partly no doubt because it galls an artist to hear people forever talk about work done decades ago, partly because he was a demanding self-critic and knew a good many of his early stories were potboilers. Moreover, the modern critical canon excluded all nonrealistic fiction as inherently inferior, and Wells was a self-made man, competitive, edgy about aspersions of inferiority. Possibly he convinced himself that imaginative fiction is less powerful or useful than the fiction of social observation. His training after all was in science, not in art, and scientists are taught to put observation first. But his calling was art, not science, and his nature was that of a visionary, a seer of the unseen, the unobservable. He could never be satisfied by the world as we see it, as it is. He had to change it, reinvent it, or find a new one.

The Time Machine, The First Men in the Moon, The War of the Worlds, The Invisible Man, The Island of Doctor Moreau—these are what the name H. G. Wells means to most of us now, and rightly so. These short novels or novellas established whole genres. They left a set of indelibly vivid images, imageries, archetypes, in the minds of generations of readers— and filmmakers, graphic artists, comic book devotees, TV sci-fi fans, pop cultists, and po-mo pundits.

Wells wrote science fiction long before it had a name. He called it "scientific romance," and later "fantasy of possibility"—better names, perhaps, than the one it's stuck with. His originality and inventiveness were astonishing. Whatever kind of science fiction you look at, you're likely to find an example of it—a first example of it—among his tales. He didn't distinguish between science fiction and fantasy because nobody did then or for years to come; but he invented a literature, because he was the first man to write fiction as a scientist. His imagination was formed and informed by the study of biology, a science in its bright dawn of discovery and expansion, and he brought that sense of limitless possibility, both playful and fearful, to his speculations and explorations of other worlds where the mind alone can go.

And then he turned to social commentary, political exhortation, and programmatic utopias, and stopped writing short stories. Almost all the stories in this volume were written and published in the last decade of the nineteenth century and the first of the twentieth, before the First World War, many of them before the death of Queen Victoria. Enough to make one reconsider the meaning of the word Victorian.

Some students of science fiction insist that its particular quality depends on its ideas alone, and that attention to literary considerations apart from clarity and narrative drive, or to character as opposed to stereotype, merely weakens or dilutes it. There are memorable stories to support this view, and Wells wrote several of them. His interest in society and psychology and his high literary standards, however, led him away from such a narrow focus on idea-driven plot.

Introducing his own selection of his short stories (*The Country of the Blind and Other Stories*, 1913), he discusses the form and his relation to it. Citing the work of Kipling, Henry James, Conrad, and many others, he calls the 1890s the high point of the short story, speaks of "lyrical brevity and a vivid finish" as its virtues, and sees hyper-aestheticism as the death of it. Chekhov had not yet been translated, to show the limitless possibilities of the form; Maupassant's bleak, tight, neat tales were the accepted model. Wells could not be comfortable with that. "I am all for laxness and variety in this as in every field of art. Insistence upon rigid forms and austere unities seems to me the instinctive reaction of the sterile against the fecund," he wrote. "I refuse altogether to recognise any hard and fast type for the Short Story." He was surely right to do so; but his almost patronising description of it as "this compact and amusing form" hardly includes Henry James's, or Kipling's, or his own best stories, though it describes the lesser ones very well.

He knew the difference, of course. In 1939, in his discussion of his revision of what is probably his finest story, "The Country of the Blind," he wrote that he had lost his tolerance for the idea story, the gimmick, the trick ending—the potboiler he had written so many examples of. "You laid hands on almost anything that came handy, a droning dynamo, a fluttering bat, a bacteriologist's tube . . . ran a slight human reaction round it, put it in the oven, and there you were." He could have gone on doing it forever, he says, but for the feeling that "not only might the short story be a lovely, satisfying, significant thing, but that it ought to be so, that a short story that wasn't whole and complete like a living thing, but just something bought and cut off like half a yard of chintz on a footstool, was either an imposture or a lost opportunity." But "the vogue for appreciating the exceptional in short stories was passing," he says, and when he tried to write stories that didn't suit the market, editors rejected his submissions, and so he "drifted out of the industry."

He had quit selling cloth by the yard at seventeen when he broke his apprenticeship. Selling words by the yard got him going as a writer, but maybe it led him to impatience with the form itself. For it is certainly untrue that the short story flowered in the 1890s and then declined into triviality; the form went on developing and flourishing right through the twentieth century. I wonder if what stopped him was not so much the editors' lack of appreciation for the exceptional as the critics' increasing restriction of literary fiction to social and pyschological realism, all else being brushed aside as subliterary entertainment. No matter how good his stories, if they were fantastic in theme or drew on science or history or any intellectual discipline for their subject, they could be dismissed categorically as "genre fiction." It is a risk every imaginative writer runs, even now; writers who crave literary respectability still hasten to deny that their science fiction is science fiction. At least Wells stood by his imaginary guns.

But he stopped firing them.

Meanwhile, *The Time Machine* has never been out of print for a hundred and some years now. And though only a few of Wells's short stories have come near that genuine literary permanence, the best of them remain vividly alive, amazingly pertinent, sometimes unnervingly prescient, as haunting as nightmares or as bright unrecallable dreams.

I chose twenty-six stories from the eighty-four collected in John Hammond's massive and invaluable *Complete Short Stories of H. G. Wells*.

I selected for excellence, of course, not as defined by the standards of realism, which have little use or application here, but generic excellence. Was the story outstanding in itself for intellectual urgency or moral passion, for some particular virtue or strangeness or beauty? Was the story outstanding of its kind, and was the kind an interesting one? Was it fruitful, vital, did it lead forward to other works of other writers? I am not one of the readers who prize only "greatness" and to whom "great" art is defined by being inimitable, unique, a dead end. I see art as a community enterprise both in place and time, and believe that art that leads to more art is more valuable than sterile excellence.

Certain stories I left out with regret; one is "A Story of the Days to Come," full of interesting stuff, but so long it would have taken up half the book. I would have liked to include some of the satirical, joking tales that Wells was good at, such as "Aepyornis Island" and "The Pearl of Love," but being light, they got pushed out of the boat.

Because almost all Wells stories are genre stories and because I value them as such, I arranged them, not chronologically, but in sections by genre or subgenre. Each section has a brief introduction, talking about what kind of stories they are, where this kind of story came from, and what it may have led to.

As for trying to sum up the stories as a whole, as a set, it's difficult. Wells is an elusive writer. Certainly one sees his distinctive style throughout the book. Many of the stories are told in a journalistic tone, easy and breezy, extremely self-confident but unpretentious, clear, moving forward at a good clip—it all seems quite simple, quite artless, which is exactly what the author wanted. He distrusted the high aesthetic manner (a charming note to his friendship with Henry James is that each man confessed he often longed to rewrite the other's stories). But he was a careful writer and tireless rewriter, keenly aware of what he was doing, sensitive and skilled in his craft. A modulation of his tone can be as effective as a key change in music.

We are often told that in stories written less to reveal individual experience or character than to entertain or inform or stimulate the imagination, plot is needed to provide structure, and action is all-important. Wells plotted cleverly, and his action scenes are vivid and suspenseful; but his true mastery, I think, was in that very difficult, underestimated, even maligned element of storytelling, visual description. Wells can make you see what he wants you to see. When this is something that does not in fact exist, a fantastic scene, a dream or prophecy, his power seems uncanny. He was—literally—a visionary. Perhaps the finest things he wrote are the wonderful lunar morning in *The First Men in the Moon* and the glimpses of the dying world at the end of *The Time Machine*, and in the short stories one comes again and again on a similarly vivid scene, a glimpse into another world, fearful or radiant or simply very strange. These visions have the authority, in memory, of something seen with one's own eyes. A squadron of airplanes over Naples (two years before Kitty Hawk!) . . . two men laughing and making faces at people who stand unseeing, frozen in time . . . a dreaming garden behind a door in a wall . . . the faces of the townsfolk in the Country of the Blind . . .

Book Reviews

Many of these pieces differ in some details from their original publication, having been edited slightly when I was preparing them for this book. The only one I changed substantially (mostly to update it) is the review of Sylvia Townsend Warner's Dorset Stories.

I dithered between chronological and alphabetical order for these reviews, and settled for the alphabet so that readers could easily find an author they might be looking for. The original published versions of most of the reviews can be found on my website, and the publications in which they first appeared are listed in the acknowledgments.

I like book reviewing, and in order to keep doing it have taken a good many chances on books I didn't know anything about till I read them. It's sad when the advance reading copy that arrives in a dense cloud of blurbs all declaring it a supreme masterpiece of gut-wrenching lyricism turns out to be a dud. But mostly I've been lucky in being asked to review a book by an author I'm already interested in, or a book that won me over even though I didn't much expect to like it.

Most of the reviews were published in the Manchester Guardian, to whose editors I am grateful for many opportunities to review good books, for wonderfully flexible, intelligent editing, and for being eight thousand miles away. The New York/East Coast literary scene is so inward-looking and provincial that I've always been glad not to be part of it; but when I lived in London I was positively terrified by the intensity of British literary cliques, the viciousness of competition, the degree of savagery permitted. That bloodymindedness may have lessened somewhat, but still, whenever I review a British book for the Guardian, I'm glad I live in Oregon.

But then, I always am, except when I'm homesick for California.

Margaret Atwood:
Moral Disorder

2006

Most collections of short stories by a single author are grab bags, but some approach or achieve real unity; it is a different unity from that of the novel, and deserves some attention. The gaps between stories, the lack of obvious continuity, preclude the supporting structures of conventional plot. If the stories tell a story, it must be read in glimpses and through the gaps—a risky gambit, but one which offers singular freedom of movement and ironic opportunity.

In such episodic narratives character, place, and/or theme replace plot as unifying elements. Elizabeth Gaskell's *Cranford* and Sarah Orne Jewett's *Country of the Pointed Firs* are both about a single town and a few strong characters. Each book seems to have begun as a "local color" story or two written for periodicals, the success of which led the author to further explorations of Cranford or Dunnets Landing, and to the realisation that she was in fact writing a work of considerable length and scope. Freed from the tyrannies of Victorian plotting, both these lovely books develop locality and character with a lightness and subtlety that was rare then, and is still rare now.

Though it seems to me a genuine form, this kind of book has no accepted name, perhaps because it's an exception rather than a rule. Many collections that pretend to unity merely fake it. That does have a name: a fix-up—a collection of short stories stuck together with some kind of expository word-glue invented after the fact, or merely arranged in hope that recurrences or similarites of place, person, or theme will hold the pieces together. Ray Bradbury's *Martian Chronicles* is an example: inter-story glosses patch over contradictions and anachronisms, but the stories don't really tell a coherent history, and parts remain far more memorable than the whole. Yet fix-up seems an unnecessarily disdainful name for that lovable book, and it absolutely won't do for *Cranford.* We need a name for a book that is truly a story told in stories. Could we call it a story suite?

Moral Disorder consists of eleven short stories. Is it a collection, a fix-up, or a suite? A suite, I think. Place, perhaps the commonest cement of the story suite, is not very important, but the stories have a single protagonist, a central character—or I think they do. She is variable, elusive, even a bit slippery. This is, after all, a book by Margaret Atwood.

Seven of the stories are told by an "I" who remains nameless, four from the third-person point of view of "Nell." It's easy to project Nell into all the stories, because they run in chronological order from childhood to age, the central figure is always female, and there are definite clues that Nell is the protagonist even when not named. Such clues are needed, for there isn't very much in the first-person stories of childhood and adolescence to connect the girl to the woman Nell—no strong sense of character or destiny, no overriding reason to think this is, or isn't, the same person. The last two stories concern a woman's experience with her father entering dementia, her mother in extreme old age. The daughter may well be Nell, the parents may be the parents of the child in the earlier stories, but I had no feeling of recognition, of rejoining the same people at a later stage of life. The book did not quite form a whole for me, an architecture, a life story however episodic. The glimpses are brilliant, but the gaps are wide.

Things happen to Nell; she accepts what happens; this is not a portrait of a powerful character, perhaps rather an intimation of experience shared by many women. So character is not a strong bond, locality ties only a few of the stories together, and if the stories are connected by theme, I haven't found what it is yet. What they have in common is a clear eye, a fine wit, and a command of language so complete it's invisible except when it's dazzling.

One story is dramatically and effectively out of place. Starting with the second story, we follow Nell through the years from her childhood with sister and parents, through the vicissitudes of semi-marriage—does Tig in fact ever divorce that ghastly wife and marry her?—the trials of amateur farming and late parenthood, and at last to her middle age, the daughter of parents at the edge of death. But the first story in the book is chronologically the last, a portrait of Nell and Tig in their own old age, when they are the parents on the edge of death. Why this reversal works so well I don't know; perhaps because "The Bad News" is a stunning opener, electric with wit, energy, Atwood's achingly keen sense of fear and pain. She has never been sharper, dryer, funnier, sadder. And there was wisdom in not putting this story last, because the last two are about dying, the end, and this one isn't, quite—not yet.

> *Not yet* is aspirated, like the *h* in *honour*. It's the silent *not yet*. We don't say it out loud.
>
> These are the tenses that define us now: past tense, *back then*; future tense, *not yet*. We live in the small window between them, the space we've only recently come to think of as *still*, and really it's no smaller than anyone else's window.

The uncomplaining, absolute accuracy of this is most admirable. "The Bad News" really has some news for its readers.

None of the other stories entirely escape conventionality, not a word I'd expect to use about Atwood. The subjects are familiar tropes of the current short story: miseries and confusions of childhood, city people learning life on a subsistence farm, dysfunctional family members, Alzheimer's. They are not quite predictable, but near it, though there is a patience, a kindness in the tone which is not common. Atwood doesn't pull any of the surprises, the narrative flights and dodges she's so good at, except in that first story. There the old Canadian couple morph quietly into an old Roman couple in a small Gallic town called Glanum, which Nell and Tig once visited as tourists. Breakfast is good whether in Toronto or Glanum, but the world is not in good shape. Terrorism, barbarians threatening the empire. The news is all bad—the news is always the same and always bad, and what are two old people supposed to do about it? This gentle, plausible slide into a fantasy that deepens reality is Atwood at her slyest and sweetest. There really is nobody like her.

Margaret Atwood: *The Year of the Flood*

2009

To my mind, *The Handmaid's Tale, Oryx and Crake,* and *The Year of the Flood* all exemplify one of the things science fiction does, which is to extrapolate imaginatively from current trends and events to a near future that's half prediction, half satire. But Margaret Atwood doesn't want any of her books called science fiction. In her recent, brilliant essay collection, *Moving Targets,* she says that everything that happens in her novels is possible and may even have already happened, so they can't be science fiction, which is "fiction in which things happen that are not possible today." This arbitrarily restrictive definition seems designed to protect her novels from being relegated to a genre still shunned by hidebound readers, reviewers, and prize-awarders. She doesn't want the literary bigots to shove her into the literary ghetto.

Who can blame her? I feel obliged to respect her wish, although it forces me, too, into a false position. I could talk about her new book more freely, more truly, if I could talk about it as what it is, using the lively vocabulary of modern science-fiction criticism, giving it the praise it deserves as a work of unusual cautionary imagination and satirical invention. As it is, I must restrict myself to the vocabulary and expectations suitable to a realistic novel, even if forced by those limitations into a less favorable stance.

So, then, the novel begins in Year 25, the Year of the Flood, without explanation of what era it is the twenty-fifth year of, and for a while without explanation of the word Flood. We will gather that it was a Dry Flood, and that the term refers to the extinction of—apparently—all but a very few members of the human species by a nameless epidemic.

The nature and symptoms of the disease, aside from coughing, are undescribed. One needs no description of such events when they are part of history or the reader's experience; a reference to the Black Plague or the swine flu is enough. But here, failure to describe the nature of the illness and the days of its worst virulence leaves the epidemic an abstraction, novelistically weightless. Perhaps on the principle that since everything in her novel is possible and may have already happened the reader is familiar with it, the author doles out useful information sparingly. I sometimes felt that I was undergoing, and failing, a test of my cleverness at guessing from hints, reading between lines, and recognising allusions to an earlier novel.

The Year of the Flood is a continuation, not exactly a sequel, of *Oryx and Crake*. Several characters from the earlier book appear, along with such institutions as God's Gardeners and the Corporations. The Gardeners, an eco-religious sect, farm rooftops, which can be defended from the gangs and marauders who infest the streets. Presented with irony and affection as seeking harmony with nature in the breakdown of civilisation, the Gardeners are a memorable invention. As for the Corporations, these aren't the dear familiar corporations that now control our governments in a more or less surreptitious fashion, because in the novel there appear to be no fuctioning national governments. The setting may be the upper Midwest or Canada, but there is no geography, no history. The Corporations, and particularly their security arm, CorpSeCorps, are in total control. As in the earlier book, all science and technology is Corporation-owned, in the service of furthering capitalist growth and keeping the populace unrevolutionary while destroying the resources and ecological balances of the planet at an ever-increasing rate. Genetic manipulation has been busy producing useless or noxious monsters such as green rabbits, rakunks, and partly rational pigs.

You can see that the world of the Year 25 is not an improvement on the world of another great realistic novel, *1984*. It is if possible even more depressing, most of humanity being dead and the few survivors scrabbling out an evidently hopeless existence. Not even Beckett could make a scene so bleak endurable for several hundred pages, so much of the novel takes place in flashbacks to as early as the Year Five, when things were bad, but not that bad, yet. And the story finds its vitality in the characters through whose eyes we see these scenes. Probably what I will remember from the book in a year's time will not be its grim events, but the two women Toby and Ren.

One of the features supposed to distinguish "popular" from "literary" fiction is the nature of the characters who enact the fiction. In a realistic novel we expect to find individual personalities of some complexity; in a Western, mystery, romance, or spy thriller, we accept or welcome conventional types, even stock figures, the Cowboy, the Feisty Heroine, the Dark Brooding Landowner. We may, of course, in any one example, get the reverse of what we expect. The supposed distinction is so often violated in both directions as to be nearly meaningless. But there is one kind of fiction where complex, unpredictable individuality is really very rare. That is satire, and satire is one of Atwood's strongest veins.

The personalities and feelings of characters in *Oryx and Crake* were of little interest; these were figures in the service of a morality play. *The Year of the Flood* is less satirical in tone, less of an intellectual exercise, less scathing though more painful. It is seen very largely through the eyes of women, powerless women, whose individual characters and temperaments and emotions are vivid and memorable. We have less of Hogarth here and more of Goya.

If there were any affectionate human relationships in the earlier novel, I don't recall them. In this one, affection and loyalty are strongly felt, loving relationships between characters are memorable. Such loyalties are affirmed, of course, against all the odds, and like everything Toby, Ren, Amanda, and the Gardeners are and do, will soon end in the brute failure of all human intentions. Yet these loyalties spring up, like the shoots of March. In this tiny green featherweight in the scales of Doom we persist in seeing a vast, irrational hope. And somewhere here, somewhere in this irrational affirmation, I think, lies hidden the heart of the novel.

That is why the hymns of the Gardeners, which are printed about every third chapter along with the sermon-meditations of Adam the Gardener, may be read as kindly spoofs of hippie mysticism, Green fervor, and religious naïveté, and at the same time can be taken quite seriously. Their hymnbook rhythms and Blakeian dodges are appropriate to their sentiments, which aren't as simple as they might seem at first sight.

> *But Man alone seeks Vengefulness,*
> *And writes his abstract Laws on stone;*
> *For this false Justice he has made,*
> *He tortures limb and crushes bone.*
>
> *Is this the image of a god?*
> *My tooth for yours, your eye for mine?*
> *Oh, if Revenge did move the stars*
> *Instead of Love, they would not shine.*

In an endnote, Atwood invites us to hear the Gardeners' hymns sung on her websites and to use them "for amateur devotional or environmental purposes." This seems to indicate that she means what they say.

But any affirmation by this author will be hedged with all the barbed wire, flaming swords, and red-eyed Rottweilers she can summon. Much of the story is violent and cruel. None of the male characters is developed at all; they play their roles, no more. The women are real people, but heartbreaking ones. Ren's chapters are a litany of a gentle soul enduring endless degradation with endless patience. Toby's nature is tougher, but she is tried to the limit and beyond. Perhaps the book is not an affirmation at all, only a lament, a lament for what little was good about human beings—affection, loyalty, patience, courage—ground down into the dust by our overweening stupidity and monkey cleverness and crazy hatefulness.

It is no comfort to find that some of the genetic experiments are humanoids designed to replace humanity. Who wants to be replaced by people who turn blue when they want sex, so that the men's enormous genitals are blue all the time? (Who wants to believe that a story in which that happens isn't science fiction?)

I found the final sentences of the book unexpected, not the seemingly inevitable brutal end or dying fall, nor yet a deus-ex-machina salvation, but a surprise, a mystery. Who are the people coming with torches, singing? In the Year of the Dry Flood, only the Gardeners ever sang. Are not the Gardeners all dead? Perhaps I missed the clues again. You must read this extraordinary novel and decide for yourself.

Margaret Atwood:
Stone Mattress

2014

In the last century, a good many people were taught that serious poets wrote only poetry, never fiction. No Goethes for the purists. At the same time, modernist critics of fiction decreed that writing imaginative literature disqualified you as a serious novelist. No Mary Shelleys for the realists. Professors and prize-givers preferred purity, so maverick writers whose talent led them to wander cross-country kept running into barbed-wire fences.

Young Margaret Atwood leapt them handily, winning the Governor General's Award early on both for poetry and fiction as well as for literary criticism. But she took on a high fence with *The Handmaid's Tale*, a brilliant example, like Huxley's *Brave New World* or Orwell's *1984*, of the near-future social-satirical-cautionary mode of science fiction. Huxley and Orwell had no problem here, but by the mid-eighties the day after tomorrow had been exiled from the precincts of Literature. Any publisher with his eyes on the prizes was terrified of the label SF. A mistress of deft evasion, Atwood has avoided it, at some cost then and since, while her flexible, adaptable, fiercely intelligent, and highly willful talent kept roaming farther from conventional realism. These days, she can play freely with genre, and it's as interesting as ever to see where she goes.

In *Stone Mattress*, her eleventh volume of short stories, she's having a high old time dancing over the dark swamps of Horror on the wings of satirical wit. She's out for the shocked laugh, and gets it, but with elegance. Her scenes and caricatures, as accurate and vivid as those of Hogarth, are almost entirely of old age. The tales run to a general pattern: people who knew one another intimately in their twenties are brought back together in their seventies to live out the variously absurd, fantastic, or dreadful aftermaths of youthful sex, illusion, and crime.

The first three tales are connected by the narrative device that allows participants in an event to recount it from widely differing, sometimes irreconcilable viewpoints. Henry James did it with characteristic subtlety in *The Turn of the Screw;* Kurosawa did it so well in film that it's often called the Rashomon Effect. Fascinating in itself, it's well suited to a modern take on the fantastic or supernatural, since all the evidence is word-of-mouth and the author never has to commit to a belief in any of it. That's important to this author; but I think she enjoyed writing her ghost story, with its scathing caricatures, its well-deserved punishments, and its fairy-tale happy ending, as much as we enjoy reading it.

Atwood has never indulged in gross cruelty to the extent many of her contemporaries do. She shuns predictability, and writes with a light hand and a dry wit. Still, these tales dwell at length not only on the feeble artifices old people may use to disguise physical decay and their fear of death, but also on their murderous fantasies. These dotards are dangerous. The common source of their bloody imaginings and actions is sexual anger, hardly a laughing matter, but Atwood maintains her light tone, and the violence won't trouble readers inured to such self-indulgence in sexual rage as the Stieg Larsson mysteries.

In the very entertaining title story, the protagonist has a sudden vulture's eye view of herself: "an old woman—because, face it, she is an old woman now—on the verge of murdering an even older man because of an anger fading into the distance of used-up time. It's paltry. It's vicious. It's normal. It's what happens in life."

Satire often walks a knife edge between controlled and uncontrolled anger, between selective and total attack, and the fiercer the indignation behind the satire, the higher the risk of its serving only to destroy. Like Swift, Atwood runs the risk of leaving nothing standing in the wake of her cleansing fire. To my mind the last tale, "Torching the Dusties," fails as comedy or as cautionary satire, offering no alternative to mindless terror, violence, and despair. "*Fun* is not knowing how it will end," a character in an earlier story thinks in a moment of insight, and I thought perhaps he was speaking for Atwood. But in this final story, the fun consists of telling us that this is how it will end, don't kid yourself, cruel Nature's out to off you, and she will. Courage and the friendship, generosity, and tenderness briefly praised in earlier passages are worthless. Mortality makes life meaningless.

Atwood calls these fictions tales, a word, as she says, that removes a story "from the realm of mundane works and days, as it evokes the world of the folk tale, the wonder tale." Fiction that reduces life to the paltry and the vicious is often humorless. But many folk tales laugh at both bloodshed and petty cruelties, and the grotesque, the dreadful, and the banal are always getting mixed together in comedy and satire.

Look at these tales, then, as eight icily refreshing arsenic popsicles followed by a Baked Alaska laced with anthrax, all served with impeccable style and aplomb. Enjoy!

J. G. Ballard:
Kingdom Come

2006

The voice that narrates *Kingdom Come* is that of Richard Pearson, an advertising man who has just lost both his job and his father. The father was the victim of an apparently random shooting at a huge shopping centre in Brooklands, between Weybridge and Woking. Pearson goes there to close down the flat and seek some postmortem understanding of the father he hardly knew. On the way he runs into various signs of racial unrest, and in Brooklands itself, described as "a pleasant terrain of comfortable houses, stylish office buildings and retail parks, every advertising man's image of Britain in the 21ˢᵗ century," he finds his father's death to be involved in ambiguities, and the town a hotbed of racial prejudice and hooliganism, led by men wearing shirts with the St. George's cross. All is not well in the pleasant terrain.

Not surprisingly, given his profession, but perhaps unfortunately for the reader, Pearson's narration is so thoroughly unreliable that his story is difficult to follow, and inconsistent sometimes to the point of self-destruction. It's often hard to read his judgments and descriptions as anything but symptoms of hysteria or paranoia, though he often writes with a specious brilliance, as when he shows us a commentator on a giant screen, "his smile dying in the blur of arc lights, authentic in his insincerity." Everyone he meets talks pretty much the way he does; here is a middle-aged solicitor describing life in Brooklands, where he grew up: "No one attends church. Why bother? They find spiritual fulfilment at the New Age centre, first left after the burger bar. We had a dozen societies and clubs—music, amateur dramatics, archaeology. They shut down long ago. Charities, political parties? No one turns up. At

Christmas the Metro-Centre hires a fleet of motorized Santas. They cruise the streets, blaring out tapes of Disney carols. Checkout girls dressed up as Tinkerbell flashing their thighs. A Panzer army putting on its cutest show." To which Pearson replies, "Rather like the rest of England. Does it matter?"

This hateful, scornful exaggeration, coupled with the affectless response, is characteristic of the tone throughout. Pearson seems to side against effete London with the dwellers in the inter-urban sprawl, the consumers to whom his advertising was directed, "the real England," yet his judgment of them is brutally snobbish: "they preferred lies and mood music," the Heathrow suburbs are "a zoo for psychopaths." This well represents an advertiser's bimodal thinking, but the hysterical note keeps sounding, as he repeatedly presents his perception of Londoners and the people of the motorway towns as two equally degenerate species seething with mutual loathing and contempt.

As he sees them, the people of Brooklands, the paradise of consumerism, have nothing to do but consume, and their consumerism is consummate, so they are bored: on the edge, longing for violence, even for madness, anything for a thrill. Hence the popularity of the bullyboys wearing the cross of St. George. These faceless multitudes whose life is shopping and spectator sport are ripe for fascism.

Along in here I thought of José Saramago's *The Cave*, which is also about a monstrous supermall, a consumerist apotheosis, but one even more sinister than the Metro-Centre, because at least some of the people it destroys are seen as human beings. They retain, as long as they can, a daily life of hard work and strong emotional bonds, and through it access to the spiritual. Saramago quotes Plato as his epigraph: "What a strange scene you describe, and what strange prisoners. They are just like us."

J. G. Ballard's motive in writing *Kingdom Come* may have been much akin to Saramago's in *The Cave*, but Ballard's narrator is inadequate: he himself has no access to work worth doing or any bond but sex; he is totally alienated. He can see the people of Brooklands only as parodies of himself. Work and family mean nothing to him, or them; consumerism itself is, he tells us repeatedly, their religion. So the dome of the Metro-Centre becomes their temple, where they fall to worshiping giant teddy bears: a scene which strains both sympathy and credulity, yet is so portentous in tone as to subvert its comic potential.

In a novel, particularly in a science-fiction novel, if you're expecting an apocalypse you're probably going to get one. Richard Pearson connives in a mini-revolution, a manufactured local outbreak of irrationality, violence, and warped spiritual fervor. The leaders of this movement barricade themselves with a few thousand hapless shopper-hostages in the great dome of the Metro-Centre, and withstand for two months the government's somewhat perfunctory efforts to unseat or outwait them. All this last section of the book moves with energy through scenes of surreal vividness. As the siege goes on, as the food in the meat markets and greengrocers rots, and the air conditioning is shut off, and the water gives out, the gradual and literal decay of existence inside the huge dome is brilliantly drawn. The narrator comes alive as everything begins dying. No doubt it's what he was waiting for all along.

After the siege, as violence and racist attacks die down, and the television reverts to household hints and book-group discussions, Pearson tells us, "Once people began to talk earnestly about the novel any hope of freedom had died." Yet a page later, the last sentence of the book is: "In time, unless the sane woke and rallied themselves, an even fiercer republic would open the doors and spin the turnstiles of its beckoning paradise." The meanings of the words freedom, sanity, and republic are here so compromised as to be meaningless. To this narrator, nothing actually means anything, nothing is what it is. But the trouble with letting a spin doctor tell your story is that you risk your reader asking him his own question: "Does it matter?"

Roberto Bolaño:
Monsieur Pain

2011

Lying on my bed, reading Chris Andrews's excellent new translation of the Roberto Bolaño novel *Monsieur Pain*, I experienced a sudden sense of unease, mixed with a vast pity for something or someone, I was not certain who or what. It may have had something to do with the continual but almost unnoticeable flickering of my reading lamp—or was it the daylight itself that oscillated strangely between the greyish sheen of a street scene in a very old film and the more ordinary light of a cloudy December Tuesday? Even more unsettling was the sense, for which I could find no specific cause, that I had read, not this book, yet something very like this book, several times before in several places, none of which I could remember. Had I perhaps seen it at the cinema? Was it in that theater on the Rue Royale, when the two Spaniards in broad hats had come in directly behind me, hurrying after me, pressing themselves so closely on me as I found my way down the dark aisle that when I at last saw a vacant seat and slipped into it my heart was beating hard and my vision was obscured? All through the film they sat behind me, smoking cigarettes that glowed like unreachable stars, while the hero of the film pursued an obscure quest through tortuous alleyways and corridors, which ended strangely enough in a hospital room whose antiseptic whiteness and perfectly delimited space seemed only waiting to give artistic emphasis to the dark silhouette which I now knew, with no desire to know why, would materialize in the doorway, or beside the bed where I lay reading . . .

———

Surrealist narrative is a literary form at war with itself; disconnection is a primary tactic of surrealism, and story is a process of making connections, however unexpected. Readers open to the autodestructive element of modern art may find the surrealist devices in *Monsieur Pain* more deeply engaging than coherent narrative. I find them curiously old-fashioned, overly cinematic, and all too close to self-parody. But this early Bolaño novel has a keen moral and political urgency that obliges me to accept its *noir* banalities. Its tortuous method of approaching the unspeakable reveals the face of evil without glamorizing it as popular literature and film so often do. By indirection it avoids collusion.

A synopsis that made sense would misrepresent the book, since all we know of "what happens" is what the narrator tells us, and he doesn't distinguish actuality from hallucination. He is Monsieur Pain, a gentle Frenchman, lung-damaged in the First World War, who makes a small living as a mesmerist in mid-1930's Paris. The woman he loves but is too shy to win brings him to the hospital where a friend of hers named Vallejo is dying of a mysterious illness, complicated by intractable hiccups. The white corridors of the Clinique Arago are labyrinthine, nightmare-like. Two Spaniards persistently shadow Pain, then bribe him not to treat Vallejo. He accepts the bribe. He returns to the clinic, but is driven from it into a (labyrinthine, nightmare-like) warehouse where his life is threatened. He follows one of the Spaniards into a theater where they watch a surrealist film containing a sequence in which he recognises a friend, a physicist, long dead; another man he knew back then joins the Spaniard, insists on renewing acquaintance with Pain, takes him out for a drink, and tells him, smiling, that he is "treating" Republican prisoners for the Spanish Fascists. Pain throws a drink in his face. He finds a way back into the dream-corridors of the clinic in a vain search for Vallejo; hiding in an empty room, he witnesses an apparently significant conversation but cannot hear it through the window. Some while later the woman he loves comes back to Paris with her new husband; she tells Pain that Vallejo is dead, and that he was a poet. The narrative is followed by a set of brief, allusive obituaries of some of the characters.

César Vallejo, considered by some the greatest South American poet, an active Communist persecuted by the government of his native Peru, lived the latter half of his life in exile; he died in Paris in 1938 of an undiagnosed illness. His wife brought in "alternative" practitioners to try to save him.

Roberto Bolaño, now often spoken of as the successor to Borges and García Márquez, left his native Chile when the dictator Pinochet took power, and lived most of the rest of his life in exile. He wrote *Monsieur Pain* in 1983, when he was thirty. He died in 2003.

From the seed of fact grows the great vine of imagination, twining and intertwining, casting shadow, bearing fruit sometimes sweet, sometimes bitter.

T. C. Boyle:
When the Killing's Done

2011

California was an island in the earliest, fanciful maps. Ecologically, the maps were right. Isolated by the ocean, the Sierra, and the great deserts, dozens of species unknown elsewhere flourished in the benign climate, until the white men came. Then, under the impact of a thousand imported exotics, native species began to decline or perish.

There are Californians today who, far from planting lawns around their desert condos, would like to uproot all the golden Spanish wild oats to let the bunch grasses of Indian days cover the hillsides again. The Forest Service, though not so purist as that, keeps up a fierce and unremitting resistance to many invasive species, not only plants but animals.

T. C. Boyle is well aware that Americans like to see everything as a war against something. Even the lonely fogbound Channel Islands off Santa Barbara can be a battlefield. And it's civil war, the worst kind, because the opponents are close kin: they both want passionately to save the island's wild creatures.

Government agents believe salvation lies in control, in careful scientific stewardship. Animal rights advocates believe human interference does more harm than good and is morally wrong. The arguments on both sides are passionate and cogent.

A typical dilemma: The Forest Service must trap or kill eagles on one of the islands. Why persecute these magnificent birds? Well, when DDT finished off the native bald eagle, which isn't much of a hunter, the carnivorous golden eagles moved out from the mainland to prey on the wild pigs thriving in the great stands of fennel that sprang up after the island was closed to sheep ranching (pigs, fennel, and sheep all, of course, destructive species introduced by the whites—themselves an invasive race). As the hordes of pigs are eliminated by shooting them, the golden eagles have nothing to eat but the one remaining native species, a charming dwarf fox. How to save the fox? Get rid of the golden eagles so the bald eagle can be reintroduced.

Animal rights activists reject such painful, partial, meddlesome solutions. It's simple: just keep hands off, stop interfering, don't kill anything. We've done enough damage. Let the animals have it their way.

And let the foxes go extinct, leave the island to the pigs? Deny our responsibility and let the harm we've done be our total legacy on earth?

This dire complexity, these insoluble questions are of course not limited to California. This is the dilemma our species faces all over the earth. It is a tremendous subject for a novel. And a tremendously dramatic one.

T. C. Boyle is not one to scant the drama. Beginning with a splendidly described shipwreck-and-castaway-survival scene, his story weaves among several generations and on both sides of the environmental issues, always clear, crisply written, fast-paced, most of it in the perpetual-motion presto of the present tense. No need to cut to the chase—it's all chase. After a while I found that the unremitting tension and stress, the rush from one nerve-wracking, painful, or gruesome scene to the next, began to cancel itself out, even to drift from tragic drama into melodrama. For readers accustomed to taking their adrenaline straight, it will no doubt be more effective.

Most of the characters we get to know are women, hard-edged, tough, and more or less sympathetic. Dave, the leader of the local animal rights activists, is a man whose rage, impatience, and contempt for human beings are the reverse side of his identification with animal freedom. Overconfident, fatally inept, intending harm to those he sees as his enemies, he brings disaster and death to his allies and even the animals he thinks he alone can save. Alma, the protagonist on the Forest Service side, is intelligent, conscientious, and likable, but so neurotic, so endlessly driven, so self-tormenting, that her stream-of-consciousness becomes almost as exhausting to read as her baneful opponent's.

There is no rest in the book, no peace. Every breakfast in the sweet California morning sunlight, every visit to the lovely, lonesome coasts and hillslopes of the Channel Islands, is weighed down with foreboding, marginalised by the threat of impending disaster. Any happiness is illusory, too brief to be meaningful. For all its energy and urgency, its historical accuracy and sweep, its excellent action writing and faultless reproduction of contemporary speech and life, the novel is heart-chillingly bleak. In that, it is an honest reflection of the mood of most people who look at what we have done to our world and seek to take responsibility for it. A story that begins with a shipwreck and ends with a rattlesnake in the dark does not leave much room for hope.

Geraldine Brooks:
People of the Book

2008

Not long after the United States invaded Iraq, our local newspaper printed a photograph I cannot forget. It showed an Iraqi man hurrying away from the library of Baghdad through a smoky, chaotic street, his arms filled, overfilled, burdened down, with books. The books—some of them large and heavy, like art books or old records of some kind—may have been rare treasures, or they may have been merely whatever he could gather up in the confusion of the burning building. He may have been a librarian, or he may have been only a reader. I know he was not a looter, because his face showed not only distress and fear, but passionate grief.

As soon as I knew it was the story of a book saved from the destruction of a library, I wanted to read Geraldine Brooks's *People of the Book*. An irresistible subject, given urgency by its timeliness and poignance by its paradoxicality: for the novel is based on the true story of an ancient Jewish codex saved from the fire by a Muslim librarian.

The Sarajevo Haggadah, pride and glory of the Bosnian collection, was spirited out of the library and hidden in a bank vault when the Serbs began to target the libraries and museums of Sarajevo in their shelling. But that was its second rescue: a half-century earlier, it had been slipped out from under the noses of the Nazis and hidden in a village mosque for the duration. In 1941 it was saved by an Islamic scholar, Dervis Korkut; in 1992, by a Muslim librarian, Enver Imamovic. A little later, one of Imamovic's colleagues, trying to carry books away from the burning library (like the Iraqi in the photograph I cannot forget), was killed by a sniper. Her name was Aida Buturovic.

The Sarajevo Haggadah is very unusual among Jewish holy books in having illustrations, like a Christian Book of Hours; these are of great delicacy and beauty. It was written and illuminated in Spain, in the mid-fourteenth century, but nothing of its early history is known. A priest spared it from the book burnings of the Inquisition in Venice in 1609 by writing in it "*revisto per mi*"—"I have reviewed/approved this"—and signing his name. Apparently we know little or nothing of how it got from Venice to Bosnia, to undergo its two hairbreadth rescues in the twentieth century.

There is certainly a story there. And Geraldine Brooks, with her background covering wars and troubles in Europe, Africa, and the Middle East for the *Wall Street Journal*, her penchant for a broad historical canvas, and her Pulitzer Prize, would seem the right novelist for the job. Her performance will satisfy many readers. The tale is full of complex twists and turns, with even a bit of mystery plot towards the end; there's sex, a rather tenuous love story, and the obligatory descriptions of acts of violence. Proceeding ever farther back through the centuries, following the codex through real and imagined vicissitudes to its origin, the alternate chapters bring in a large cast of historical characters. The central story, however, moves forward in time, and concerns a contemporary Australian expert in rare books, a smart sophisticate named Hanna Heath. She is brought over to Sarajevo to analyze the (fictional) Haggadah, and falls for the (fictional) librarian who rescued it. We follow the adventures of the book back through five centuries, alternately with pursuing Hanna's professional duties, her difficulties with an unloving mother, her discovery of her own unexpected ethnic heritage. The story sprawls, but it is all firmly planned and plotted—possibly too firmly.

Hanna's chapters, told in the first person, are full of dialogue and written in a sprightly, crisp, journalistic style, thoroughly readable and serviceable, if without distinction or aesthetic quality as prose. Unfortunately this self-confident sureness of touch vanishes with the first step back in time, to Yugoslavia in 1940, where the protagonist is a Jewish girl who joins the Partisans. The style gets clunkier. The grinding of axes can be heard. By the time we are in Barcelona in 1492, dialogue has descended to the level of Bulwer-Lytton—"I know not what it is you imagine that I have done!"—and narration has become that heavy mixture of useful information with predictable behavior and generalised description which weighs down so many historical novels like stones in the pocket of a coat.

Full of action but with no leavening of humor, no psychological revelations, no vivid language to focus description, the chapters grind on. Most unhappily for an historical novel, there is little sensitivity to the local color of thought and emotion, not enough of the openness to human difference that brings the past alive.

Brooks expends a good deal of anxious effort trying to bring a modern sense of justice and ethical judgment into places and ages where it is an anachronism. People call such anxiety "political correctness," a term that once had meaning but now usually reflects only a reactionary sneer. Brooks's earnest good will deserves respect, but the fact is, a novel can get away with anachronism only when it is completely invisible, and her efforts to right old wrongs are only too visible. In the same way, a kindly feminism informs her efforts to invent women who were important to the creation and existence of the precious book. That's a tall order, among the old rabbis, but she persists; and so we find that the artist of the lovely illuminations was a woman, and a black one at that. This is not in itself impossible; the explanations are plausible; I'd like to believe it—but I can't. The person, the artist, the world of the artist, have not been made real enough to allow me to believe it. It's just wishful thinking. It has not taken on the fierce reality of true fiction.

So in the end I wonder whether this might not have been a better book if, foreswearing invention, the author, an experienced journalist, had simply followed the true and amazing story of the Sarajevo Haggadah. I wish someone could make a story or a poem of Aida Buturovic's life and death, for I know I will never know the story of the Iraqi with his arms full of books and his face full of anguish.

Italo Calvino:
The Complete Cosmicomics

2009

The summer reading I like best is either a lovely long fat novel to lie down with and get lost in, or a lovely lot of short stories, like a basket of summer fruit, to come back to and eat one or two at a time, savoring fully. Here, from Italo Calvino, is a great big basket of stories—nectarines, apricots, peaches, figs, everything.

It's a compendium of the volume *Cosmicomics* (published in English in 1968), seven newly translated stories from *La Memoria del mondo* (1968), all the stories from *Time and the Hunter* (1969), four from *Numbers in the Dark* (1995), and a couple of uncollected pieces. It's a joy to have all the Cosmicomics within one cover, and a handsome cover it is, and a well-made book. More than a third of the stories were entirely new to me, and will be to most readers in English; some of them are jewels. The translations, by William Weaver, Tim Parks, and Martin McLaughlin, are entirely satisfactory, and Mr. McLaughlin's introduction couldn't be better as a guide to these dazzlingly idiosyncratic tales.

What was Italo Calvino? A prepostmodernist? Maybe it's time to dispense with modernism and all its prefixes. A young Resistance fighter for the Communists during the Nazi occupation of Italy, Calvino became and remained a consistently original writer of intellectual fantasy. And what is a cosmicomic, this form he invented midway in his career? Clearly a subspecies of science fiction, it consists typically in the statement of a scientific hypothesis (usually genuine, though sometimes not currently accepted) which sets the stage for a narrative, of which the narrator is usually a person called Qfwfq. Thus "All at One Point" begins:

> Through the calculations begun by Edwin P. Hubble on the galaxies' velocity of recession, we can establish the moment when all the universe's matter was concentrated in a single point, before it began to expand in space. . . .
> Naturally, we were all there—*old Qfwfq said*—where else could we have been? Nobody knew then that there could be space. Or time either: what use did we have for time, packed in there like sardines?

Observe, please, the sardines. They are characteristic of and essential to Calvino's method and style. The story unfolds from this opening perfectly logically, at least if your definition of logic includes, as surely it should, not only modern astrophysics but Xeno's paradox, Borges's Aleph, and the Mad Hatter's tea party.

Calvino's later works may well be considered not as stories in the conventional sense but as *contes*: narrative illustrations of an intellectual apperception, an idea or theory, even a conceit. A favorite Enlightenment vehicle, the *conte* lends itself to satire and comedy; Voltaire's *Candide* is a masterpiece of the type. It presents caricatures rather than characters, irony rather than empathy. Personality and emotion may creep quietly in and exert their power, but the form can also be bloodlessly cerebral. Calvino's *contes* play word games with science, with time, space, and number; and in some of them the game is all there is. A game-loving reader, one perhaps fascinated by Wittgenstein or Eco, will find the pieces from *Time and the Hunter* especially satisfying; those of us more clogged by mortality may find their radical abstraction sterile. And Calvino's imagination is nothing if not radical. In "The Chase," he cuts to the chase so literally that the pursuit isn't the climax of a thriller movie, but is the whole story—the world reduced to a highway, emotion reduced to suspense, so completely without context or personality as to suggest (the pun is inevitable) a kind of autism.

Calvino's *Invisible Cities* derives in this same way from an idea, a notion; but the notion of old Marco Polo going back to China to tell the old Khan about the cities he did *not* see on his journeys is so inherently comic and poetic, so infinite in suggestion, that it guided the author into perhaps his most beautiful book. And if some of the Cosmicomics are a bit geeky, most are thoroughly entertaining, and some attain the true Calvinic sublime: intelligence, humor, poignancy, irony distilled to the purely luminous.

Their topics are exhilaratingly immense, the uttermost reaches of space and time, into which warmth and humor enter through all kinds of gaps, quirks, and tricks. Calvino's airy, dry, clear prose dances over the light-years, bringing forth homely and vivid images everywhere. Such are the sardines; such is the stone sky above those who dwell inside earth, through which "sometimes a fiery streak zigzags through the dark: it's not lightning, but an incandescent metal snaking down through a vein."

To me the one fault in this prose is its joky or satirical convention of unpronounceable names. If I can't say or hear "Qfwfq" (kefoofek?), how can I hear the cadence of the sentence it occurs in? Here Calvino's abstracting bent threatens language itself, reducing it to the literally unspeakable symbology of mathematics. That game gets chancy. But we breeze on, borne by the good humor and aplomb of the narrator, especially the ubiquitous, unquenchable Qfwfq, and enchanted by his friends and relations—all the people who were all there at the beginning, because where else could they have been, such as his grandfather, old Colonel Eggg, who moved into our solar system with his wife just as it was forming. "In the four billion years they've been here, they've already settled in more or less, got to know a few people," but their neighbors the Cavicchias are leaving, going back to the Abruzzi, and Grandmother would like to move about a bit too, go see her mother in the Andromeda Galaxy, maybe, but it's not the same thing, Grandfather protests, and they bicker about it, they bicker forever, on to the end of time they go, with "'you always think you're right' and 'it's because you never listen to me' without which the history of the universe would not have for him any name or memory or flavor, that eternal conjugal bickering: if ever it should one day come to an end, what a feeling of desolation, what emptiness!"

Calvino's take on duality, the existence of opposites, is almost entirely sexual. It does not result in a synthesis but an eternal process, like the yin-yang figure, represented quite well by conjugal bickering. Qfwfq is male, whatever form he happens to be in at the moment, a falling atom, a cosmic voyager, or (in the beautiful story "The Spiral") a tiny mollusc. As a rule there is also a female entity, whose essence is not only difference but disagreement, resistance, escape: the unpossessable, unloving beloved. Because we are never in her point of view, the Calvinic cosmos is skewed to the masculine principle. For me his ongoing metaphor of the everlasting and limitlessly extended Italian family is more endearing and more useful. But he develops his gendered dualism richly and with powerful feeling in such stories as "The Stone Sky" and its rewrite "The Other Euridice." Where there's authentic desire the male sees rivalry; and so the duality expands to the eternal triangle—here truly eternal.

Calvino was ahead of his time in so many ways that only now, twenty-five years after his death, is his work widely perceived not as marginal because it is fantasy but as a landmark in fiction, the work of a master. When he was writing, science fiction was not to be spoken of in the presence of the literary, and comic books were if possible even less acceptable. Few literary critics could imagine discussing them seriously until the late nineties. If they paid any attention to the name Calvino gave these stories, it was to emphasize one implication, the cosmic comedy. But he unmistakably meant us also to think of the lightning approaches, the leaps and vast simplifications, of graphic narrative drawn in frames, cartoons, the comics. And one story, "The Origin of the Birds," plays directly with this image, directing the reader in a very characteristic fashion: "It's best for you to try on your own to imagine the series of cartoons with all the little figures of the characters in their places, against an effectively outlined background, but you must try at the same time not to imagine the figures, or the background either."

So, there we are, given perfectly conflicting instructions. Perhaps if we could follow them we might arrive somewhere near the condition of "negative capability" which Keats believed the most fruitful of all. I have a notion that Italo Calvino lived a good part of the time there.

Margaret Drabble: *The Sea Lady*

2006

Each of Margaret Drabble's eighteen or nineteen novels has been an accurate, honest record of its time in the idiom of its time, and yet she has never been truly fashionable. A sharp critical intellect keeps her keenly aware of trend, and she's never bucked it; but the qualities for which I value her fiction could not be satisfactorily called modernist, nor are they postmodern now. Of course I'm trying to avoid the word old-fashioned, because I fear Drabble herself thinks it the kiss of death; and yet what is one to say? A compelling narrative impetus, essentially straightforward though entertainingly subtle; a moral burden, clear though mostly unstated; acute and amusing observation of society, gender, manners, fashions; strongly individual characters, whose character is probably their destiny. Lord, am I talking about Jane Austen?

A while back, Drabble seemed to be going a bit astray, hipped on some pseudo-issues such as the fascination that serial murderers are supposed to have for all of us; I thought her novels suffered accordingly. It is a pleasure to read *The Sea Lady* and find again the canny, cagy, unfooled, intransigent author of *The Needle's Eye*.

To get the caviling over with, I'll register my objection to one character, or voice, or persona, or whatever, in *The Sea Lady*—a Public Orator, male, who appears sporadically in a self-conscious pose to comment on the story, combining the metafictional interfering author, the Thackerayan aside to the reader, and a faint whiff of Bunyan. Some of the passages about him are eloquent:

> . . . the powers of the Orator are limited. They have been
> limited to the forethought, to the planning, to the invitation,

to the setting of the stage, to the choice of the venue, to the public confrontation. After that, the actors have this terrible freedom. They can write their own script. The Orator's formal script is already written, but they can write their own informal interchanges, as they meet in a crowded room, and as they climb the painful cobbled steps. This is risky, this is terrible.

So it is. It is also revealing. But I'm not certain that the revelation is relevant. It serves to emphasise the characters' artificiality while asserting their autonomy, and thus to protect the author from critical accusations of soft-heartedness; but having fearlessly subtitled her story "A Late Romance," she might as well have braved it without the Orator. He is, incidentally, related to (but cannot be identified with) one of the actual characters, to whom I have some objections also; this character resurfaces far too late, and unconvincingly. Ockham's razor might spare him, but would shave the Orator quite away. There is no need to multiply entities when you've got hold of two such good solid ones as Ailsa and Humphrey.

Ailsa is the Sea Lady, whom we first meet dressed in silver sequinned scales. "She gleamed and rippled with smooth muscle, like a fish. She was boldly dressed, for a woman in her sixties," and she's a bold woman—a brazen hussy of the intellect, a star in the showbiz of the mind. She is wearing her fish scales to present a literary prize, after which she will drive north to receive an honorary degree at a small university. She is the same Sea Lady who loved and married a man who loved fish and the sea, a marine biologist; they divorced and have not seen each other for decades, but as it happens (not by chance), he will be traveling north by train to receive an honorary degree at the same ceremony. They are converging.

Ailsa is genuinely brilliant and also a fake, maybe a bit of a monster, a mermaid on dry land. Humphrey is the real thing, both feet on the ground, an excellent scientist with a strong moral sense, a kind, responsible man. She is all performer, driven by competition; he has forfeited top honors in his field by refusing to treat science as a competition for recognition. Both have had success and yet have had to settle for somewhat dubious rewards. But the two of them also have a history, and not a simple one. Long before they were married long ago, they knew each other as children, in that same small northern city by the sea, just after the end of the Second World War.

The depth and weight of the story, its ballast, its bottom, are in the pages that relate Humphrey's two summers as a child in Ornemouth and Finsterness. The flexible, steady accuracy of the narration in these chapters is marvelous; the story is utterly engrossing. Identification with the child's point of view all too often leads to the whining falsities of *The Catcher in the Rye,* but Drabble has always been able to write as an adult about children. Her generous and unsentimental truthfulness to the condition of childhood is very rare. Hump is a nice boy, and he has one wonderfully happy summer—not an easy thing to write about, happiness. The betrayal, anxiety, and dubious gains of the second summer are more predictable, yet ring equally true.

So satisfying are these hundred pages that the rest of the book has a problem matching them, particularly as the direction of the narrative is trickier, moving back and forth. Humphrey grows up into a really nice man—again not an easy thing to write about—but when he and Ailsa, who is not a very nice woman, but an entertaining one, first meet again as adults and fall in love, the episode fails to engage on the deep level of the Ornemouth summers. It's all right, as lust goes. But novelistically, it isn't much more than an interlude between the dense, brilliant reality of the beginning—children on the beach—and the guarded ambiguity of the end, with the sixty-year-old smiling public man and woman, receiving their accolades. And, perhaps, finally, their true rewards.

Carol Emshwiller:
Ledoyt

First published in 1997, revised in 2002, and revised again for this book

Looking over the New Fiction shelf at the library one day in 1997, I saw *Ledoyt*, by Carol Emshwiller. Emshwiller? I thought—*my* Emshwiller? She wrote a new book that's been out for two years and I never heard about it?

I shouldn't have been surprised. Emshwiller's readers know her to be a major fabulist, a marvelous magical realist, one of the strongest, most complex, most consistently feminist voices in fiction. But her books, mostly published by a good small press in San Francisco, Mercury House, don't get wide attention. Part of the problem may well be her calm originality. Most reviewers prefer pigeons that fit in holes and rabbits that redux. Emshwiller's like a wild mixture of Italo Calvino (intellectual games) and Grace Paley (perfect honesty) and Fay Weldon (outrageous wit) and Jorge Luis Borges (pure luminosity), but no—her voice is perfectly her own. She isn't like anybody. She's different.

Before I get to *Ledoyt* (which is different) I want to talk a little about the other Emshwiller books (which are all different).

Before 1990 I knew her work only from science-fiction publications. She isn't categorisable as an sf writer, but she knows how to play brilliant games with sf themes. *Verging on the Pertinent* (from Coffee House Press, 1989), the first of her books I read, is a collection of fables, witty, cool, scary. After reading it I thought of her as an impressive and sophisticated writer whom I admired without exactly liking—though I did love the first story in the collection, "Yukon," about a woman in the Far North who runs away from her husband and spends the winter comfortably with a bear and then meets her true love, who is an Engelmann spruce tree, or a man very like a spruce tree, named Engelmann. . . . So often in Emshwiller stories you can have it the way you want it. She doesn't make you have it the way she wants it. For all her formidable wit, she is a kind writer. And a surprising number of her stories have happy endings. At least they do if you want the ending to be happy. I am not sure Mr. Engelmann is *really* the heroine's true love, but it seemed that way to me last time I read the story. It may seem quite different the next time.

In 1990 came *Carmen Dog*, a novel about women turning into animals and animals turning into women, perhaps the funniest and the cruelest of her books, a sort of feminist *Candide*. The kindness of the innocent heroine, Pooch, triumphs over cruelty in the end, which is happy; at least it is if you want it to be. Even Pooch's children turn out well, "setters, and all male." Why this book isn't a feminist classic I don't know. Maybe it is. Maybe that's why people haven't heard about it. It should be a required text on gender in all high schools and colleges.

I taught *Carmen Dog* in a literature class at San José State University in the spring of 2001. That is, I got permission to Xerox the first three chapters for the class, since Mercury House had let the book go out of print and didn't seem interested in the fact that we needed fifteen copies. The class loved it so much that they demanded I get permission for them to xerox the rest of the book, which they'd found several copies of. Teaching it made me see that it is better even than I had thought, and there is no cruelty in it. Truth, yes. And funny? Lord!

After *Carmen Dog* came the stunning collection *The Start of the End of It All*, in which both her range and her voice have widened, deepened. The comparison to Borges becomes inevitable with such stories as "The Circular Library of Stones" or the haunting "Vilcabamba." And so does the contrast with Borges. In Emshwiller's fables, while the invention is as magistral, the element of human pain is less distanced. And her humor is wilder than Borges's. The title story of this collection is a magnificent example of what happens to science fiction when a real feminist gets hold of it. It's about aliens coming to earth, yes, but has nothing whatever in common with gooey-minded stuff like *Close Encounters* and *E.T.* The heroine, like most Emshwiller heroines, is obliging and trusting and has very low self-esteem, being one of "the rejected, the divorced, the growing older, the left out." An Alien, or several of them, named Klimp, trick(s) her into giving birth to his (its) (their) offspring, a lot of tiny little fishy Aliens; but her cats eat all of them but one. She keeps it and names it Charles after her father, or possibly Henry, and indulges in no more illusions about the Aliens. It is a perfectly happy ending if you want it to be, or not at all if you don't; but either way it is extremely and profoundly funny.

All right, so this was the Carol Emshwiller I thought I knew, this kind, scary, funny, feminist fabulist. I picked *Ledoyt* (Mercury House, 1995) off the New Fiction shelf and stared at the cover: not Queen Kong climbing the Empire State Building, not a bird-dog-woman, nothing wild and imaginary, but a hand-tinted photograph of a very young woman in old-fashioned Western riding gear, reading a letter, in a desert.

And the cover is a fair introduction to the book. *Ledoyt* is different, as I said—from its author's other books and from most contemporary novels. It does belong in a certain fragile and discontinuous tradition of novels by or about women in the Far West in the late 1800s and early 1900s. But first of all I want to say that it is a love story.

We tend to consider love stories as common, a simpleminded genre stuffing the Romance shelves, rarely rising to art in the hands of a Brontë or Austen. But how many stories are, in fact, about love? I never asked the question till I gave "a love story" as an assignment to a writing workshop. From that group I got fourteen stories about lust. Next time I tried it, I got eleven lust stories, two hate stories, and one love story about a woman who loved her niece.

Given all the kinds of loving we do, it's odd that we use fiction so often to explore love only as sexual desire or as an abusive, exploitive, or obsessional relationship employing sexuality as a means to power.

Ledoyt is a love story. It's about the passionately fulfilled but never secure love of a married couple for each other, and the passionately angry, rejecting love of a young girl, Lotti, for her stepfather, her mother, and her young half-brother. Family love, that voyage across a shoreless, uncharted sea of shipwrecks and sunken treasures. What a story it makes! How infinitely more interesting it is than any position Madonna can be photographed in! And how close such a story comes to the love life most of us actually live—the unromantic, endless adjustment and disappointment and readjustment, the blind cruelty and blind tenderness, the knots and complications and tangled nets, the rage and loyalty and rebellion, the ordinary passions of ordinary people trying to live with one another, trying to love one another.

At the center of the story are Ledoyt, the dirty, gentle cowboy who keeps trying to run away from his luck because he can't believe in it, and young Lotti, who sets herself afire and shoots a man and draws horses with mustaches that are portraits of Ledoyt . . . Ledoyt, who married her mother, Oriana. Oriana, raped by her respectable fiancé, ran away, came West, and had the daughter who's going to wreck the family and run away from her. A lot of the history of our country consists of people running away. It doesn't mean they weren't good people. Some of them.

Then there's the setting. Those who live in the eastern half of the country tend to see cowboys on the range and ranches in the sagebrush as props for macho movies, not as the setting for a serious novel. You mean real people live out there?

Emshwiller's Sierra-slope California of 1905 is far, far from Louis L'Amour and on another planet from Hollywood; but it's right up the road from Mary Austin's *Land of Little Rain.* This is one of the Americas where "success" has no meaning, a country of dryland farming and hardscrabble cattle ranching, where each loner knows the next loner. These are people with low expectations, tough, peculiar failures and runaways, desert people. In this impassively dangerous and beautiful landscape, human acts and relations take on the importance of any voice or gesture that breaks deep stillness. But Emshwiller doesn't rhapsodise desert life. She knows the country as a rancher knows it, as land, not scenery; she knows its people as individuals, not archetypes. She knows how to listen to its silences, and theirs.

My family on my mother's side, Far Westerners from the mountain and desert states, were people like these, and Emshwiller has them absolutely right. Young Lotti keeps a diary, which recurs through the novel. Reading it, I kept thinking of my great-aunt Betsy, born in Oregon in 1874. This sounds like Betsy, I thought. Betsy would have known this girl. Betsy *was* this girl. It's still a rare experience for a Westerner to find her people in fiction, to hear them talk the way they talked. There were women writers early in the century who knew them; Mary Hallock Foote, whose work Wallace Stegner appropriated without credit in one of his novels, was one. H. L. Davis's *Honey in the Horn* and Molly Gloss's *The Jump-Off Creek* have an implacable honesty about Western place and character. Writers like Carolyn See, Judith Freeman, Deirdre McNamer, and Alison Baker are bringing this tradition up to date. At last, and slowly, and mostly by women writers, the West is being won.

But Emshwiller, whose stories are so New Yorkish and sophisticated, who teaches writing at NYU, how does she know all about my great-aunt? By being a first-class novelist, I guess. Fiction writers do, after all, use the imagination, which is what makes them different from memoirists. Emshwiller knows the setting of her novel by heart, knows what life was like on a homestead ranch, knows what side you get onto a horse from. In a photograph at the back of the book, she's laughing as she hefts a businesslike saddle towards a handsome Appaloosa. But the background, trees or bushes, could be a creek bottom near Barstow, could be Long Island, could be anywhere. All I'm sure of is, she knew what she wrote about in *Ledoyt*, and it was worth writing about, and nobody else has ever written anything quite like it.

I'm sorry to report that as of this writing, *Ledoyt* is still out of print. And if you look it up at the place everybody thinks you have to buy books from these days, you may get what I got: the title *Ledoyt*, but a description of a book about Belarus. So there we are again—up the Amazon without a paddle. I can only hope some publisher will have the sense to reissue *Ledoyt*: a fierce and tender portrait of a girl growing up fierce and tender; a sorrowful, loving portrait of a man whose talent is for love and sorrow; a Western, an unsentimental love story, an unidealised picture of the American past, a tough, sweet, painful, truthful novel.

Alan Garner:
Boneland

2012

Boneland is an adult sequel to the two books for children Alan Garner published in 1960 and 1963. Colin and Susan, in *The Weirdstone of Brisingamen* and *The Moon of Gomrath*, are twins of about twelve, rushing about on nonstop miraculous aventures, enduring sleeplessness, danger, and pain, and accepting supernatural events with almost superhuman placidity. At the end of the second book, Susan appears to be destined for an otherworldly fate or role.

At the beginning of this third book, Susan has vanished. Her brother Colin has aged some thirty or forty years, and their author nearly fifty.

I had to wait seventeen years between books to see where the story of my own Earthsea must go, and the whole series took thirty-three to write. Fifty years is a long time between books; yet it seems perfectly right and natural that Alan Garner should need five decades to gyre back round to where he began, the legend-haunted landscape of Alderly Edge, to be able follow his story deeper into the human psyche and the dark backward and abysm of Time.

Colin has become a brilliant astrophysicist, ornithologist, and all-round savant with five or six master's degrees, as well as being an outstanding cook, carpenter, and social misfit. He has total recall of everything that has happened to him since the age of thirteen, but has lost all memory of the years before that, along with his sister and his intrepidity. The almost phlegmatically fearless child has become an anguished, supersensitive, self-absorbed man whose incoherent obsessions are driving him mad.

Colin's search for his sister and his sanity are a true Quest, for the well-being of the world is also at stake. Descendant of men who danced and sang on Alderly Edge to keep the stars in their courses and bring the sun back from winter death, Colin is a shaman, heir of the shamans of the Ice Age and ages long before. He needs to find his own balance because his job is to keep the balance of the world. The rocks and caves of a reef of Triassic sandstone in Cheshire are the axis of the balance, the navel of the universe, the center that must hold.

That center, of course, is also in a cave in Delphi, on an island in the Klamath River of California, in a thousand places on earth, and in the Earth itself as revealed to the astronaut Rusty Schweickart on a walk in space—wherever human beings feel the depth of their connection to the world and take it as a sacred responsibility.

Yet this universal connection is felt as deeply local. *This* place is the sacred place. More mythmaker than fantasist, Alan Garner names his chosen, actual landscape minutely, feature by feature, stone by stone, relishing the old place names and the grand vocabulary of geology, weaving the words into a litany of confirmation, the endless repetition that keeps the end from coming, the rhythmic dance on the world's edge that maintains the world. Alderly Edge is the scene of a timeless ritual that must be reenacted over and over by ignorant and ephemeral mortals. Personal tragedy and redemption are subsumed in the cosmic vision.

No wonder that the people of his story are less characters than masks, types, archetypes. But as imaginative literature reclaims the territories forbidden it by modernist realism, and moves back from Elfland towards the outskirts of Manchester, it treads on dangerous ground. Readers looking for more than mere adventure expect characters whose behavior and reactions are humanly comprehensible. The child twins Colin and Susan were semi-characterless actors in a fantasy tale. The man Colin is both a severely disturbed radio astronomer and the man chosen from his generation to "look after the Edge"—and how to reconcile these roles in a character in a modern novel? How are the psychic sufferings of a man so anachronistically fated and so emotionally crippled to be made comprehensible?

The author's success hinges partly on his division of the character into two—the twenty-first-century scientist Colin and an unnamed Stone Age ancestor. But in the end, his success must depend on the reader's willingness to be teased through an imaginative labyrinth by allusions, hints, puzzles, and tricks such as unascribed dialogue and undescribed location. The process of Colin's healing, the stages of therapy, the un-nesting of image within image, is fascinating, but the narration demands that the reader let the author manipulate and control, just as Colin is manipulated by the analyst.

And she in the end appears to have been a witch or goddess, who disappears in a puff of smoke. In a serious novel, this is risky business.

Alan Garner can count on the trust and admiration of his readers to see him through it. My trust and admiration, though great, weren't always sufficient. No rereading has yet given me a clue to the meaning of the first eight lines of *Boneland*. Well, I'll get it, one of these days. Is the all-wise, wisecracking, motorcycle-riding psychoanalyst the Witch-Crone or the Moon Mother? Is Susan one of the Pleiades? Well, OK. Is truth, as Garner would have it, not attainable through knowledge, only through belief? Well, maybe.

Where all the teases and all the risks pay off, for me, is in the shadow story of the man who "looked after the Edge" so long ago, the solitary artist-shaman of the Ice Age. These sections of the book are told in a charged, elliptical, symbolic, highly concrete language: "He cut the veil of the rock; the hooves clattered the bellowing waters below him in the dark. The lamp brought the moon from the blade, and the blade the bull from the rock. The ice rang."

You figure out what it's all about gradually as you go along. It's not mere puzzle-solving; as with reading poetry, learning another language, learning to see and think differently, the demands and rewards are intense and real. It is this element of the book, in which the obsessions come into focus and a true balance is glimpsed, that will bring me back to *Boneland*, knowing I'll find there what no other novelist has ever given us.

Kent Haruf:
Benediction

2014

The Colorado of the mind, and the posters, is all peaks and picturesque ski lodges. But if you ever drive into Colorado from the east, you may begin to wonder where they keep the Rockies. The slope of the plains rises imperceptibly, immense, monotonous, with an ugly little town now and then. The American West goes beyond all picturesqueness, and its sublimity is not superficial.

One of those ugly little towns, Holt, was invented by the novelist Kent Haruf. Readers of his three novels *Plainsong, Eventide,* and *Benediction* know the place now, street by street, citizen by citizen. I find that Haruf's characters, like Pierre and Natasha or Huck Finn, inhabit my mind permanently; they're people I think about. Their conversation is dry and plain, with an easy Western cadence, and the author's narration is the same. The absence of quotation marks around speech gently emphasizes this continuity. It is a restrained voice, a quiet music.

The passions of the people of Holt, many of them loners by nature, subject to the repressive conventionality of small-town America and all the restraints of poverty, ignorance, and relentless hard work, break through sometimes in violence, sometimes in acts or attempted acts of outreaching compassion. The violence is common in novels at present, the compassion less so. Haruf handles human relationships with fierce, reticent delicacy, exploring rage, fidelity, pity, honor, timidity, the sense of obligation; he deals with complex, barely stated moral issues, pushing perhaps towards an unspoken mysticism. Occasionally he risks sentimentality, and once or twice, I think, falls into it, but in the Holt novels as a whole, his courage and achievement in exploring ordinary forms of love—the enduring frustration, the long cost of loyalty, the comfort of daily affection—are unsurpassed by anything I know in contemporary fiction.

Benediction is best read as what it is, the third of three novels linked by some recurrence of characters but chiefly by the extraordinary presence of the town and its countryside, built up incrementally, detail by detail, in each book. They are three different stories, but they have cumulative power. The story of *Benediction*, like its title, suggests closure. But life in Holt is going to go right on, for the sense of continuity in time is as strong as the sense of location in place.

The earlier books supplied vivid action and some more conventionally "Western" doings, such as a scene in *Eventide* of moving range bulls out of a corral. That scene, ending in the death of an old man, carries a shock like the last sentence of the Waterloo chapter in *Vanity Fair*. *Benediction* is quieter; in it, too, an old man dies, but it's a long-drawn-out death, and Dad Lewis isn't a cattle rancher, just a shopkeeper. He owns the hardware store in Holt. He's not likable, not very interesting—a narrow, grouchy old guy dying of cancer.

Memoirs and fictions relating the relentless course of a disease or a dementia are legion these days, and the dismal familiarities are all here; but Dad Lewis's dying reveals not only the banality and humility of physical suffering, but an unusually open, daylight approach to mystery, and a humor so dry it's almost ether.

There's unfinished business on Dad's conscience. His ghosts—his dead parents, his lost son—come and sit on wooden chairs by his bed and talk with him. They're all just as ornery as he is. His father, an old hardscrabble Kansas farmer, says to him,

> Well, you sure got you a real fine nice big house here. You done all right that way, didn't you. This is a real nice big pleasing satisfying house you got here.
>
> I worked for it, Dad said.
>
> Well sure. Of course. I know, the old man said. Had some luck too, I believe.
>
> I had some luck. But I worked hard. I earned it.

> Yeah. Sure. Most people work hard. It's not only that now, is it. You had you some luck.
>
> Goddamn it, I had some luck too, Dad said, but I earned the luck.

His bitter, inconclusive conversations with his son—who may or may not be dead, Dad doesn't know, though he refuses the possibility—reveal the all too ordinary tragedy of their relationship: inexpressible love, unattainable forgiveness. Dad Lewis wrestles with his ghosts as Jacob with the angel, trying grimly, vainly, not to let them go until they bless him.

The narrative circles out from and back to this central figure, weaving a complex, rich texture of sub-stories, personalities, generations. Haruf writes about girls and women with tenderness and without idealisation, as individuals. He has an unjudgmental sympathy with the agonies of adolescence, and an unblinking eye for coarseness and hypocrisy. His skill at showing affectionate nonsexual relationships, and at describing the relation of parents and children from the point of view of both, is as uncommon as it is welcome.

Haruf is in fact a stunningly original writer in a great many ways. The quality of his originality goes right under the radar of much conventional criticism. He doesn't posture or raise his voice. He talks quietly, intimately, yet with reserve, as one adult to another. He's careful to get the story right. And it is right, it's just right; it rings true.

Kent Haruf:
Our Souls at Night

2016

Writing about the everyday is a tough job. The extraordinary, the thrilling, the transgressive provide automatic glamor, but it takes a brave author to try to describe lives that are so commonplace as not even to be extraordinarily unhappy. And happiness—not sexual satisfaction, not reward of ambition, not ecstasy, not bliss, just day-to-day happiness—has practically vanished from fiction. That may be because we distrust it, seeing it as sentimentality, confusing the real thing with the fake. Indeed, it's not easy to write about. To ring true, description of even the humblest kind of fulfillment and contentment must be written in awareness of human inadequacy and cruelty and the always imminent possibility of illness, ruin, death. One false word can make it all incredible.

I don't think there's a false word in Kent Haruf's *Our Souls at Night*. Nor, for all the colloquial ease and transparency of the prose and the apparent simplicity of the story, is there a glib word, or a predictable one.

Ordinarily the circumstances of the writing of a novel aren't of much interest to me as a reader, but in this case, I am moved, even awed, to consider that the book was written while the author was dying. It is a report from the far edge of life, the edge of darkness, made in the consciousness of responsibility. Haruf is bearing witness. Having gone farther than we have, he wants to tell us what matters there. His knowledge of his situation, and my knowledge of it as I read the book, made me appreciate the rare privilege of being with a person who is past the need to say anything but what needs to be said.

The voice is quiet. All the darkness is there, but we're looking at the light. A lamp in a bedroom in a small town in Colorado.

———

Haruf's novels are all set in that small town, Holt. The first two were fairly conventional. In the third, *Plainsong*, he found his own voice: profoundly American in its cadences, Western American in its unexpected drollnesses and its calm, dry reticence. *Plainsong* and the novels that followed it are, like Willa Cather's, eloquent of the lonesomeness of that vast country, the paradoxical constriction of people's lives there, and the fragility. Violence, never gloated over as a spectacle, is brief, inevitable, and shocking. Children are always among the characters, drawn with extraordinary realism, compassion, and intensity. The young people are restless, nervy, unguided. Older men do their jobs and keep their defenses up. Women generally keep things running, though now and then one goes to pieces or suddenly runs off to Denver. But there is joy also, hard joy—the pleasure of risk, the pleasure of responsibility. Among these people tenderness is sheltered, cherished like a seedling tree as it slowly puts down deep roots to reach the water.

Holt is a long way from New York, farther perhaps than London or Prague. To many Eastern Americans, Western America means only cactus and Hollywood, a film set for Westerns, not for literature. Haruf's fidelity to the glamorless and untrendy Holt may have played into the parochialism of urban critics to keep his thoughtful, subtle, skillful work from the attention it deserves. Perhaps he didn't mind. Not playing the hunger games of success, not undergoing the mechanical hoopla of the PR celebrity factories, he could go on stubbornly being Kent Haruf, doing his job, keeping his defenses up. He could go on writing about how hard it is to go on doing what you see as right when you aren't sure how to do it, or even whether it's right—how hard we are on one another and ourselves, how hard most of us work, how much we long for and how little we mostly settle for.

This is all solid, satisfying novel stuff, and in this last book something very rare has been added to it. Many novels have been about the pursuit of happiness, but this one is luminous with its actual presence.

"And then there was the day when Addie Moore made a call on Louis Waters." So the story begins. Addie, a widow, has come to ask her widower neighbor if he'd consider coming over to her house sometimes to sleep with her.

"What?" says Louis, naturally a bit taken aback. "How do you mean?" And she says, "I mean we're both alone. We've been by ourselves for too long. For years. I'm lonely. I think you might be too. I wonder if you would come and sleep in the night with me. And talk."

So the light comes on in the bedroom on Cedar Street, in Holt, Colorado. And a happiness is very cautiously, courageously, tenderly achieved. Not, however, in the way we might expect, but on quite complex terms, involving quite a few of the other citizens of Holt. Perhaps happiness is less predictable than misery, since it partakes of freedom. Like freedom, also, it's never secure; it can't be forever. But it can be real, and in this beautiful novel, we can share it.

Tove Jansson:
The True Deceiver

2009

After the enduring and international success of her Moomintroll fantasies, the Finnish author-artist Tove Jansson, in her sixties, began to write realistic adult fiction. It has taken a while for these books to get much attention outside Scandinavia. On the patronising assumption that books for children are nice—i.e., morally bland and stylistically infantile—critics, reviewers, and prize juries often dismiss those who write them as incapable of writing seriously for adults, a prejudice which, transferred to painting, not incidentally plays a part in the plot of *The True Deceiver*.

Anyone familiar with any of Tove Jansson's works knows it would be unwise to dismiss or patronise her work on any grounds. Her books for children are complex, subtle, psychologically tricky, funny, and unnerving; their morality, though never compromised, is never simple. Thus her transition to adult fiction involved no great change. Her everyday Finns are quite as strange as trolls, and her Finnish village in winter is as beautiful and dangerous as any forest of fantasy.

If a transformation has taken place, it is in the nature of her writing. The language is more than ever lean, taut, minimalist. These adjectives, however, describe a good deal of modern narrative prose—the modishly anorectic style, well suited to thrillers, police procedurals, and the existential noir, but very limited in range. Jansson's range, though effortlessly controlled, is great. Her spare exactness can express not only tension and stress but deeply felt emotion, expansion, relaxation, and peace. Her description is unhurried, accurate, and vivid, an artist's vision. Her style is not at all "poetic," quite the contrary. It is prose of the very highest order. It is pure prose. Through its quiet clarity we see unreachable depths, threatening darkness, promised treasures. The sentences are beautiful in structure, movement, and cadence. They have inevitable rightness. And this is a translation! Thomas Teal deserves to have his name on the title page with Tove Jansson's. He has pulled off the true translator's miracle.

I wish I could quote whole pages; a paragraph must do:

> If it got really cold, it didn't make sense to go on working. The shed wasn't insulated, and the stove was barely able to warm it enough to keep their hands from stiffening. They locked it up and went home. But on the seaward side where the boats were launched, the doors had a latch that was easy to open. Mats would go out on the ice with his cod hook and when no one was in sight he'd go into the boat shed. Sometimes he'd go on with his work, usually details so trivial that no one noticed they'd been done. But most times he just sat quietly in the peaceful snowlight. He never felt cold.

The main characters are Anna Aemalin, a successful illustrator of children's books, and Katri, whose only love and ambition is for the younger brother left in her care, Mats, a shy, slow, gentle fellow. Then there are honest Liljeberg the boat-builder, the wise Madame Nygard, the malicious storekeeper, a little horde of village children, and Katri's dog. Nameless, silent, and yellow-eyed, the dog is yellow-eyed Katri's creature. And she flatters herself on her own wolfish superiority to other people: "My dog and I despise them. We're hidden in our own secret life, concealed in our innermost wildness."

No one in the village seems to be married, and the relationship that will form between the two solitary women, Katri and Anna, is not sexual, though it is intensely passionate, fiercely unstable, destructive, and transformative.

Anna, far wealthier than Katri, keeps her parents' house piously unchanged, and illustrates little books for which the publisher provides the text. Her paintings are marvelously truthful depictions of the forest floor, patterns of leaf, twig, moss, lichen . . . to which she adds the cute bunnies of the publisher's texts. She spends much time answering letters from her child readers, and none in looking after her business interests. She sleeps, sleeps all winter until spring comes and she can see the living ground and paint it.

Wolfish young Katri, determined to provide security for her brother, and also the fishing boat that is his one heart's desire, fakes a robbery of Anna's house in order to make her afraid to live alone, and pushes her way into Anna's service and confidence. Before long she appears to be in full control and has thrown out all the old furniture and the comfortable lies that let Anna sleep. But Anna, awake now, is not the bunny rabbit she seemed, any more than Katri is truly the wolf. The unfolding of their story through vivid contrast and interplay of truthfulness and deceit, purity and complexity, ice and thaw, winter and spring, makes the most beautiful and satisfying novel I have read this year.

Barbara Kingsolver: *Flight Behavior*

2012

Some of the finest American novels were written at least partly in the hope of effecting moral change. From *Huckleberry Finn* and *Uncle Tom's Cabin* through *The Grapes of Wrath* and beyond runs a clear and brilliant arc of explicit concern with poverty and social injustice. Barbara Kingsolver's *Flight Behavior* is a worthy new member of that company, its concerns embodied in the vivid characters of a novel written with passion and intelligence. What is new is that her scathingly accurate depictions of societal imbalance are closely interwoven with urgent concern about environmental imbalance—the ongoing catastrophe that no serious writer will be allowed to ignore much longer.

Many reviewers, predictably dismissing Kingsolver as earnest but naïve, or scolding her for not knowing where monarch butterflies winter, evidently don't know how to read a writer so gifted at seeing and portraying both sides of a social dilemma and so adept at invention based firmly on knowledge. This scientifically trained novelist uses imagination to illuminate reality, and irony to transcend irony. The conventionally baroque and grotesque "Southern novel" in her hands gains the breadth and aplomb of South American magic realism.

Describing *Flight Behavior* for British readers is a problem. Particularly in its humor, it's very American, regional, dialectical—an equivalent of those very British novels that Americans read while wishing they could catch the implications and nuances and knowing they don't. To the ear that recognises them, the cadences are perfect. When the heroine's friend says, "Here's the thing. You looked bookoo hot. Can I borrow that sweater?" or when her mother-in-law says, "Lord Almighty, the girl is receiving grace!"—will the complex indications and references of the language carry across the Atlantic? I can only hope so, because the implications are fiercely revealing, and the nuances often very funny.

I had the opportunity to ask the author if there was an aspect of the book she felt critics had missed so far. She pondered briefly and said, "Class." Another problem for me: American class definition is so much vaguer and less conscious than in England. All the same, poor is poor, and Kingsolver is right: reviewers have talked about the butterflies, not the characters, ignoring the stunning complexity of the novel's achievement in showing how social factors—class, education, privilege, religion—control individual interaction with the processes we call Nature, the world we live in.

These days, many Americans proclaim that they "do not believe in" global warming, or evolution, or science. What has led to such foolish, perilous denial? To lay it to ignorance, stupidity, Republicanism, or Southern redneckism is to evade the question in a particularly arrogant and cowardly way. Kingsolver tackles it head on, because she knows and respects the people she writes about, the vivid, vulnerable, beleaguered, unconsidered hicks who have no credit in any sense of the word, and who get little help and a great deal of disinformation when they try to understand the world and their place in it.

The heroine and viewpoint character of the story has lived her twenty-some years in the "worldwide entrapment of bottom feeders," as she calls it—not hungry but living on boxed mac and cheese, pinching every dollar yet never out of debt, secondhand car, secondhand clothes. Her mother named her Dellarobia in the hopeful notion that the name was biblical. It turned out to mean a wreath of acorns and such glued onto cardboard. When she finds it may refer to an Italian artist, Dellarobia feels better about it, but generally speaking, she doesn't feel very good about herself. She doesn't feel deserving or entitled. She feels inadequate and unworthy. She wanted to go to college, but got pregnant and had to marry Cub, who pretty much lives up to his name. She miscarried that baby but had two more, now six and two years old. Overwhelmed, seeing no way out, she has decided to run off with the handsome telephone man. In the first chapter of the book she's on her way to meet him through a dark fir forest when the hillsides of trees around her catch fire, blazing up in orange flames, burning unconsumed. And she receives grace.

> "Jesus," she said, not calling for help, she and Jesus weren't that close, but putting her voice in the world because nothing else made sense. . . . The sparks spiralled upward in swirls like funnel clouds. . . .
> Unearthly beauty had appeared to her, a vision of beauty to stop her in the road. For her alone these orange boughs lifted, these long shadows became a brightness rising.

Films of monarch butterfly gathering-places in Mexico or California show us a shadow of that brightness. The scene of the miracle soon becomes exactly that, a place of pilgrimage—particularly after the nearest TV station sends elegantly coiffed and booted Tina out to interview bewildered Dellarobia. Posed for the photographer among the swirling clouds of thousands of butterflies, she confesses that she'd been about to throw her life away when she saw that "here was something so much bigger. I had to come back and live a different life."

The photograph goes viral on the internet: the Madonna of the Butterflies. And her father-in-law, who can't understand who the hell has the right to stop him from logging his fir trees to help cover his debts, finds himself the villain of a lurid environmental drama.

TV Tina returns to interview Dr. Byron, the lepidopterist who has come to study this unprecedented (and in fact highly ominous) phenomenon of monarchs wintering so far from their ancestral migratory routes. Dellarobia is understandably smitten with the scientist, the first man who ever noticed she has a mind. He respects her, teaches her, gives her a job, and is kind to her kids. But under the relentless obtuseness of Tina's questions, he loses his careful detachment. It's a fine confrontation: Tina blinking and asking, "Are we talking about global warming here?" and cutting the camera off as soon as the scientist says, "Yes, we are"—her repeated glib rephrasings that trivialize whatever he says—his increasingly fierce refusals to evade or concede. It's what we never see on TV because, if it happens, it isn't aired. Tina and the cameraman storm out to destroy the film, the scientist tears his hair in shame at blowing his one great chance to present his side of the story, and Dellarobia's friend Dovey holds up her smartphone. "Yo, guys," she says. "Don't worry. I got it all. Posting it now. YouTube."

It's a fine moment of simple dramatic satisfaction. The book is full of such unpretentious pleasures. But the deep and lasting satisfaction of it is in the quiet, implacable unfolding of its great theme: our need, our desperate need as human beings, to begin to live a different life.

Chang-Rae Lee:
On Such A Full Sea

Published in the Guardian, *February 2014*

Dystopia is by its nature a dreary, inhospitable country. To its early explorers it held all the excitement of discovery, and that still fills their descriptions, keeping them fresh and powerful—E. M. Forster's "The Machine Stops," Yevgeny Zamyatin's *We*, Aldous Huxley's *Brave New World*. But for the last thirty years or more, Dystopia has been a major tourist attraction. Everybody goes there and writes a book about it. And the books tend to be alike, because the terrain is limited and its nature is monotonous.

The most familiar view of it is a wild landscape, more or less catastrophically ruined or neglected, in which human settlements exist widely separated from each other and cut off from nature, other species, sometimes even the outer atmosphere. These enclaves—underground or in domes or behind walls—are human hives, controlled by government and routine, living a regimented, sheltered, safe, highly unnatural, often luxurious "utopian" life. Those inside the enclaves consider those living outside them primitive, lawless, and dangerous, which they are, though they also often hold the promise of freedom. So Dystopia has a hero: an insider who goes outside.

Chang-Rae Lee's guidebook to the country is, as one would expect from a professor of creative writing, full of ingenious variations on predictable themes, and written with such complex subtlety of point of view as to give it at least the appearance of a new understanding of the place. It follows the usual inside/outside pattern. A vague entity called the Directorate maintains two kinds of enclave: crowded and industrious worker-class colonies produce the necessities for upper-class colonies called Charters, where people live in lavish and competitive luxury. Outside these (somehow) protected zones is anarchic wilderness, called the counties. The narrator-guide is a first-person-plural voice that represents and speaks for the people of B-Mor (Baltimore), a colony of Asian-ancestry workers who grow food for the Charters. This "we" voice is also inexplicably able to know and relate the journey and the emotions of the hero who goes outside.

A good many things in the novel were inexplicable to me, such as how and when North America came to be like this, what happened to nation and religion, how raw materials are produced, and how, without trains or good highways, they manage to have coffee, gasoline, electronic devices, food in plastic pouches, neoprene suits, plastic throwaway dishes and implements—unsustainably high-tech luxuries that we of 2014 enjoy thanks to our immense global network of industrial production. But in a broken, sporadic civilization, where does all this stuff come from?

Neglect of such literal, rational questions in imaginative fiction is often excused, even legitimated, as literary license. Because the author is known as a literary writer, he will probably be granted the license he takes. But social science fiction is granted no such irresponsibility, and a novel about a future society under intense political control is social science fiction. Like Cormac McCarthy and others, Lee uses essential elements of a serious genre irresponsibly, superficially. As a result, his imagined world carries little weight of reality. The whole system is too self-contradictory to serve as warning or satire, even if towards the end of the book the narrator begins to suspect its insubstantiality.

The hero is a young woman named Fan, pregnant by a young man named Reg. Uniquely immune to the one scourge of the Charter colonies and the wild counties alike—a group of fatal diseases known as C—Reg is taken away by the Charters so they can study him and find the secret of his immunity. Fan then leaves her home colony and sets out to find Reg, with no idea where he is and no plan of how to get there or how to survive in the savagely unsafe and incoherent outside world. She trusts to her amazing physical prowess and her amazingly sharp wits. Maybe she just relies on being a superhero—a quality that will indeed get you safely through anything. Her superheroism is colored by a tinge of saintliness ascribed to her by the elusive first-person-plural narrator, the voice of the industrious, modest, patient workers of her home hive. Perhaps she represents their virtues. I could believe in those virtues, but I could not believe in Fan.

Lee's prose is suave and canny; his story flows; events are vividly described, particularly as they verge into grotesque folktale violence and exaggeration; there are pleasant contemplative moments. Readers who find anachronism and implausibility easy to swallow will enjoy the story and perhaps find in it the fresh vision, the new take on dreary old Dystopia, that I could not.

Doris Lessing:
The Cleft

2007

A Roman scholar of the age of Nero has a mysterious manuscript from ancient times—times that he considers ancestral to his world, though they differ strangely from Roman, or even human, history and myth. *The Cleft* is his translation of this document, with his comments and occasionally a modest bit of autobiography.

Somewhere, sometime, creatures like a cross between women and walruses, called Clefts, heaved about on a seashore and had babies. They conceived by an unspecified mechanism of parthenogenesis, since there were no males. They did nothing but wallow, give birth, suckle, and occasionally sacrifice a young female by pushing her off a high rock, also called the Cleft. It was an idyllic life.

But suddenly, somehow, one of the females had a baby with a spigot rather than a cleft. Ruled by unthinking instinct as they were, the walrus-women were upset. As more of them bore such monsters, they dimly perceived that trouble lay ahead—change, progress, even perhaps the dawn of something like (although not awfully like) intelligence. They tried discarding their male infants, and mutilating them, and so on; but they kept having them, and large eagles kept carrying the babies off and depositing them safely in a valley just over the hill. There some eventually survived, nourished by a single, extremely patient, and highly lactiferous doe.

After a while these males grew up, and a female who went over the hill found them and discovered sex. Just sex. Nothing in the story so far has indicated that these creatures know love, affection, or friendship, or have any community feeling more developed than that of a school of fish. And, as in other speculative fiction by Doris Lessing, free will is not an option. People do not choose or decide anything, but are driven by imperative, ineluctable orders from Nature or God or some people from another planet. Thus impelled, and having become slenderer and more terrestrial, the young Cleft women desert the hideous fat old walrus-women and start keeping house for the men. Of course they go on having babies. The men neither keep house nor have babies, but do brave and adventurous things.

Eventually—the passage of time is deliberately vague—some men, led by a man named Horsa, set off by raft and coracle to explore beyond their world-island. Since the unruly mob of little boys that tag after them is on foot, the men of the fleet hug the shore, landing every night to be with the boys and some young women who have also come along for sex. Why they use boats at all is unclear, but at last they sight a farther shore, and Horsa sets sail for it with a single companion, and is thrown back by a storm. The whole exploring party then blunders its way overland back to the original colony. There some of the young men, for no particular reason, destroy the great rock called the Cleft, and Horsa and the leader of the women, Maronna, move the colony up the coast. And so the story ends.

There are a few other names—Maire, Astre, and Maeve (as puzzlingly Celtic as Horsa is puzzlingly Anglo-Saxon)—but there are no characters: the author scrupulously refrains from anything characteristic at all. Description is in the most resolutely general terms. The climate is warm. The landscape has trees, caves. There are wild animals. Nothing vivid, no details.

Perhaps Doris Lessing believes inexactness is typical of myth, or that lack of local color gives a parable more universal applicability. I can only disagree, as I find the power of myth often lies in its startling immediacy, and follow Blake in believing that "All Sublimity is founded on Minute Discrimination."

I call the tale a parable, but hesitantly, because I can't believe it says what I think it says. It appears to be as prescriptive as Desmond Morris and more essentialist than Freud himself. Anatomy is destiny. Gender is an absolute binary. Women are passive, incurious, timid, and instinctively nurturant; without men they scarcely rise above animal mindlessness. Men are intellectual, inventive, daring, rash, independent, and need women only to relieve libido and breed more men. Men achieve; women nag. Much of the presentation of this is familiar from the literature of misogyny. The "Old Shes" are described (vividly, for once) with loathing and disgust. The escapades of boys are made much of, the doings of girl-children are ignored.

Now this, of course, may be supposed to be the voice of the Roman scholar, who seems a decent fellow in his autobiographical musings, but who is, after all, retelling the story from a man's viewpoint. He's aware of that, and often speaks of it. Yet where does that leave us? It merely makes it impossible to read the text either as irony or as satire.

There are some strange omissions. Our Roman would wonder at men who never fought, showed no signs of being warriors, and kept no discipline over their sons—all very unmanly by Roman standards. Living in the days of Greek influence, he might also have wondered why homosexuality is mentioned only as a temporary expedient for boys without access to women.

If we are offered the story as an origin myth of human sexuality and gender, it is unacceptable. It is incomplete; it is deeply arbitrary. I'd be happy to be shown that I misunderstood it, for as it is, I see in it little but a reworking of a tiresome science-fiction cliché: a hive of mindless females is awakened and elevated (to the low degree of which the female is capable) by the wondrous shock of masculinity. A tale of Sleeping Beauties—only they aren't beautiful. They're a lot of slobbering walruses till the Prince comes along.

Donna Leon:
Suffer the Little Children

2007

Before I started to write this review of the sixteenth mystery in Donna Leon's Commissario Guido Brunetti series, I reread the first, *Death at La Fenice*, curious to see if there was a great difference. I was happy to find the first not at all tentative, and the latest in no way stale or perfunctory. Leon started out with offhand, elegant excellence, and has simply kept it up.

There is, to be sure, the problem of all long-continued series—do the characters age in tandem with the writing of the books, or do they exist in a kind of timeless present? Leon's topics have kept up to date, closely related to Italian history and politics since 1992; but the Brunetti children, apparently trapped in eternal adolescence, are increasingly left out of the stories. That is a pity, for Raffi and Chiara are most engaging characters, and I hoped to see the marriage of their parents evolve through time. The portrait of a family—along with the subtle and vivid picture of Venice, and the enticing descriptions of what Venetians eat— is at the heart of Leon's books, giving them the warmth and vitality that balances out the darkness of their concerns.

Of course they are mysteries, with a crime and an ingenious solution, though seldom the rational, comforting, penny-drop solution of the whodunit. The crimes in Leon's books are sometimes rather against humanity than an individual; the moral problems raised may be completely unsolved by arrest or punishment; and the criminals may be less criminal than their abettors in big business and government.

One can in fact read the books as a guide to Italian corruption, inertia, favoritism, nepotism, and cynicism. Leon, an American, has lived in Italy only since the eighties, but she seems completely Italian in the cold, resigned clarity of her view, and in the apparent ability, which she shares with her principal characters, to enjoy daily existence very much and love her city passionately while in bleak despair about the government, the future, and life in general. Her website tells us that her books are translated into twenty languages, but not into Italian. She says this is to save her from local celebrity, but Venice is not a very literary city, and I doubt she'd be much bothered. The reason for her reticence must go deeper. I wouldn't blame her if she doesn't want the Questura to know what she's been saying about them.

She's even harder on the Carabinieri, though, in *Suffer the Little Children*. The Italians have a surfeit of police organisations, which trip over one another in the dance of cross-purpose rivalries ending in frustration that is the supreme achievement of bureaucracy. My impression is that the Carabinieri, still carrying a taint of Mussolini, are the least popular of these entities, though their uniforms are the grandest. At any rate they don't come off very well here, stomping into private homes and carrying off babies to be dumped in orphanages.

But the baby in this story was illegally adopted. The Carabinieri commit a moral outrage, but in pursuit of a serious crime. The interlocking complexities, political and emotional and ethical, that surround the adoption schemes and the police actions, and Brunetti's slow, patient search for the motivations behind it all, form an exemplary Leon plot. For those of us to whom plot is less interesting than story, the fascination lies in the easy narrative movement through the web of relationships in which Brunetti lives, the complexities of his ties with fellow policemen and women, with old friends and informers, with his wife and her family. And there is equal delight in his intense and complex bond with his extraordinary city, its calles and canals, its palaces and poverty.

My favorite passage in the book is a brief taxi drive in inland city traffic, as experienced by two Venetians. They find the automobile and the landscape it has created for itself as exotic as most of us find the gondola, but infinitely more awful. "My God," says the usually imperturbable Signorina Elettra, "how can people live like this?" And Brunetti answers, "I don't know." I wonder if any of us knows.

Yann Martel:
The High Mountains of Portugal

2016

The High Mountains of Portugal, in Yann Martel's novel of that name, turn out to be grassy uplands rather than high mountains; and the book turns out to be three stories rather than a novel. The stories, connected ingeniously, vary greatly in tone and quality. The first two display so little of the author's narrative skill that they may offer more temptation to stop reading than to go on. Liking the last part of the book much better, I could wish that it stood alone.

In Martel's best-selling *Life of Pi*, the author-within-the-story tells us that he went to India with the intention of writing a novel set in Portugal. Then he met the Indian who told him the tale of Pi, and Portugal was forgotten. It's recollected in the first part of this book, sometimes in great detail: "He heads off down Rue São Miguel onto Largo São Miguel and then Rua de São João da Praça before turning onto Arco de Jesus"—a sort of street rosary that may delight initiates of Lisbon, but to others is made interesting only by the fact that the protagonist, Tomas, is walking backwards, and that he always does so. After some elaborate rationales for walking backwards and a farcical encounter with a lamppost, we learn that he walks with "his back to the world, his back to God," not because he is grieving for the sudden, recent death of his wife, his child, and his father, but because "he is *objecting*."

How much of this, other than the street names, is the reader to accept as plausible? While I'm reading a story I want to be able to suspend disbelief; the more questions of authorial reliability force themselves on me, the weaker the hold of the narrative. This is a naïve approach to fiction, granted, but a tough one, since intellect, cleverness, charm, wit, tact, even fact cannot conceal incredibility. The importance of plausibility to realistic fiction is obvious, but it may be even more important to fantasy, where its failure dumps the reader out of the book onto the cold hillside where no birds sing.

However, if a writer works on the principle that fiction isn't true, and the reader accepts that principle, then anything goes, and Tomas can walk backwards clear across Lisbon as easily as he could walk forward. Surrealism is very like wishful thinking, you get to make up the rules as you go; the operative word is "somehow." So a man who habitually walks backwards can continue to hold a job as assistant curator in the National Museum of Ancient Art. He can recognise from a passage in a seventeenth-century diary that a certain sculpture found on an island in the Gulf of Guinea "would do nothing less than turn Christianity upside down." Though he has no idea what the sculpture is and only the vaguest notion where, he sets right off to locate it, walking backwards, of course, until provided a "brand new fourteen-horsepower, four-cylinder Renault" touring car, which he doesn't know how to drive, but drives on through a scenario of more or less amusing ludicrousness to the High Mountains of Portugal, where he finds the object of his quest.

The second section of the book takes place in Lisbon some thirty years later, in 1938 (the novel abandoned for the sake of Pi was to be about Lisbon in 1939). The tale meanders via disquisitions on religion to an autopsy, described with extraordinary grossness, at the end of which surrrealism prevails entirely and a living woman is sewn inside the dead man's body along with an ape and a bear cub. The themes of religion, of grief, and of animals connect the story to those that precede and follow it.

I haven't hesitated to reveal events, because in the absence of causality plot evaporates; when everything is a surprise nothing can be a surprise. The third story, the last part of the novel, works on a different and deeper level. Despite some vast, casual unlikelihoods, it's far more considerate of the reader's wish to be allowed to believe what's happening; it more successfully connects event with emotion and distinguishes miracle from mere unreason. The narration is less rococo; scenes aren't played for mere farce or shock. The theme of the animal, the relation of human and animal, has come to predominate, and on this subject Martel is an original, strange, and subtle thinker.

It's a timely subject of thought. We're fortunate to have brilliant writers using their fiction to meditate on a paradox we need urgently to consider—the unbridgeable gap and the unbreakable bond between human and animal, our impossible self-alienation from our world. Karen Fowler's novel *We Are All Completely Beside Ourselves* (shortlisted for the 2015 Man Booker Prize) handled the relationship of ape and human realistically, with a powerful sense of the tragic potential. Martel is happier, more easygoing, and his semi-surreal, semi-absurdist mode is well suited to exploring the paradox. The moral and spiritual implications of his tale have, in the end, a quality of haunting tenderness.

China Miéville:
Embassytown

Published in *the* Guardian, *April 2011*

Some authors fill a novel with futuristic scenery and jargon and then strenuously, even stertorously, deny that it's science fiction. No, no, they don't write that nasty stuff, never touch it. They write *literature*. Though curiously familiar with the tropes and conventions of the despised genre, they use these so clumsily, they so blithely ignore the meaning of terms, they reinvent the wheel with such cries of self-admiration, that their endeavors seem a doomed effort to prove that one can write a novel without learning how.

China Miéville knows what kind of novel he's writing, calls it by its name, science fiction, and exhibits all the virtues that make it an intensely interesting form of literature. It's a joy to find this young author coming into his own, and bringing the craft of science fiction out of the backwaters where it's been caught lately between the regressive drag of publishers marketing to a "safe" readership and the bewildering promises of change and growth offered by postmodernism in all its forms and formlessness. *Embassytown* is a fully achieved work of art.

Only the trash forms of science fiction are undemanding and predictable; the good stuff, like all good fiction, is not for lazy minds. Where the complexity of realistic novels is moral and pyschological, in science fiction it's moral and intellectual; individual character is seldom the key. But Miéville's characters are deftly sketched, and his narrator-protagonist, Avice, is a subtler portrait than she seems at first. Nothing in her behavior offers conventional signals of femininity . . . or unfemininity . . . an indication that gender may be differently constructed when humanity finds itself dealing with genuine Others.

There are men right now who have never learned how to talk to women. How will we talk to somebody *really* different—aliens? The Ariekei of *Embassytown* are immensely unlike us. The problem of communication, the nature of language and of spoken truth, is the novel's core.

When everything in a story is imaginary and much is unfamiliar, there's far too much to explain and describe, so one of the virtuosities of sf is the invention of box-words that the reader must open to discover a trove of meaning and implication. The imaginative leaps involved in decoding such inventions and appreciating their wit can give a reader much pleasure. China Miéville sets the bars rather high, but most of his neologisms come clear with a nice shock of revelation. My favorite is the immer, which is to our space-time reality as the sea is to our lands: therefore, to travel through space is to immerse. Other elegant images follow, for this is a book by a writer who loves language. And then there are new twists on ordinary words: such as Avice's realisation that she is a simile. Before she could speak the Ariekei language, they made her part of it, a figure of speech, like our boy who cried wolf. She is the girl who ate what was put before her.

The Ariekei want similes because their language, which is innate, does not permit lying. Like Swift's Houyhnhnms, they cannot speak that which is not. This contradicts the nature of language as *we* know it—language is a wonderful vehicle for untruth and perhaps a necessary vehicle for invention, the leap to the not-yet-existent. But why should all language be like ours? The Ariekei have got on very well with only truth, cultivating a high biotechnology that Miéville describes with gleeful poetry, the living houses with their parasitical furniture, the great farms lurching over the countryside behind their keepers. . . . I wondered how the Ariekei thought of making such creatures if they can think only of what is, but that question may be indirectly answered: it seems they crave that which is not, the unthinkable untruth, the lie.

Our species has put a colony on their planet, and we are certainly well qualified to teach them how to lie. They are eager to learn but no good at it at all. A different kind of human Ambassador is sent to Embassytown, one who can give them what they want—or an intoxicating imitation of it, a misuse of their language producing a kind of false lie. Such paradoxicals, once heard by the truth-tellers, act on them like heroin or meth—utterly destructive of their grip on reality, and fatally addictive.

The picture of a society shaken, shattered, wrecked to the foundation by a universal drug addiction infecting even the houses, even the farms, for they are all biologically akin, is apocalyptic vision on the grand scale—curiously beautiful, alien in every vivid detail, yet psychologically and socially only too familiar. Science fiction, like all fiction, is a way of talking about who we are.

The story, at first a bit hard to follow, very soon attains faultless impetus and pacing. If China Miéville has been known to set up a novel on a marvelous metaphor and then not know quite where to take it, he's outgrown that, and his dependence on violence is much diminished. In *Embassytown*, his metaphor—which is in a sense metaphor itself—works on every level, providing compulsive narrative, splendid intellectual rigor and risk, moral sophistication, fine verbal fireworks and sideshows, and even the old-fashioned satisfaction of watching a protagonist become more of a person than she gave promise of being. And all along we thought she was only a simile.

China Miéville:
Three Moments of an Explosion

2015

Much contemporary fantasy is quite violent, perhaps in an attempt to win the respect of people who assume fantasy is all fairies and fluff; but I doubt if that's why so much of China Miéville's work is so in-your-face gruesome. More likely he's meeting the expectations of a readership used to the endless kill-count of sensational films and electronic games, and is quite bloody-minded enough to enjoy doing so. But, knowing him as a writer avowedly committed to Marxist principles of social justice, with an intense sensitivity to contemporary moral and emotional complexities and a thoughtful mind that finds expression in lucid, cogent talks and essays, I wonder if he uses the horrific at least partly as a brilliant barrage of blanks concealing a subtler, deeper engagement with the dark side.

Brilliant: you can't talk about Miéville without the word, whether it's intellectual brilliance, as in "The Limits of Utopia," an essay that opens genuinely new ways to think about our future, or the dazzle of his prose, as displayed in this new collection of stories. Stylistic brilliance often implies some coldness, a spectator pose. The reader's not expected to identify and suffer with the characters, but to watch the fireworks go off, and gasp, and say Wow! And indeed some of these stories are pure fireworks. A whizbang, a starburst, a bright configuration of unpredictable, momentary elegance—gone. Many writers, and many readers, ask no more.

Fortunately for plodders like me, it's not all pyrotechnics. The writing, never less than excellent, takes many tones throughout the twenty-eight stories, some showy, some not. Pastiche, when present, is so skillful it can go unnoticed. Subjects of real weight are handled with unobtrusive ease but never glibly and never diminished by facetiousness. There are even a few characters one can, surreptitiously, suffer with. None, however, to rejoice with. Happiness is not currently on the Miéville menu.

But his wit dazzles, his humor is lively, and the pure vitality of his imagination is astonishing—even in a trendy gross-out such as "After the Festival" (zombies, rotting meat-masks), more so in tales that develop creepy concepts such as feigned symptoms of illness becoming genuinely contagious ("The Bastard Prompt"), or a school of psychiatry that routinely uses murder as a cure ("The Dreaded Outcome"). These are essentially horror stories, self-circumscribed by the curious objectives of the genre. Readers who don't find being scared or disgusted satisfying as an end in itself will prefer the more ambitious stories, such as "Covehithe," which with marvelously unnerving poetic justice describes wrecked and sunken oil rigs clambering back up onto land to suck more oil from the earth and returning to the ocean to spawn. With such a subject, in its playful yet deeply disturbing reference to the ill times we have brought upon the world, the author is arousing not a pleasurable make-believe shudder, but the real fear we'd rather pretend we don't feel, a fear that is not simply irrational.

Brilliance is often in concision. As I read "The Rope Is the World," I kept imagining the 500-page science-fiction novel it could so easily have been, crammed full of detailed scientific and technological arcanities, with a complex plot involving the machinations of the powerful and the fate of cosmic enterprises or empires, routinely punctuated by descriptions of sexual activities. But Miéville didn't take the easy route. He wrote it all in five pages.

The offhand density is superb:

> Initial outlays were clearly gigavast, but lifting one ton of cargo out beyond everyday gravity to orbit by elevator was this or that many times cheaper—some absurd margin— than doing so by rocket, by shuttle, by alien indulgence. Now that the space elevators, the skyhooks, the geostationary tethered-dock haulage columns, were shockingly feasible, research projects were all human-spirit this and because-it's-

there that. As if, faced with them, the mere savings were as vulgar as they in fact were.

This is science fiction to the nth. To unpack all that would take hours, and the result would be blah.

The next story, "The Buzzard's Egg," is told in the quiet, rambling voice of an ignorant old slave who serves in a temple/prison for idols taken in war—captured gods. He, their priest and jailer, is himself a prisoner. Alone, he talks to his latest god-prisoner. This one-sided conversation or confession or meditation is the whole story. I found it fascinating, full of suggestion and implication, and beautiful.

The last, long piece, "The Design," has a characteristically inventive and unsettling subject, contrasting with the plain, clear, unhurried Stevensonian prose it's told in and the repressed emotion of the teller that finds voice only once. But my favorite of all these tales is "The Rules," two and a half pages long. Read it. You won't regret it, or forget it.

David Mitchell:
The Bone Clocks

2014

On the July day that I sat down to write a review of a novel due to be published in September, I learned that it had just been nominated for the Man Booker award. This rather took the wind out of my sails. I felt as if I should say "Bound for glory!" and leave it at that.

Certainly the book invites the prediction. In its almost six hundred pages of metafictional shenanigans in relentlessly brilliant prose, *The Bone Clocks* hits lots of hot buttons, from the horrors of the Iraq War to the Eternal Battle of Good and Evil to the near-future downfall of our civilization. It aims unerringly and from many directions at success. At one point it even reviews itself, and the temptation to quote is irresistible:

> One: [the author] is so bent on avoiding cliché that each sentence is as tortured as an American whistleblower. Two: the fantasy sub-plot clashes so violently with the book's State of the World pretensions, I cannot bear to look. Three: what surer sign is there that the creative aquifers are running dry than a writer creating a writer-character?

The review is too nasty to be just, but its self-protective mockery does provide a good example of an outstanding quality of the book: self-consciousness. In its vast inventiveness, its exploitation of trendy pop-cult stereotypes (soul-sucking vampires, anyone?), its jaunty hops between holocausts, the novel reminded me of Michael Chabon's *Kavalier and Clay* and *The Yiddish Policeman's Union*; but where Chabon is genuinely freewheeling, Mitchell's daring is somehow anxious. He watches his steps, always. Reading Chabon, I'm carefree; reading Mitchell, I feel cautious, uncertain. The story is narrated in the first person by five very different voices, at six different times from 1984 to 2043; among them a fifteen-year-old girl writing in the general tone of a Young Adult thriller, a consummately self-parodic prick (whose first novel was called *Desiccated Embryos*) writing in Anglo-Mandarin, and a semi-immortal body-shifter. I find these radical shifts of time and person difficult, and though willing to suspend disbelief, am uncertain when to do so. Am I to believe in the hocus-pocus of the secret cult of the Blind Cathar in the same way I am to believe in the realistic portrayal of the death agonies of Corporate Capitalism, or should I believe in them in different ways?

But what does it matter? It's just a novel, innit?

Well, maybe. But how many novels is it?

Maybe it's one and I just don't see how it hangs together. Or maybe its not hanging together is the point and I don't get it. There you are: anxiety in the writer makes the reader anxious too.

In its temporal leaps, and in that the narration is stream-of-consciousness (or stream-of-selfconsciousness), *The Bone Clocks* can be compared to Woolf's *The Years* and *The Waves*. But *The Years* is told in the past tense, and the voices that tell *The Waves* are always framed by it: *Jinny said, Louis said.* In *The Bone Clocks*, a novel deeply concerned with Time, there is virtually no past tense.

Present-tense narration is now taken for granted by many fiction readers because everything they read, from internet news to texting, is in the present tense, but at this great length it can be hard going. Past-tense narration easily implies previous times and extends into the vast misty reaches of the subjunctive, the conditional, the future; but the pretense of a continuous eyewitness account admits little relativity of times, little connection between events. The present tense is a narow-beam flashlight in the dark, limiting the view to the next step—now, now, now. No past, no future. The world of the infant, of the animal, perhaps of the immortal.

While learning how it is that some of the characters are indeed more or less immortal, we get a glimpse of a scene that to me stands out in silence from the jangle of dazzle-language and the kaleidoscopic tumult of brilliant imagery and filmic cliché. We see it again just before an extended climactic orgy of violence. Nothing in the plot appears to depend directly on this vision or refer back to it; yet I came away from the book with the sense that it is the center, the still center, of all the frenetic action.

> 'The Dusk,' says Arkady, 'between life and death. We see it from the High Ridge. It's a beautiful, fearsome sight. All the souls, the pale lights, crossing over, blown by the Seaward Wind to the Last Sea. Which of course isn't really a sea at all. . . .'
>
> . . . a west window offers a view over one mile or a hundred miles of dunes, up to the High Ridge and the Light of Day. Holly follows me. 'See up there?' I tell her. 'That's where we're from.'
>
> 'Then all those little pale lights,' whispers Holly, 'crossing the sand, they're souls?'
>
> 'Yes. Thousands and thousands, at any given time.' We walk over to the eastern window, where an inexact distance of dunes rolls down through darkening twilight to the Last Sea. 'And that's where they're bound.' We watch the little lights enter the starless extremity and go out, one by one by one.

Sketchy as it is, this has to me the quality of a true vision. For all the stuff and nonsense about escaping mortality by switching bodies and devouring souls, death is at the heart of this novel. And there lies its depth and darkness, bravely concealed by all the wit and sleight-of-word and ventriloquistic verbiage and tale-telling bravura of which David Mitchell is a master. Whatever prizes it wins or doesn't, *The Bone Clocks* will be a great success, and it deserves to be, because a great many people will enjoy reading it very much. Even if I'm not quite sure what it's all about, I know it's a whopper of a story. And in it, under all the klaxons and saxophones and Irish fiddles, is that hidden, haunting silence at the center. Behind the dazzle of narrative fireworks and verbal Klieg lights is the shadow that maybe makes it true.

Jan Morris:
Hav

2006

When *Last Letters from Hav* was published (and nominated for the Booker Prize) in 1985, Jan Morris's well-deserved fame as a travel writer, and the unfamiliarity of many modern readers with the nature of fiction, caused unexpected dismay among travel agents. Their clients demanded to know why they couldn't book a cheap flight to Hav.

The problem, of course, was not the destination but the place of origin. You couldn't get there from London or Moscow. But from Ruritania, or Orsinia, or the Invisible Cities, it was simply a matter of finding the right train.

Now, after twenty years, Jan Morris has returned to Hav, and enhanced, deepened, and marvelously perplexed her guidebook by the addition of a final section called "Hav of the Myrmidons." To say that the result isn't what the common reader expects of a novel is not to question its fictionality, which is absolute, or the author's imagination, which is vivid and exact.

The story is episodic, entirely lacking in action or plot of the usual sort; but these supposed narrative necessities are fully replaced by the powerful and gathering direction or intention of the whole book. It lacks another supposed necessity of the novel—characters who, while they may represent an abstraction, also take on a memorable existence of their own. Like any good travel writer, Morris talks to interesting people and reports the conversations. And people we met in the first part of the book turn up in the second part to take us about and exhibit in person what has happened to their country, but I confess I barely remembered their names when I met them again. Morris's gift is not portraiture, and her people are memorable not as individuals but as exemplary Havians.

This lack of plot and characters is common in the conventional Utopia, and academics and other pigeonholers may stick *Hav* in with Thomas More and Co. That is a respectable slot, but not where the book belongs. Probably Morris, certainly her publisher, will not thank me for saying that in fact *Hav* is science fiction, of a perfectly recognisable type and superb quality. The sciences or areas of expertise involved are social—ethnology, sociology, political science, and above all, history. Hav, the place, exists as a mirror held up to several millennia of pan-Mediterranean history, customs, and politics. It is a focusing mirror; its intensified reflection sharply concentrates both observation and speculation. Where have we been, where are we going? Those are the questions the book asks. It poses the questions through the invention of a place not recognised in the atlas or the histories, but which, introduced plausibly and without violence into the existing world, gives us a distanced, ironic, and revelatory view of everything around it. The mode is not satiric fantasy, as with the islands Gulliver visited; it is exuberantly realistic, firmly observant, and genuinely knowledgeable about how things have been, and are now, in Saudi Arabia or Turkey or Downing Street. Serious science fiction is a mode of realism, not of fantasy; and *Hav* is a splendid example of the uses of an alternate geography. If, swayed by the silly snobbery of pundits as contemptuous of science fiction as they are ignorant of it, you should turn away from Hav, that's a shame and a loss—very easily prevented and turned to pure gain by reading the book.

It's not an easy book to describe. Hav itself is not easy to describe, as the author frequently laments. As she takes us about with her in her travels of discovery, we grow familiar with the delightful if somewhat incoherent Hav of 1985. We climb up to its charming castle from which the Armenian trumpeter plays at dawn the great lament of Katourian for the knights of the First Crusade, the *"Chant de doleure pour li proz chevalers qui sunt morz."* We visit the Venetian Fondaco, the Casino, the Caliph, the mysterious British Agency, the Kretevs who inhabit caves up on the great Escarpment through which the train, Hav's only land link to the rest of

Europe, plunges daily down a zigzag tunnel. We see the Iron Dog, we watch the thrilling Roof Race. But the more we learn, the greater our need to learn more. A sense of things not understood, matters hidden under the surface, begins to loom, even, somehow, to menace. We have entered a maze, a labyrinth constructed through millennia, leading us back and back to the age of Achilles and the Spartans who built the canal and set up the Iron Dog at the harbor mouth, and before that to the measureless antiquity of the Kretevs, who are friends of the bear. And the maze stretches out and out too, half around the world, for it seems that Havian poetry was deeply influenced by the Welsh, and just up the coast is the westernmost of all ancient Chinese settlements, which Marco Polo found uninteresting. "There is nothing to be said about Yuan Wen Kuo," he wrote. "Let us now move on to other places."

Achilles and Marco Polo aren't the half of it. Ibn Batuta came to Hav, of course, all the great travelers did, and left their comments, diligently quoted by the Havians and Morris. T. E. Lawrence may have discovered a secret mission there; Ernest Hemingway came to fish and to carry off six-toed cats. Hav's glory days of tourism were before the First World War and again after it, when the train zigzagged through its tunnel laden with the cream of European society, millionaires, and right-wing politicians; but whether or not Hitler was actually there for one night is still a matter of dispute. The politics of Hav itself in 1985 were extremely disputable. Its religions were various, since so many great powers of the East and West had governed it over the centuries; mosques and churches coexisted amicably; and indeed the spiritual scene was so innocuous as to appear feeble—a small group of hermits, reputed to spend their days in holy meditation, proved to be cheerfully selfish hedonists who simply enjoyed asceticism. And yet, and yet, there were the Cathars. Late in her first visit, Morris was taken in darkness and great secrecy to witness a sitting of the Cathars of Hav, a strange ritual conclave of veiled women and cowled men. In some of them Morris thought she recognised friends, guides, the trumpeter, the tunnel pilot . . . but she could not be sure. She could not be sure of anything.

On her return twenty years later, some things appear to be all too certain. The old Hav is gone, destroyed in an obscure event called the

Intervention. The train is gone, a huge airport is under construction. Ships come in to a destination resort called Lazaretto! (the punctuation is part of the name) of the most luxuriously banal kind, where, as a middle-aged lady tourist remarks, one feels so safe. The strange old House of the Chinese Master is a burnt ruin; the new landmark is a huge skyscraper called the Myrmidon Tower, "a virtuoso display of unashamed, unrestricted, technically unexampled vulgarity." The English Legate is at least as sinister and much slimier than his predecessor the English Agent. Most of the city has been rebuilt in concrete. The troglodytic Kretev are housed in hygienic villas, and the bears are extinct. The age of postmodernism has arrived, with its characteristically brutal yet insidious architecture and propaganda, its reductionist culture of advertisement and imitation, its market capitalism, its factionalism and religiosity forever threatening terror. Yet we find pretty soon that Hav is still Hav: the maze, the labyrinth, is still there. Even the elevator of the Myrmidon Tower is indirect. Who in fact is running the country—the Cathars? But who are the Cathars? What does the M on the Myrmidon Tower stand for?

Jan Morris says in the epilogue that if Hav is an allegory, she's not sure what it is about. I don't take it as an allegory at all. I read it as a brilliant description of the crossroads of the West and East in two recent eras, seen by a woman who has truly seen the world, and who lives in it with twice the intensity of most of us. Its enigmas are part of its accuracy. It is a very good guidebook, I think, to the early twenty-first century.

Julie Otsuka:
The Buddha in the Attic

2011

Some of us on the boat were from Kyoto and were delicate and fair, and had lived our entire lives in darkened rooms at the back of the house. Some of us were from Nara, and prayed to our ancestors three times a day, and swore we could still hear the temple bells ringing. Some of us were farmers' daughters from Yamaguchi with thick wrists and broad shoulders who had never gone to bed after nine.

This passage may give a clue as to how Julie Otsuka's book is to be read. She calls it a novel. It is closely and carefully based on factual histories. There are novelistically vivid faces, scenes, glimpses, voices, each for a moment only, so you cannot linger anywhere or with anyone. Information is given, a good deal of it, in the most gracefully invisible manner, and history is told. Yet the book has neither a novel's immediacy of individual experience, nor the broad overview of history. The tone is often incantatory, and though the language is direct, unconvoluted, almost without metaphor, its true and very unusual merit lies, I think, in that indefinable quality we call poetry.

Writing a long narative in the first person plural is a risky business. It brings up questions that don't come to mind with the familiar first or third person singular. For one thing, the reader identifies easily with an "I" narrator or a "he/she" protagonist, and though some critics sneer at sympathetic identification and some novelists delight in frustrating it, it remains a fundamental element of the pleasure of story. But it's hard to identify strongly with a whole group, even if one is interested in it as a group, and even if its members are individually sympathetic.

And "we" sets up two groups: We and They/You. Some languages make the distinction between the inclusive "we" meaning "I and all of you" and the restrictive "I and others not including you." The "we" of *The Buddha in the Attic* is an artificial literary construct that does not include an "I." The group supposed to be speaking are Japanese "picture brides" of the early twentieth century. Women married by proxy to Japanese men working in the United States were shipped across the Pacific to husbands whom they had seen, and who had seen them, only in a photograph. The arrangement was made for men who had no other way to get a wife, and for women, mostly young and very poor, who hoped for a better life in golden California. The practice was continued for some decades; the group in the novel appears to have come over shortly after the First World War.

The picture brides had no way to know that American racial prejudice would isolate them with their husbands and that for the rest of their lives they would be "we" only to one another, we the Japanese in America. To white Americans they would always be Them.

That is Otsuka's justification for telling the story in an unusual and difficult way, and it is a powerful one. And effective: it makes the point without stating the point.

On the ship, traveling in steerage, the women really do form a group, however disparate. When they get to the promised land, they are scattered, each to her husband, and the husbands are emphatically "they," not "we."

> That night our new husbands took us quickly. They took us calmly. They took us gently, but firmly, and without saying a word. . . . They took us flat on our backs on the bare floor of the Minute Motel. . . . They took us before we were ready and the bleeding did not stop for three days.

Later, as they go on with their hard, poor lives, slaving at "stoop labor" in the fields of California, working in the kitchens of the labor camps or of middle-class employers, the absolute otherness of the whites still doesn't join them with their husbands. Even when their children are born, though at first they are very close, always, heartbreakingly, they too are not "us."

> In early summer, in Stockton, we left them in nearby gullies while we dug up and sacked onions and began picking the first plums. We gave them sticks to play with in our absence and called out to them from time to time to let them know we were still there. *Don't bother the dogs. Don't touch the bees. . . .* And at the end of the day when there was no more light in the sky we woke them up from wherever it was they lay sleeping and brushed the dirt from their hair. *It's time to go home.*

Before long, as the children grow taller than their fathers and forget their Japanese and will speak only English, as they eat hugely, drink milk, dump ketchup on potatoes, become ashamed of their parents and will not bow to them, the gap widens—"with each passing day they seemed to slip further and further from our grasp." The children are joining the Others, the white Americans.

But then comes the Japanese attack on Pearl Harbor.

Otsuka tells of the months of increasing hostility and suspicion the Japanese Americans lived through, their fear, their incredulity, before they were summarily dispossessed and deported to detention camps as enemy aliens. In its agonised poignancy and restraint, this may be the finest passage of the book.

I am sorry that after it, in the last chapter, she suddenly changes her narrative mode, ceases to follow her group of women. The point of view changes radically, and suddenly "we" are the whites: "The Japanese have disappeared from our town."

I was twelve when "the Japanese disappeared" from my town, Berkeley. My unawareness, my incomprehension of the event at the time, has troubled and informed my mind for many years. It's up to me, as a white American, to deal with that ignorance and denial. Julie Otsuka can't do it for me. I can only wish she had gone all the way with her heroines into the exile from exile, to those bitter desert and mountain prison-towns, where few of "us" went even in imagination, until those who returned began to bear witness.

Salman Rushdie:
The Enchantress of Florence

2014

From the sea of stories our master fisherman has brought up two gleaming, intertwining prizes—a tale about three boys from Florence in the age of Lorenzo de' Medici, and a tale of Akbar, greatest of the Mughal emperors, who established both the wondrous and short-lived city Fatehpur Sikri and a wondrous and short-lived policy of religious tolerance. Both stories are about story itself, the power of history and fable, and why it is that we can seldom be sure which is which.

Fabulous as his life was, Akbar was a historical figure; and one of the young Florentines is Niccolò Machiavelli, our byword for political realism. But Niccolò's friend Argalia flies on the peacock wings of the novelist's invention to become the bosom friend of Akbar before returning to fight for a lost cause in Florence. Some characters are the inventions of other characters: Queen Jodha and Qara Köz, the Enchantress, are Akbar's daydreams of the Perfect Wife and the Perfect Lover, brought into existence by tale-tellers and artists and Akbar's all-powerful desire and obsession, and accepted by his people, "such occurrences being normal at that time, before the real and the unreal were segregated forever and doomed to live apart under different monarchs and separate legal systems."

This brilliant, fascinating novel swarms with gorgeous young women both historical and imagined, beautiful queens and irresistible enchantresses, along with some whores and a few quarrelsome old wives—all stock figures, females perceived solely in relation to the male. Women are never treated unkindly by the author, but they have no autonomous being. The Enchantress herself, who makes puppets of everyone, has no real self but exists—literally—by pleasing men. Akbar calls her a "woman who had forged her own life, beyond convention, by the force of her will alone, a woman like a king." But in fact she does nothing but sell herself to the highest bidder, and her power is an illusion permitted by the man.

In a marvelous scene Akbar's wife and mother come to show his imaginary wife Jodha how to release him from the Enchantress's spell, and in so doing are reconciled with Jodha in a moment of hilarious feminine solidarity. But the Enchantress appears, Jodha vanishes, and the women are defeated by the man's obsession. Indeed, the men in the book are as hormone-besotted as adolescents. All their derring-do, their battling for cities and empires, comes down to little more than a bed with a young woman in it. Machiavelli becomes a disappointed middle-aged lecher whose middle-aged wife "waddles" and "quacks" while he looks at her with loathing. But then, suddenly, for a page or two, we slip into her soul, we feel her anger at his disloyalty, her hurt pride as a woman, her unchanged pride in him and his "dark sceptical genius," her puzzlement at his failure to see how he lessens himself by scorning what he has that is treasurable and honorable. For that moment I glimpsed a very different book, almost a different author. Then it was back to the dazzling play of fancy and the all-powerful dreams of men.

The swashbuckling Argalia's adventures, linking the Florentine and the Indian strands of the double tale, are full of Rushdian charm and extravagance but descend too easily into facetiousness (such as four giant albino Swiss mercenaries named Otho, Botho, Clotho, and D'Artagnan). These exploits are less interesting than the misfortunes of Machiavelli or the mind of the Emperor Akbar.

Rushdie's Akbar is imperious, intelligent, and very likable, a marvelous spokesman for his author. The historic Akbar tried to unite all India, "all races, tribes, clans, faiths, and nations," a powerful dream indeed, though doomed to perish with him. What winds were blowing in the late fifteenth century to waken that emperor's syncretic vision, even as Europe began to free itself from the Church's control of ideas? "If there had never been a God, the emperor thought, it might have been easier to work out what goodness was." Goodness might lie not in self-abnegation before an Almighty but in "the slow, clumsy, error-strewn working out of an individual or collective path." Lord of a theocratic, absolutist society, he glimpses harmony not as the enemy of discord but the result of it: "difference, disobedience, disagreement, irreverence, iconoclasm, impudence, even insolence might be the wellsprings of the good."

Akbar is the moral center of the book, its center of gravity, and provides its strongest link to the issues which have concerned Salman Rushdie in his works and his life. It all comes down to the question of responsibility. Akbar's objection to God is "that his existence deprived human beings of the right to form ethical structures by themselves." The curious notion that without religion we have no morals has seldom been dismissed with such quiet good humor. Rushdie leaves ranting to the fanatics who fear him.

Driven from his magical city when its lake goes dry, Akbar gravely foresees his defeat: "All he had worked to make, his philosophy and way of being, would evaporate like water. The future would not be what he hoped for, but a dry hostile antagonistic place" where people would hate and kill "in the great quarrel he had sought to end forever, the quarrel over God"—the quarrel our fanatics are still so enthusiastically pursuing.

But there is another theme to the book: "Religion could be rethought, reexamined, remade, perhaps even discarded; magic was impervious to such assaults." Akbar in his splendid city, like the Florentines in theirs, inhabited a world of magic "as passionately as they inhabited the world of tangible materials." This is the great difference between them and us. We have separated the real and the unreal, put them in different kingdoms with different laws.

Like all serious fantasy, Rushdie's story erases this division by making us realists inhabit, for the span of our reading, the realm of Imagination, which is controlled by but not limited to observation of fact. This is the land of story, where word makes be: the child's world, the ancestral, prescientific world, where we are all emperors or enchantresses, making up the rules as we go along. Modern literary fantasy is given a paradoxical intensity, sometimes a tragic dimension, by our consciousness of the other kingdom we inhabit, daily life, where the laws of physics cannot be broken, and whose government was described by Niccolò Machiavelli.

Some boast that science has ousted the incomprehensible, others cry that science has driven magic out of the world and plead for "reenchantment." But it's clear that Charles Darwin lived in as wondrous a world, as full of discoveries, amazements, and profound mysteries, as that of any fantasist. The people who disenchant the world are not the scientists, but those who see it as meaningless in itself, a machine operated by a deity. Science and literary fantasy are intellectually incompatible, yet both describe the world. The imagination functions actively in both modes, seeking meaning, and wins intellectual consent through strict attention to detail and coherence of thought, whether one is describing a beetle or an enchantress. Religion, which prescribes and proscribes, is irreconcilable with both of them, and since it demands belief, must shun their common ground, imagination. So the true believer must condemn both Darwin and Rushdie as "disobedient, irreverent, iconoclastic" dissidents from revealed truth.

The essential compatibility of the realistic and the fantastic imagination may explain the success of Rushdie's sumptuous, impetuous mixture of history with fable. But in the end, of course, it is the hand of the master artist, past all explanation, that gives this book its glamor and power, its humor and shock, its verve, its glory. It is a wonderful tale, full of follies and enchantments. East meets West with a clash of cymbals and a burst of fireworks. We English speakers have our own Ariosto now, our Tasso, stolen out of India. Aren't we the lucky ones?

Salman Rushdie: *Two Years, Eight Months, and Twenty-Eight Nights*

2015

A "colossal fragmentation of reality" occurred in the twentieth century, Salman Rushdie has said, and his novels enact and display that fragmentation with terror and glee. His new novel, *Two Years, Eight Months, and Twenty-Eight Nights*, assures us that reality has been crumbling more colossally than ever lately and is about to come completely unglued. An even worse storm than any last winter will be followed by eschatological lightning strikes and local failures of gravity as the Dark Ifrits begin to take advantage of the weakening of the fabric of the everyday.

The cumbrous title transcribes a certain number of days into years and months, but not the four weeks that should complete it, because the word *Nights* is needed to suggest the original Thousand and One. Rushdie is our Scheherazade, inexhaustibly enfolding story within story and unfolding tale after tale, with such irrepressible delight in doing so that it comes as a shock to remember that, like her, he has lived the life of a storyteller in immediate peril. Scheherazade told her thousand and one tales to put off a stupid, cruel threat of death; he brought the threat upon himself by telling an unwelcome tale. So far, like her, he has succeeded in escaping. May he continue to do so.

At the idea of trying to summarize the plot, I shriek and fall back fainting upon my seraglio couch. Rushdie has a fractal imagination. Plot buds from plot, endlessly. There are at least a hundred and one stories and substories, and nearly as many characters. All you need to know is that they're mostly highly entertaining, amusing, and—but I won't say ingenious, because a good many of the characters are in fact genies.

Genies in English, jinn in their own language. The dilapidation of reality has affected the wall between our world and Peristan, the world of the jinn, leaving slots and slits through which they can slip.

Their existence in Peristan is one of almost ceaseless sexual intercourse in surroundings of total luxury. Still, some of them, finding this as boring as some of us might, have always liked to sneak over here to entertain themselves by meddling with our little mortal lives. The male jinn are creatures of flame, the jinnia of smoke. They have great powers of magic, not so great powers of intellect. Willful, impulsive, and unwise, one of them gets trapped over here every now and then, imprisoned by a spell in a bottle or a lamp.

We haven't seen any jinn for a while, because their passages into our world were sealed up about a thousand years ago, not long after the greatest jinnia princess, Dunia, had a love affair with the philosopher Ibn Rushd in Andalusia. The outcome was a slew of descendants distinguished by their lobeless ears and the trace in them of fairy blood. For that's what Peristan is in English—Fairyland.

The main plot—the outermost Chinese box—is constructed around a philosophical feud between the rationalist Ibn Rushd and the pious Ghazali of Iran, who placed the power of God above all earthly causes and effects. Ibn Rushd tried to reconcile reason and humane morality with God and faith, a kindly God and an unfanatic faith. He challenged Ghazali. His reward was disgrace and exile.

I met Salman Rushdie many years ago, long before the fatwa, but I can't remember if he has lobes to his ears. In any case, certain parallels are clear. This book is a fantasy, a fairy tale—and a brilliant reflection of and a serious meditation on the choices and agonies of our life in this world.

The choices are presented simplistically, comic-book style, as absolute Good and Evil. The agonies are presented, disaster-movie style, as catastrophes so awful that readers who don't want to think about them can shrug them off. Rushdie is a generous, good-natured writer who'd rather woo and seduce his readers than reduce the truth to gall and brimstone and make them swallow it.

All the same, the frontispiece of the book is the Goya engraving that stands at the very entrance of the modern age: "The sleep of reason engenders monsters." The monsters here engendered, however playfully imagined, are not imaginary.

The strongest male figure among the many in this book is Mr. Geronimo, a gardener. Physically and emotionally he's a vivid character, likable for his strength and modesty and his homesickness for the city of his childhood, Bombay (which to him will never be Mumbai). There are strong women in the book, a Mayor, a Lady Philosopher, but they're pretty much cartoons. The novel's heroine and protagonist is female, which I think is a first for Rushdie, and I wish I didn't have a problem with her. It's not that she isn't human; you can't ask a fairy princess to be anything but what she is. But you can ask her not to think like a man.

Bearing children by the litter, seven to nineteen at a time, is certainly a practical engineering approach to leaving a large number of offspring, but not one many women would choose. We don't see Dunia nursing her babies (it would interesting to know how she did it) or anything of her certainly busy motherhood. When she returns to earth after a thousand years, it is to defend "her children"—but this means her remote descendants, a scattered group of earlobeless people whom she calls the Duniyat, asserting her authorship of a lineage.

The usual name for this authorship is paternity. Its importance to men among the Mediterranean and Arabic peoples is very great. More generally, while women are likely to value their actual children and their status as mother over any abstract idea of lineage, men often consider their children, particularly sons, most valuable as maintaining the paternal bloodline. This gender difference may reflect biological imperatives, male mammals being motivated to reproduce their genes, females to nurture the gene-bearers.

Dunia's a mammal all right, but her loving heart and her numerous litters can't keep me from suspecting that—like so many other kickass, weapon-wielding warrior women—she's a man in drag.

In the terrible period called The Strangeness, beginning about right now, the dark jinn, the great Ifrits, will try to destroy humanity with all their arts of magic and unreason, and Dunia will summon her Duniyat, with their drop of jinn blood, to defend us with the same arts.

So we have the War between Good and Evil, with supervillains and superheroes (my favorite is Natraj Hero, a.k.a. Jimmy Kapoor of Queens, New York), conducted according to the best precedents. According to precedent, and a bit anticlimactically, the Good Guys win. The last of the mighty Dark Ones, Zumurrud, is imprisoned in a blue glass bottle by the Lady Philosopher, the rest of the jinn retire to Peristan, and Dunia closes the passages between the worlds in a final act of supermaternal self-sacrifice.

Towards the end of the book, we find that our descendants of the next millennium have abandoned conflict as a way of life. They peacefully cultivate their gardens rather than their bigotries and hatreds, having found that "in the end, rage, no matter how profoundly justified, destroys the enraged." But . . . Of course there has to be a but.

Contemporary sophistication declares that peace is boring, moderation is bleh, happy is sappy. Defying sophistry, Rushdie imagines a contented people, but only by depriving them of dreams. No visions, no nightmares. Their sleep is empty darkness.

The implication is that our human gift of imagining can't exist without the hatred, anger, and aggressiveness that lead to such human behaviors as warfare, conscious cruelty, and deliberate destruction. To imply that only the dark jinn in us can give us dreams and visions may be one way of admitting the essential balance between the creative and the destructive within us.

But it's also, I think, a capitulation to the idea, so powerful in twentieth-century literature, that the slow processes of creation are less interesting, less *real*, than the catastrophic dramas of destruction. And this leaves us right back where we are now. If cultivating our garden stultifies our minds, if using reason prevents our seeing visions, if compassion enfeebles us—what then? Back to conflict as our default solution? Cultivate hatred, anger, violence, reinstate the priests, politicians, and warmakers, and finish destroying the Earth?

I wish we could abandon this false alternative, which neglects the possibility of more imaginative uses of both the light and the darkness in us.

So the very end of the story was, to me, a letdown. But it may not be so to others. And I like to think how many readers are going to admire the courage of this book, revel in its fierce colors, its boisterousness, humor, and tremendous pizzazz, and take delight in its generosity of spirit.

José Saramago:
Raised from the Ground

2012

For the last couple of centuries, novels have been written mostly by middle-class writers for middle-class readers. Novels about the very poor, the oppressed, peasants, aren't generally written by or for the people they are about. Thus they tend to have a distanced, sociological air, while being at the same time terribly depressing—revelatory, grim, unhopeful, and of necessity brutal. The two great American novels of the oppressed, *Uncle Tom's Cabin* and *The Grapes of Wrath*, are saved from that minatory coldness by the authors' passion for justice and their loving respect for their protagonists. The same is true of José Saramago's early novel *Raised from the Ground*—with a tremendous bonus: the author is writing about people he grew up with, his own people, his family.

The temptation I can only partly resist in this review is to let José Saramago write it. This is how he opened his Nobel Prize lecture in 1998:

> The wisest man I ever knew in my whole life could not read or write. At four o'clock in the morning, when the promise of a new day still lingered over French lands, he got up from his pallet and left for the fields, taking to pasture the half-dozen pigs whose fertility nourished him and his wife. My mother's parents lived on this scarcity, on the small breeding of pigs that after weaning were sold to the neighbours in our village of Azinhaga in the province of Ribatejo. . . . In winter when the cold of the night grew to the point of freezing the water in the pots inside the house, they went to

the sty and fetched the weaklings among the piglets, taking them to their bed. Under the coarse blankets, the warmth from the humans saved the little animals from freezing and rescued them from certain death. Although the two were kindly people, it was not a compassionate soul that prompted them to act in that way: what concerned them, without sentimentalism or rhetoric, was to protect their daily bread, as is natural for people who, to maintain their life, have not learnt to think more than is needful.

Living and working with his grandparents as a boy gave him the experience that underlies this novel, its inspiration, its motivation, and its tone. In the Nobel talk he summarised it thus:

> Three generations of a peasant family, the Badweathers, from the beginning of the century to the April Revolution of 1974 which toppled dictatorship, move through this novel, called *Risen from the Ground*, and it was with such men and women risen from the ground, real people first, figures of fiction later, that I learned how to be patient, to trust and to confide in time, that same time that simultaneously builds and destroys us in order to build and once more to destroy us. [Margaret Jull Costas, his trusted translator, gives us the title as *Raised from the Ground*, and the family name remains in Portuguese, Mau-Tempo.]

Saramago left journalism and began writing novels late in his life, as if a fine old apple tree should suddenly grow heavy with the golden fruit of the Hesperides. This novel, published in 1980, when he was fifty-eight, is and is not an "early work." It hasn't the complex depth of many of his later books, and its style is still fairly conventional (there are periods, and paragraphs), but the narrative voice is unmistakable: a mature, quiet voice, conversational and easy, often ironical or endearingly humorous, that flows forward always weaving and interbraiding with itself, seeming to hesitate or wander but never losing impetus, like a big river running through a dry land.

The breadth of his thought and sympathy, the difficult balance between the patience and trust he speaks of and his passionate political conviction, give the novel a wider focus than most such testimonies of human injustice. In a passage that describes the beating of a man held as a striker, the place of torture is not, as usual, seen as a a place apart, an unspeakable secret—because nothing can be kept secret. Nothing human is outside nature. Everything is connected. Everything can be spoken. Everything can speak. An ant on the floor sees the man and thinks, "His face is all swollen, his lips cut, and his eyes, poor eyes, you can't even see them for the bruises, he's so different from when he first arrived." When the guards throw water on the victim, we follow the water on its long travels through the depths of the earth, into the clouds and rain, into the earthenware jug from which it is "poured from on high onto a face, an abrupt fall, abruptly broken as it runs slowly over lips, eyes, nose and chin, over gaunt cheeks, over a forehead drenched in sweat . . . and thus it comes to know this man's as yet still-living mask."

Though he includes so much in his vision, Saramago knows what to leave out. How well he knows it, and how rare that knowledge is! He never plods. No flat lists of details. None of the mechanical dialogue that clogs so much contemporary narrative. None of the luxurious lingering on suffering, misery, torture, that's hailed as gritty realism and pitiless truth-telling, but is more often, for both writer and reader, a self-indulgence in sadistic fantasy. The only fantasy in this novel could be seen as its unexpectedly hopeful ending. Saramago had a very high regard for truth; I think he chose to stop the story on a high point, not because he believed the ideals of social justice would ever be fulfilled—I'm not sure he "believed in" anything, in that sense—but because he judged a rational hope more useful than despair, and because he sought beauty in his art. His great book *Blindness* makes the same turn to the light at the end. But then *Seeing* turns away again. . . . He knew what darkness is.

Death in modern novels is almost habitually violent. People used to die in novels the way they mostly do in real life, prosaically and inevitably, without being shot, knifed, blown apart, or otherwise murdered; but we like our fictional deaths seen as spectacle, not felt as an experience we're going to share. There's a death scene near the end of this book; it's just a man, after a lifetime of overwork and some damage from torture, dying of old age at sixty-seven. We see his death through his own eyes. I think it beats any death scene in any novel I know. Saramago's truth-telling arises from a rare combination of intelligence, fierce artistic courage, and intense human tenderness.

In his Nobel talk he said,

> The only thing I am not sure of having assimilated satisfactorily is something that the hardship of those experiences turned into virtues in those women and men: a naturally austere attitude towards life. . . . Every day I feel its presence in my spirit like a persistent summons: I haven't lost, not yet at least, the hope of meriting a little more the greatness of those examples of dignity proposed to me in the vast immensity of the plains of Alentejo. Time will tell.

Time now gives us English-speakers the chance to see how well he worked to serve and deserve such greatness in this early novel. We already know how faithfully he followed that austere and summoning spirit through all his work.

José Saramago:
Skylight

Published in the Guardian, *June 2014*

José Saramago submitted the manuscript of *Skylight* to a Lisbon publisher in 1953. Receiving no response at all, and apparently never seeking one, he was plunged, says his wife, Pilar del Rio, in her introduction, "into a painful, indelible silence that lasted decades." He did, however, make a reputation as a journalist and editor before he returned to writing fiction in 1977 with the deceptively titled *Manual of Painting and Calligraphy*. In 1989, having published three novels, he was at work on a fourth when the publisher to which he had sent *Skylight* wrote him that they had rediscovered the manuscript and would take it as an honor to print it. He went at once and brought it home. His wife tells us that he never read it and said only that "it would not be published in his lifetime." We must assume that he said nothing about what was to be done with it after his death.

An old humiliation might be at the root of his neglect of the manuscript; or perhaps, given his late second start, he didn't want to spend time and thought in a return to this more conventional early work. In any case, I think his wife's decision to publish it now was sound. Not only does it illuminate the slow development of a radically original artist, but it is an interesting novel in its own right. The translator is the irreproachable Margaret Jull Costa.

Had the manuscript been accepted, and successful, would Saramago have kept the fine indifference to opinion that let him gradually discover his own incomparably idiosyncratic idiom, style, and subject matter? No telling.

Paragraphed and punctuated conventionally, *Skylight* follows a familiar fictional formula: a set of characters thrown together in one place at one time: in this case, a small working-class apartment house in Lisbon around 1950. Six flats; fifteen people, ten of them women. None of them is financially very secure and some are barely getting by; their lives are fragile, frugal, hard. Adriana and Isaura just manage to support their mother and aunt. In the evening all four women listen with yearning intensity to Beethoven on the radio, while young Claudinha next door plays jazzy ragtime. Claudinha's parents are unhappy in marriage. Emilio the salesman and his Spanish wife loathe each other. Brutish Caetano and diabetic Justina, haunted by the loss of her child, go past hatred into open violence.

The explicit sexuality of the book (which may have kept it from being considered for publication in Salazar's Portugal in 1953) is remarkable now only because it is so compassionate. Saramago's sympathy with the two sisters whose sexual desire can find no outlet is deep and subtle, as is his respect for Lidia, a kept woman who, while despising her keeper, respects her own professionalism in the most despised of professions. By a stunning reversal of erotic power, Saramago even manages to redeem the tiresome, pornish cliché of a woman responding to rape with passion.

Frustration, moral squalor, insecurity, all in close quarters, inevitably breed competition and malice. Moving from character to character, the loosely plotted story includes a good deal of meanspirited evildoing, quite in the tradition of Balzac and the naturalists. It also includes considerable dry humor, and at least one tranquil domestic scene revealed suddenly as almost visionary:

> Then they had supper. Four women sitting round the table. The steaming plates, the white tablecloth, the ceremonial of the meal. On this side—or perhaps on the other side too—of the inevitable noises lay a dense, painful silence, the inquisitorial silence of the past observing us and the ironic silence of the future that awaits us.

The strongest character in the book is Silvestre the cobbler. In later Saramago novels careful, honest workmen like him will appear, always significant, always wearing their significance lightly. Silvestre is married to Mariana, "so fat as to be comical, so kind as to make one weep"—a thoroughly good marriage of calm-souled, generous people. The reactionaries who now control his country crushed Silvestre's fierce social and political hopes, but not his spirit. He is a patient man, and his patience, his contentment, come across as far more than mere accommodation to defeat.

On the edge of poverty, Silvestre and Mariana rent their spare room to a lodger, Abel. He's about the age of the author of the book, thirty-one or thirty-two, and it's hard not to read him as to some degree a portrait of the artist as a young man. Purposefully avoiding close connection or commitment to anyone or anything, Abel appears a literary type of his time: the young writer who holds himself aloof, guarded, perceptive, inherently superior, essentially joyless. Though he wins his arguments with Silvestre, Abel strikes me as younger than he thinks he is and perhaps not as wise as he thinks he is. Are his existentialist poses a bit self-indulgent? Silvestre earned his disillusionment the hard way, staking himself on committed radical action. Abel isn't going to waste his life on illusions. But where will his non-commitment take him? Is he a realist reserving himself to act when action can succeed, or an idealist denying his own paralysis?

In their last argument Abel gets the last word, in fact the last words of the book: "The day when we can build on love has not yet arrived."

In the final silence after this statement I sense an unspoken refutation or qualification, which is the fact of Silvestre's life, a hardworking, responsible life built, in the most modest, limited, practical way, on love.

Sylvia Townsend Warner: *Dorset Stories*

2006

A whole region or domain of English literature is populated by great eccentrics. I imagine a hilly, spacious landscape of farm and forest, with no cities or main roads, but many beautiful, isolated houses, each occupied by a hermit of genius: Thomas Love Peacock, George Borrow, Forrest Reid, T. H. White, Sylvia Townsend Warner. . . . It is not that these writers were unaware of the literary fashions and techniques of their time, not at all; they knew quite well where the bright lights were, but they preferred to cultivate their garden.

Such purity of aim keeps their work singularly fresh, but puts it at risk both during the author's life and after. Fictions that can't be conveniently shoved into publishers' or critics' pigeonholes get such diminishing labels as "marginal" or "feminist" or "regional," which permit professors to ignore them and pundits to snub them. And Sylvia Townsend Warner's work suffered an extra measure of estrangement. In the 1930s, the *New Yorker* very cannily asked her for first refusal of her stories, and the arrangement lasted till her death in 1978. The large circulation and literary cachet of that magazine ensured that she became well known as a story writer in America. But in England, though the stories were reprinted in collections by British publishers, she appears to have been considered chiefly as a novelist, and her novels were mostly not published in America. This division of her reputation was surely harmful in the long run. Whatever the cause, her books seldom found publishers who kept them in print.

When I heard that Black Dog Books was about to publish a collection of her Dorset stories, under that title, I couldn't wait to see it. If any of her volumes of stories were in print in England, they hadn't made it over to the States; here, her reputation very largely died with her. Indeed, it's surprising that she ever was a *New Yorker* star, her work being very British in tone, style, locale, and sense of humor.

I had the great good fortune to be introduced to Sylvia Townsend Warner late in her life, in her damp, tobacco-smoke-varnished Naiad of a house, which was in Maiden Newton, on the river Frome, and also, from time to time when the river flooded, in it. She was very old, very tired, very kind. I told her I couldn't remember the name of her story about the family who go on a picnic and end up wandering along a footpath—a middle-aged man playing a fifty-pound music box; a lady carrying a birdcage; a girl dressed as Gainsborough's portrait of Arminella Blount; and a cadaverous small boy in a bloodstained Indian shawl. Because we've been following the perfectly plausible story, we have thought nothing odd at all about the music box, the costume, the birdcage, the blood— until the marvelously funny final reversal of point of view.

Sylvia laughed, remembering the story, but she couldn't remember its name or what book it might have been collected in. (It is "A View of Exmoor," in *One Thing Leading to Another*—which might well be the collective title of all her stories.)

That is one of her most gently funny tales. Others are less gentle; some are unbearably cruel. The very late stories about elves, collected as *Kingdoms of Elfin*, are among the strangest of her works; there is a lordly, icy, anguished indifference in them that chills the blood. Critics who confuse fantasy with whimsy and believe that only realism can deal with pain and cruelty should be exposed to Townsend Warner. She can cast a cold eye with the best of them.

So I was hoping for a selection of major stories that might reestablish Townsend Warner's reputation on the level it deserves. The *Dorset Stories* are not that. They are short occasional pieces, semi-memoirs, and minor tales, mostly from the 1930s and 1940s, only a couple of them developed fully as short stories. Many are mildly or not so mildly satirical, and quite funny; several have a dry, understated poignancy that lingers long in the mind. They are well chosen, and wisely arranged to give a certain narrative unity. The book is handsome, elegantly presented, and Reynolds Stone's woodcuts are in excellent harmony with the text. It is a charming book, and though too slight to serve well as an introduction to her work, will be a treasure to those who already know her. And I recommend it to anyone who would appreciate a wry glance at village life and character, not unkind, but—like all her writing—drastically unsentimental, undeceived.

After this review was published, I found that in 1988 Viking and in 2000 Virago had published a *Selected Stories*, giving a good sample of her shorter work, including "A View of Exmoor," the great story of incest called "A Love Match," and "On the Stroke of Midnight," perhaps her most unflinching statement of the impossibility of escape, the inevitability of loss and grief. Yet so little notice was taken of these collections that I didn't know, in 2006, that they existed.

Her first novel, *Lolly Willowes*, reprinted from time to time, is a dazzling display of the extraordinary wit and tough-mindedness of her fantasy; her historical novel *The Corner That Held Them* is harsh and splendid in its realism. She, who wrote an unsurpassable biography of T. H. White, was as fortunate in her biographer, Claire Harman. And then there are her poems; her letters, full of wit and fire and charm; and her diary, the record of a generous mind, a fiercely observant eye, and an intransigently faithful heart.

Jo Walton:
Among Others

2013

The beautifully titled novel *Among Others* is, I suppose, a fairy tale, since there are fairies in it, or anyhow beings called fairies. They aren't visible to everyone, yet can affect the lives of people who don't see them, or don't believe in them. In that, they play in modern industrial England something like their role in the folklore of the past. They don't, however, fit conventional notions of fairylikeness. They aren't the tall Fair Ones who carry you off under the hill, nor yet the tiny Peaseblossoms and sprites the Victorians loved, and they are most definitely not Tinker Bell. Descriptions suggest that the great illustrator Arthur Rackham was one of the people who could see them:

> In the same way that oak trees have acorns and hand-shaped leaves and hazels have hazelnuts and little curved leaves, most fairies are gnarly and grey or green or brown and there's generally something hairy about them somewhere. This one was grey, very gnarly indeed, and well over towards the hideous part of the spectrum.

Mori, the protagonist and narrator of the novel, has always seen and known the fairies. Though she'd like them to be Tolkien's Elves, they aren't gracious and powerful, but frustrated, marginal, somehow diminished. Some of them are probably ghosts. They are untamed, uncivilized, and unpredictable. They speak Welsh, mostly. They don't answer to any name, but if asked properly they can grant wishes. They are like fragments of the Wild, surviving only where a trace of woodland survives, haunting whatever remains of the unhuman—old parks, preindustrial untilled places, forgotten roads out past the edges of towns and farms.

Among Others does not, however, make the trite equation of Wilderness with Magic, for several quite commonplace-seeming human beings in the story also have supernatural powers. The knowledge of how to ask the fairies to grant a wish is one kind of magic, but there are others, some much nastier.

Bringing supernatural events into ordinary modern life—in this case, Oswestry in 1979—isn't an easy business for a novelist. The realists left us with the notion that "fantasy" is acceptable only when presented as about or for children. But there's nothing inherently childish about the overlapping of the natural with the supernatural, and many novels written for adults even in the heyday of realism involve that overlap. The first that came to my mind was the subtle and charming *Lady into Fox*. In David Garnett's story, as in many others, the supernatural element is simply there, not explained, not discussed—a good aesthetic ploy, for if it is discussed, the author has to tackle both plausibility and causality head on.

Most fantasies evade both these great and very challenging opportunities to make the impossible plausible, to give magic accountability in a realistic setting and moral and emotional weight in a modern novel. Jo Walton accepts the double challenge and meets it with courage and skill. She shows how easily the effects of a magic spell can be seen and explained away as perfectly natural, and how every action that brings about real change must be *paid for*—a reciprocity as absolute in the world of Three Wishes as it is in the world of Newton's Third Law.

The narrative is the diary of fifteen-year-old Mori, but Mori as an adult is implicitly present, and this stereoptical vision greatly enriches the book. Mori writes with style and reads obsessively, mostly science fiction. Some readers of the novel will be floored by her critical comments, enthusiastic or disapproving, about authors they may never have heard of. This strikes me as only fair; since we no longer have a common literary culture many readers are floored by references to classical authors they've never been introduced to. Anyhow, given the chance, Mori devours Plato as eagerly as she does Heinlein or Zelazny. Her critical notes, delivered with the energetic conviction of her age, are a delight. I was glad to learn that T. S. Eliot is brill.

Having suffered a lot of major damage, physical and psychic, Mori sees her reading as "compensatory." In fact, books give her passion and her fierce intelligence their only access to larger realities of art and thought. Books are almost enough to get her through separation from everyone she has loved, the pain of a smashed pelvis, the suffocating pettiness of the girls' boarding school that her three very respectable and very strange aunts have sent her to, and the uncanny attacks of an insane witch, her mother. But even reading fails her at last, and in search of some companionship, some human warmth in her life, she resorts to working magic.

Among Others is a funny, thoughtful, acute, and absorbing story all through, but in the magic bits it is more than that. When Mori realises that perhaps her new friends did not choose to offer her friendship but were forced to do so by the spell she laid upon them, her moral anguish is that of anyone who honestly faces the responsibility of power; and it is not soon or easily resolved. The heart of the book is a scene in the Welsh hills where Mori obeys the fairies' command to help the souls of the dead go into the darkness on All Souls Eve. In the crash that crippled Mori, her twin sister was killed, and the sister's soul comes to the gate of darkness now and clings and clutches and will not let Mori let her go. In this passage, haunting in its reticence and its drama, all the anguish of loss and need gathers almost intolerably, and as in some old ballads the quiet, factual narration deepens the inexplicable experience, making strangeness real.

Jeanette Winterson:
The Stone Gods

2007

It's odd to find characters in a science-fiction novel repeatedly announcing that they hate science fiction. I can only suppose that Jeanette Winterson is trying to keep her credits as a "literary" writer even as she openly commits genre. Surely she's noticed that everybody is writing science fiction now? Formerly deep-dyed realists are producing novels so full of the tropes and fixtures and plot lines of science fiction that only the snarling tricephalic dogs who guard the Canon of Literature can tell the difference. I certainly can't. Why bother? I am bothered, though, by the curious ingratitude of authors who exploit a common fund of imagery while pretending to have nothing to do with the fellow authors who created it and left it open to all who want to use it. A little return generosity would hardly come amiss.

The Stone Gods opens rather unfortunately with such meaningless flourishes as the "yatto-gram" and some fancy writing—"Eggs, pale-blue-shelled, each the weight of a breaking universe." Most of that gets done with early on, and Winterson settles into telling her story, which is complex, interesting, and doom-laden. There is an excess at times of the device known to science-fiction writers as "As you know, Captain . . ." Realistic fiction, dealing with the familiar, seldom needs such a device, but imaginative fiction may have to explain what a hobbit or a light-year or a limbic pathway is; and so we get dialogue beginning, "Oh, Spike, you know the theory," followed by a lecture on the theory. But even in the lectures Winterson's tone is lively. Her wit varies from flashy to flashing, her highly mannered, crackling dialogue moves things right along, the surface of her tale scintillates. Underneath it, as in every fable telling us that the future will be much worse than we thought, things are deadly serious.

"What is it about?"
"A repeating world."

So the narrator Billie Crusoe tells us, talking about a book she's picked up in the Tube, called *The Stone Gods*. So, yes, we are doing metafiction. And beyond that, it's hard to discuss the story without entirely giving away the central conceit, which Winterson develops teasingly, gradually. Delayed revelation is an essential effect in the book, and I don't want to spoil it. But since there are some apparently arbitrary initial confusions, I want to assure other readers that it does all add up. We will come to see the connections. We will understand why, from the interplanetary cataclysms of the first section, we are shifted so abruptly to the visit of Captain Cook's ship to Easter Island, and from that taken suddenly to a near-future London, and also why certain characters have the same names though they don't inhabit the same space-time.

Some of these significantly hidden connections are made with truly charming inventiveness. In the first section, the reduction of the robot Spike to a mere head is grotesquely sad; in the last section, Spike's existence as a mere head that doesn't have its body is grotesquely funny, particularly when Spike succeeds, as I think no other detached head has, in having sex. And when Billie Crusoe finally finds her Man Friday, the ironic comedy is fine.

At times Winterson seems to think poetical invention excuses fictional implausibility or incoherence. A farmhouse, with hearth fire, beside a willow-hung river complete with iris and moorhens, could not possibly exist in the terminally exhausted world of the first section. But since this image of the farm is essential to the book, it is essential that we be able to believe in it.

Bursts of emotion may be forgivable, given the dire events recounted and predicted, but they may also be overwrought. I felt this particularly in the Easter Island section, the central section and hinge point of the book. The history of that island and its people, as it has been pieced together in recent years, is in itself so appalling, and so appallingly apt an image of human misuse of our world, that it needs no heightening to make it hit home. But here it is all mixed up with a love story which is asked to carry far too much weight. Sentimentality, the product of a gap between the emotionality of the writing and the emotion actually roused in the reader, is very much a matter of the reader's sensibility; to me, both the love stories in the book are distressingly sentimental.

Still, despite the gaspy bits, the purple bits, and the lectures, *The Stone Gods* is a vivid cautionary tale—or, more precisely, a keen lament for our irremediably incautious species.

Stefan Zweig:
The Post Office Girl

2009

Artists work so hard, expending themselves with such unselfregarding energy, that it seems unfair to demand of them that they also be sick. But the nineteenth-century notion that genius is illness laid the onus of malaise on artists, particularly writers and composers. Before long, if you didn't poison your teenage brain with absinthe or withdraw to a cork-lined room, you were expected at least to indulge in alienation, alcoholism, bullfights, or suicide. German and Austrian artists started with an unfair advantage, in that their whole society was fairly toxic. Mahler, Richard Strauss, Thomas Mann, even Rilke: men of immense talent immersed in a cultural neuroticism, a wooing of perversity, disease, and death. Now, at this distance, their work appears stronger as it yields less to the mystique of hypersensitivity, ceases to swoon over the sick hero-self, and reports with sober clarity on their keen perceptions of a world out of balance. Mann's story "Disorder and Early Sorrow," the tiniest of household dramas, catches an entire historical moment in a few vivid, tender pages. On a larger scale, with a darker palette but comparable emotional power and control, Stefan Zweig's novel *The Post Office Girl* tells us a dark fairy tale of Austria in 1926.

The book is an anomaly in Zweig's work. His fame was based on highly "psychological" biographies and to a lesser extent on novels written in a high-strung, rather overwrought style. *The Post Office Girl* was not published, perhaps not finished, during his lifetime. Evidently he wrote most of it in the thirties, took the manuscript with him when he fled Nazism to Brazil, and was perhaps still working on it there before he killed himself in a suicide pact with his wife in 1942. Forty years later it was published in German, and now, thirty years after that, in English.

There is nothing dated about it. It strikes no self-conscious poses; the language is straightforward, precise, delicate, and powerful. The flow of the story, now lingering, now fast and lively, is under perfect control. A postmodern reader expecting linear exposition and descriptive passages to lead to "old-fashioned" resolution is in for a shock. Perhaps because the book is a work in progress, perhaps because Zweig's conception of it was essentially ambiguous, there is no closure at all. The moral desolation of the novel is unsparing, accurate, and absolute. It is far beyond cynicism. It is as irrational and unanswerable as Dostoyevsky.

The story begins in a dreary Austrian village, where Christine, whose bourgeois family fell into poverty during the First World War, barely supports her sick mother through her soulless job in the post office. Suddenly comes a telegram from the aunt who went to America before the war—and Christine is transported to the magical world of a luxury hotel in the Alps, where wishes she never knew she had are granted before she makes them. This long section of the book is marvelously written, bright as mountain air, vivid with delight. But the delight begins to be excessive, verges on hysteria. And so the reversal comes—again, wonderfully told, unforgettably real. Back down into the ashes, Cinderella.

And there she meets her Prince, Ferdinand, a bitter, bad-luck veteran of a lost war and a Siberian prison camp. Where can these two make a life together or find a life worth living?

Christine's world consists of irreconcilable extremes—hopeless need, obscene wealth—and she, wildly volatile and helplessly impressionable, is tossed between these extremes with no chance of establishing selfhood. The villagers, even the kind, ugly schoolteacher who adores her, are hopelessly coarse, cowardly, and humdrum; loathing them, she behaves as they do. In the Alpine hotel, the wealthy guests live solely for the immediate gratification of physical pleasure; adoring them, she learns within a day to behave as they do. There is no middle way in her world. There is no middle class. What Lao Tzu called "the baggage wagon" is simply not there. Nobody has a profession, they merely scrabble after money. Nobody looks beyond self or has the faintest spiritual striving or intellectual interest. All that, it seems, was burned away by the war and the dreadful postwar years of inflation and famine. Christine exists in an unspeakable poverty of mind and spirit.

Is this deprivation, this absence, what made Hitler possible: the void that Nazism filled? Missing from Christine's world is the immense and apparently unremarkable middle element of life, the moderation of the middle class, whose ethical standards she follows by rote, but without any standard of intellectual or spiritual honesty to support the muddled, ordinary decency that adolescents rage at, sophisticates sneer at, saints surpass, and warriors, if they can, destroy.

The ultimate goal of war is to make slaves. Ferdinand the ex-soldier/ex-prisoner knows that. He knows he has been not only permanently damaged but permanently enslaved. At the end of the story he plans a desperate effort with Christine to escape the bondage they both live in. But at what cost? Perhaps they can buy justice, but can they steal freedom? What I see in their future, if they have any—and I don't want to see it, because after all Christine is so vulnerable, so pitiable, so likable—is the two of them standing wide-eyed and enthusiastic amid vast massed crowds, screaming *Heil, Heil, Heil.* But that is only what I see. What you may see, the author of this beautiful, risk-taking novel leaves up to you.

The Hope of Rabbits:
A Journal of a Writer's Week

Hedgebrook is a writers' retreat with a difference: it accepts only women. As Gloria Steinem said of it, it's not a retreat, it's an advance.

Gender segregation, like any segregation, is open to question as to its motives. I attended a women's college that was embedded like a seed pearl in a gigantic male oyster. I taught at Mills and Bennington, and many times at the great writing workshop The Flight of the Mind, and I attended or taught at many mixed-gender schools and workshops. My judgment is based on experience. I hold it self-evident that so long as we live in a man's world, as we still do, women have a right to create enclaves of learning or work where, instead of obeying or imitating what men do and want, women can shape what they do, how they do it, and why they do it, in their own way and on their own terms. No enclave is the whole reality, no exclusivity is entirely rightful, but when a great injustice prevails, any opportunity of counteracting it, undoing it even temporarily, is justified. Intellect and art have been so wholly owned by men, and that ownership so fiercely maintained, that no woman can assume society will simply grant her a rightful share in them. Many women still find it difficult, even frightening, to name themselves thinkers, makers, to say I am a scholar, a scientist, an artist. A place where such fear has no place, and a period of time given purely to doing one's own work, is for many men a perfectly reasonable expectation, for many women an astounding, once-in-a-lifetime gift.

The six cottages of Hedgebrook, in a beautiful farm-and-forest on the coast of Whidbey Island, north of Seattle, have offered that gift to many of us. (If you want to know more about it, the website is Hedgebrook.org.) I was kindly invited there over twenty years ago to come for a month. I chose to go only for a week. I had never been at any kind of writer's colony before, never wanted to—a room of my own in my own house had always seemed quite enough. But I was curious, now, about what this one would be like, and the timing was good. I had been having intimations of a new story that felt as if it might be a long one, a novel or at least a novella. What would it be like to work on it all day every day for a week, without any distractions, without grocery shopping or house cleaning or making dinner—alone for twenty hours a day or more?

What follows is the record I kept of what it was like.

This diary and the novella were written in bound notebooks, possibly the last long pieces of prose I composed entirely by hand. I don't want to rant about the suppression of teaching cursive writing in American schools, but I'm very glad I was taught it. Remembering writing outdoors at Hedgebrook and elsewhere, I think about the humane pace of longhand, and how one is constantly looking away from the notebook at things around it, near or far, changing position as one sits, doodling in the margin while working out a transition, half-consciously noticing the slant of the sunlight, the advance of shadows, the color of the sky: fully absorbed in the work, and yet open to the surrounding world, as we are not when working at a computer screen. A good pen or pencil and a well-made notebook are a genuine climax technology: simple, sustainable, fixable, lasting, and extraordinarily adaptable. It seems a pity to throw it entirely away by omitting to teach people how to use it, simply because a new, wonderful, and infinitely less sustainable technology has come along. I hate to think of a writerly great-grandchild silenced in the midst of a story by the failure of her power source, dumb as an unplugged machine. Well, she'll swear, and find a pencil, and start laboriously printing, and presently reinvent cursive. Nothing, not even our incalculable wrongheadedness, can keep human beings from telling stories.

DAY 1. 20 April 1994.

12:30 pm.

I am sitting in bright sunlight on the little front porch of Cedar Cottage at Hedgebrook. Linda picked me up at the Alexis in Seattle and drove me here, crossing on the Mukilteo ferry—silky water; a sea lion catching a fish and then playing about; fog low on the mainland, hiding the Cascades behind us; but as we approached Whidbey Island the snowy Olympics stood above the clouds, and there is no fog here on the island. The sun's hot, brilliant on the grass, making the shadows of the trees all round very dark. A tiny, dusty lizard under the porch wants to come out into the sunlight, but is scared of me.

I am apprehensive, feeling strange to the place, despite a kind welcome. The usual nervousness about being among people I don't know, forgetting names, being awkward. Plus an unusual apprehension: Seven days with no obligations, no routine, no society except at dinner time—but not exactly vacation days, not holiday: workdays for the real work, without any distractions except those I invent. This is austere, this prospect. A Shaker week, silent, celibate. A week of listening where there are no sounds (but the birds and the wind). A test? Will I pass it? Will I be able to keep the woodfire going to keep my Cedar Cabin warm, when the clouds and rain return? Will I be able to keep my own fire going?

Not wanting to use this week for "trivial pursuits," I did not bring the material for an essay I must write about Cordwainer Smith—not a trivial writer, but it didn't seem appropriate work for this week. I decided that I should hope to be blessed by a story, and should hold the days free for that. And if I am not blessed, I have several heavy books to read. I will read seriously, I said, not skim and gobble, for once. So I have Lévi-Strauss and Clifford Geertz, Garcilaso de la Vega el Inca and Bernardo Diaz, and Sanday on Gender, and Leanne Hinton on Californian Languages: surely enough! For novels I have only Angélica Gorodischer's, in Spanish, and my Spanish dictionary; and Joaquin Miller's *Life Amongst the Modocs,* which Dan Crommie lent me. I didn't bring anything easy. My choices were stern, austere. Will I be sorry?

I brought a tiny sketch book and colored pencils, but no camera. Nothing easy.

Lunch came in a pretty basket: two kinds of pasta salad. Greens would have been nice and something in the way of juice, but I guess one gets one's own juice and stuff in foraging for breakfast after dinner. Water seemed fittingly austere.

But how perfectly beautiful it is, this little clearing of mown green grass ringed in by dark firs and bright, new-leaved, April-blossoming shrubs and trees! What utter luxury, to sit here like a lizard in the sun!

5:10 pm.

A little rabbit: the longest I've ever watched a wild rabbit (I was indoors in the windowseat). Brindle brown-grey, with flour-dust along the flanks, and the white scut elevated now and then. A healthy young rabbit, glossy fur. The great, black eyes, light-circled, are still visible from three-quarter-back view, so that Her Elegance can see what's behind her as she grazes in the grass like a nervous little cow. Slender, reddish hind legs. She stands, the nose twitching and wiggling, one front paw dangling; she hops on; tucks her hindquarters under like a cat (like my cat, whom I miss).

Denise showed me about after lunch—the farm, the paths and pools. We heard the he-goat scream. Recently he had to have his penis cut off because of bladder stones, and now pees forcefully backwards through a tube; and the vet had to clear the tube, which evidently hurt. Beautiful herb and vegetable gardens, an orchardlet, berry bushes, root cellar, greenhouse—the dream farm. Oh money what wonders you perform (and how rarely are you so well spent). Beyond the farmhouse lie the wetlands and Useless Bay, a most endearing name, and blue land over the water—part of this or another island or the mainland, I don't know.

I drew and colored a picture of Cedar Cottage as the ring-encircled sun faded into white sky and the temperature dropped; now, as the sun crosses my windows to the right behind the trees, it has cleared up again a good deal; but I don't trust it to be fair. Now westering sunlight shines through the small young pale-apricot-color leaves of a sapling maple, and dapples the grass again. I am in my windowseat with a shot of whiskey; must leave for dinner in a short while. I have read the kind effusions of women who have stayed in this cottage in the record-books kept here. I felt somewhat unworthy; cynical; bad. We women do work so hard at keep the weaving from unravelling!

A rabbit just traversed the grass in a charming loping hurry—same one? Only rabbits know.

8:20 pm.

Dinner at the farmhouse table—rice and beans, cottage cheese and fruit, a lovely mushroom filo triangle, and green salad; wine and coffee—With the other residents—one young and black from Brooklyn, one from

Calcutta, one Native Hawaiian; one young and Asian-American—and Linda, the manager, and Nancy Nordhoff, the founder. Laura cooks, eats, serves, clears. One resident is away.

I walked the paths after a tiny spatter of rain—first north to a lovely black pool, and along the east perimeter; to the supply house, where I called Charles at home; then on round the northwest perimeter, back to the black pool, and home. It is strange, there are so many paths, and between them the forest is so thick, evergreens and currant and salmonberry and a laurelly tall shrub with white panicles—elder, that's what it is—I thought at one moment of the Sleeping Beauty's hedge— the red salmonberry flowers nodding down from high above me on their thorn-furred stems. Yet it is all within a fence, and all only 33 acres. You can get lost and never be lost. It is dreamlike. The little cottontails are everywhere, quite fearless. A great contestation of crows above my roof broke up at my approach, swooping off blackly.

Twilight now, and nearly clear. Very still. Evening bird remarks. The white, sweet-clove-scented, ball-shaped flower clusters of the shrub just facing the windowseat windows grow whiter as the light fades.

DAY 2. 21 April.

11.45 am.

I hoped to rise at dawn, but lay instead till 7:30 in the broad loft-bed as the day brightened in the beautiful arched window with its tulips of colored glass. I sought my story. I did tai chi. I made my breakfast of granola, banana and orange juice, and tea, and ate it in the windowseat, which is where I think I will spend the week.

I didn't bring the laptop, because Charles wanted it for the coast and because I decided I didn't want the baggage of it, either physical or psychic; I brought three notebooks, this being one of them. I'm glad I did, so that I can write in the windowseat with the triple window all along beside me to the right and another narrow light at my feet, so I have the sky and trees, the white-flowered shrub, a fine romantic stump sheltering a rhododendron, and always the hope of rabbits.

After story-planning, I leapt up to walk before the rain—it threatens, though blue patches still show; the wind is strong in gusts from the south, not cold; I haven't yet lighted the woodstove. I went down past the waterfall pond and round by the goats, whom I gave a twig apiece of elder, which they stood up politely for, gazing from their goat eyes; walked west along the Millman Road to where it rises to Double Bluff Road, the only route down to the beach—a goodish walk it must be. I hope it doesn't rain so I can't walk, as I love that alternation of writing and walking. I found two fine stones on the roadside among many pretty granites and interesting composites and generally good pebbles. And a tuft of rabbit fur by the farm driveway; a hawk at dawn? Came home by the pond with its lovely bronze statue of two otters under a great dark cedar. Two white seashells in the leafmould—an offering, surely.

5:30 pm.

Scribbled story, sun came out, I took off sweater, moved out onto porch; mowers mowed lanes of grass down vistas of forest; I drew the Blasted Stump that leans so picturesquely in the SE of my windowseat view (I drew it sitting on the same hummock, or Tussock, that I drew the house from); I scribbled more; the sun went in, and so did I.

Now have read some more Lévi-Strauss and sewed a little on my difficult Mimbres birds and geometries, having some whiskey. I wait for rabbits. Only flies come. But a fine, young, coppery-colored lizard came out from under the porch and glared balefully, fearlessly at me, just as I went in. This must be the lizard Denise inquired after. It has a fine new tail. The one I saw yesterday was dusty and a bit scrubby looking; it had lost its tail, and was very small. This one was maybe four inches long. Well, maybe three.

DAY 3. 22 April.

7 am.

By going to bed at 9:30 I woke up at 5:30, and listened to the birds' dawn chorus (not numerous, but sweet) and saw the treetops in the charm'd magic casement. So I was up before six and finding it clear, the brightness showing through the trees behind the house, went out with my boots on (it rained a little in the night and the dew is very heavy) and did tai chi exercises on the only flat bit of Cedar House's clearing, and then went walking, thinking it would be fine to see the Black Pond at the break of day. I wandered a while before I found it. What it is, east and north of the house, is a Labyrinth—a true, random one, where all the paths lead into other paths and branch away from them and reconnect. A rabbit started me on my wanderings, a fierce brave rabbit as in Beatrix Potter; it really didn't want to run away, moving in short, grudging little runs, and then I'd catch up to it again, till finally it left the path in one disdainful lollop over a bush into the darkness of the undergrowth, gone. I finally found the Black Pond again. I saw my reflection in it, edging cautiously onto moss on the spongy rim, leaning over. Trees and sky reflect perfectly in it, the black water making a mirror. My head was a black, uneven round, featureless. It is an uncanny little pool. I guess it feeds all the other, lower, livelier pools, with their waterfalls and duckweed.

At dinner last night A. joined us; she had been in town for sonograms of the baby she is carrying. She and B. are both black, beautiful, and pretty young. I am by far the oldest. L., who has four children in Hawaii, leaves today. As we walked back from dinner and stood at the parting of the paths under the trees, she told me her children's names and what they mean and how they imply the child's destiny, what that child must do in life.

It is utterly silent now. This will be a silent day; we don't meet for dinner, but will have it brought with lunch, as Laura has to drive two residents into town. I will cultivate silence. Maybe I will not cultivate it but leave it fallow.

I'm curious to have a weather forecast, but hate the idea of turning on the radio, spoiling, polluting the pure silence. I only did so once, for less than a minute.

9 am.

The rabbits *use the paths.*

Should wild things use paths? But after all they make their own, why not use ours.

9:30 am.

A large, dark rabbit has made himself Guardian of the path to the woodhouse. He sits, erect or in classic bunny pose, ears erect, motionless, in the middle of the path. Occasionally he patrols it for a few feet. Then he returns to his post.

From the rear they are like little short-legged deer. The behavior is very like deer: the grazing, the motionless alertness, surveillance. I live with a small predator, at home. It is interesting to watch small prey.

He's off guard now, grazing just out of the sun near the Blasted Stump. He doesn't "nibble," he grazes. Big leaves of grass go in very quickly, twitching up and down as he chews, like spaghetti.

The light ring around the great, dark eye is also deerlike, and the leaf ears.

5 pm.

Unease of the gut and a bad taste in the mouth grew in me today and have kept me close to the cottage and perhaps depressed my mind. I wandered about in mid-afternoon and drew the view south from the largest, lowest pond, over the cattails, to Deer Lagoon and blue Useless Bay; then came home and sat out, finishing Lévi-Strauss, reading a good bit of Geertz, and a little Gorodischer, and wrote more, on and off, at my story; very 'productive' and industrious, but lacking vitality and spark. "I work as a cow grazes," Käthe Kollwitz said of herself when her children were grown. I feel a bit like that, with nothing in my present life but the work; I would (I think) really prefer some regular variety, not necessarily company, at least not of strangers, but of other work—physical work— to cook, or clean, or garden, or something, at a regular time, or for a regular length of time, daily. As it is, I walk; but today didn't feel fit to walk far, and so am a bit stale. Being outside ever since eleven in the variable sunny, hazy, breezy, mild day has been very good, though my tail is tired from sitting on the hard porch. Both lizards visited. Dinner will be alone, here, tonight; I'll try to call Charles, who was out last night. The story alas is very slow and circumstantial—probably overly so.—I thought it would be nice to write short things, tiny stories, here; but what I have hold of is the tail of a very large, long creature. It seems a mild one, so far. A vast lizard?

Two walking sticks stand by the door, one just a weathered branch, the other a marvelously polished, dark-yellow staff about four feet long, tapering, with a few knots, fairly straight: is it yew wood? The door of Cedar House is of yew, its journal-book says. It is also yellowish, incredibly smooth and grainless, very beautiful. [Nancy later said the staff was probably rhododendron wood.]

I suddenly realised that I can get rid of the flies in my windowseat windows, which come in the door and buzz and distract me, by opening the windows. The flies fly out. *Ma che stupidezza!*

8:20 pm.

Two rabbits just outside the windowseat window—One has a good sprinkling of white in its fur, I would say an old rabbit, but do wild rabbits get old? The other darker—my Guard, I think. Intensely purposeful, the neat quick warm bodies move and halt in the twilight grass on narrow, delicate feet.

A female California quail was scratching in a ground feeder outside the farm kitchen window when I washed my dinner dishes, among house finches, chickadees, sparrows. The graceful oval body looked quite large among the little birds. She scratched and pecked vigorously. I love to see quail being quail, they are so full of quailness.

DAY 4. 23 April.

9 am.

Three great crying geese flew south over the trees, croaking clanging.

10 am.

Two deer, following the path from the north, stepping cautious with their delay-walk, nibbling shoots here and there, very watchful. I would guess a doe and last year's fawn. Brown coats, black tails whisking. The great leaf ears turning and alert, shot through with sunlight, and the chin-whiskers full of sunlight.

Everyone uses the same paths here.

Digestion still off but improving. I woke at six and lay till seven, storydreaming/lazing. Sleep is pure and dark here.

Elisabeth passed her exams. I talked with Charles and Theo last night.

5:25 pm.

Wrote till eleven, then went down to see about the work party—this is Saturday. They were all about, volunteers, alumnae. I joined the weeders in the garden. We cleared a bed of all but a few lettuces and a poppy or two. Then lunch, picnicking about. A lovely day, cool this morning but the warmest yet I think, a clear sky till nearly five. I came back to get my cap and sunscreen, returned to weed again, the edge of the garden by the fence next to the potatoes. I worked till a bit past three, with great pleasure in good company, talking about writers, books, and movies. Felt enough was enough and came back and had a good shower in the beautiful bath house (and put my dirty dirty shirt in the dirty clothes basket to take home. I sponged my jeans—they have to last a few more days.) Met an alumna and her mother on the path, and showed them Cedar House.

Sat out and reread the morning's work, too buzzy to write more. Read Gorodischer, and started a whiskey at five. A very good day! I really needed the physical work. How could this be managed at a place like this? so that there was some real work to be done, but only by those who wanted to do it? A "garden party" at a certain hour of the afternoon? A list of volunteer jobs kept posted? So that nobody felt obliged, but could have a work-break if they wanted? It would be difficult to handle.

DAY 5. 24 April.

11:45 am.

It began to rain along with dawn, and has rained steadily since. I lighted the stove for the first time—though it's not cold, it's dank, and I wanted the cheer and the bother of it, too. Just relighted it. It lights fast, draws a gale, and eats its little bits of wood like crazy. If I go on feeding it I'll have to squelch out and get wood today.

I'm on page 25 of the story.

Thought of calling the book *Making Souls* instead of *Love is Love*. It is as much about "religion" as it is about sex, if not more. [Later: The book this story is in ended up as *Four Ways to Forgiveness.*]

Doesn't look like any chance of physical work or walk today, unless I want to get very wet, and then how to dry wet clothes? I think the cabins wouldn't be diminished by a little wall heater, with the woodstove for glory.

At dinner last night Jennifer cooked, with her fat fair baby Nash, replacing Laura; B. was there, and a newcomer/returner, L.; and J., whom I got to know a little better. She came from another writer's retreat in Texas to this one; I don't know if I like her, but suspect that if I did I would very much, but it would take a while. Yesterday, A. walked back from the gardens with me and we talked. She is five months along and was not feeling very well. She is beautiful and appealing, with a direct, mature sweetness.

DAY 6. 25 April.

ll:45 am.

The sun gradually came out, yesterday—I went for a road walk, east then west, at two. I went down and investigated the gate which my friend Judith said one could ignore the No Trespassing sign on to get down to the shore of the Lagoon; there was absolutely no ignoring it; I think the fences have been added since J. was here. I got quite warm though it was cloudy; and by evening it was perfectly clear, and cooler.

At dinner G. from India was still away, which is too bad because she looked so nice. Connie the gardener joined us; I liked her; she has grey hair, a bond. B. read us a story after dinner, the first time we have stayed together in the evening—a vampire love story, feministically correct, as far as a vampire story can be! A. is still not feeling very well. L. seems shy but well-disposed. J. made a criticism of a word in B's story and then gave way to a charming embarrassment. I can't tell arrogant from shy, when they're so young! Or maybe ever?

I picked up some nice stones on Millman Road on my walk, and arranged them on the big rocks beside my doorstep, where the blue spike flowers, whatever they are [adjuga, dummy!] make such a show and glow of purple-blue that welcomes me through the trees; the bees and bumblebees are always at them. I think, will the next person here like stones?

Tried to get to the Dark Tarn, after calling Charles about eight pm; missed it again—and again—and then finally almost fell into it. It is a fascinating place, with its black perfect mirror of the trees and sky, and no stir of its surface at all but the slight rings spreading out quick and silent from an insect touch. The night-heard frogs are down at Waterfall Pond. The ducks mostly hang out on those lower, sunny ponds. Black Pond is lonesome.

So far I have finished Lévi-Strauss, who had a considerable influence on my story; read parts of Clifford Geertz; read Leanne Hinton on Californian Indian languages; am avoiding Sanday, which might interfere with my story; started Garcilaso de la Vega last night. Geertz on common sense is good, and he has far more common sense than Lévi-Strauss—but L-S starts the mind—my mind, anyhow. He gets wheels turning I didn't know were there. All his mythology however seems almost insane to me—the substitutions are like Freudian interpretations of "meaning," a series of reflecting mirrors reflecting mirrors, with no standpoint outside from which to say Hold, enough!—Geertz is ineffably Ivyleague, a pity; it makes him smart-alecky sometimes, and though he is quite right to point out the curious reversal of fortune in so many academic careers, from the Big School as a graduate student to the Little School for the career, his assumption that Princeton is Paradise is appalling in an anthropologist. I was ashamed to read it. Those people really do believe in the hierarchy of intelligence and merit—I guess they have to? Of course better scholars are likely to come from the centers of scholarship than from the outskirts, it's a matter of critical mass; but the preening, the snobbery, the prejudice, and the absolute indifference to the fact that, aside from specialised scholarship made available by wealth, there is *no difference in the students* at all: that's unforgivable in an educated mind. It reveals a deep fault in the education. I suppose that's really why I didn't read the book methodically—I rather dislike Clifford Geertz. I don't like being taught by a snob. Whereas Lévi-Strauss, for all his touching faith in a good boys' lycée and the École Normale Supérieure, is not a snob, and I delight in learning from him. I can handle aristocrats, I just can't take parvenus. Ha!

5:25 pm.

The curious comparison followed: Geertz is to Lévi-Strauss as a raccoon is to a unicorn.

Well!

Lunch was brought in the basket with the pretty cloth by the pretty Jennifer. Her smile is welcome after Laura's overworked look, which makes me feel guilty—though Laura has a lovely smile which I caught a couple of times at dinner (from which she removes herself as much as Jennifer joins in). Jennifer is an "easy" person, Laura is not. The lunches are a bit odd. A marvelous green salad today, and a vegetable soup made from last night's shepherd's pie, with chicken; no bread. Never. Bread is not eaten, and drink is up to you. I have taken to taking an egg and English muffin for my breakfast, and thank goodness Judith told me to bring tea. There's herbals but no tea at all, only vile "decaf." The decaf coffee, on the other hand, is lovely, at night after dinner.

It went on being nice, and I scuttled off to the ponds and tried a sketch of the Far Blue Towers, which I assume are downtown Seattle, and another one of the reeds in Waterfall Pond.

I am nearing the end of my story, which may be accommodating itself to my time here—I suspect it of doing so. But it's 41 pages now and should not go on forever, surely? It leaps about strangely, as it is. I think I know what it's about and then I am not certain. I had some insights when I tried the little low place with its little low window, at the east end of the cabin, at the foot of the ladder to the loft, to the right of the door. The woman who showed her mother this cabin on Saturday said that's where she mostly wrote in her cabin when she was here. It seems a bit dark to me, and odd, but it is a good space; from anywhere one gets beautiful views and angles on the rest of the cabin, and the view from there is particularly fine. It just would seem odd to me to stay in the dark, with the windowseat offering me all the glade, the trees, and sky. And the rabbits. Two last night, very methodical rabbits.

One more full day. The "test" aspect got passed in all senses by Saturday; in the writing aspect, by the second day. I feel some lingering reservation, which may well be nothing more than Charles's negativity about my coming here, acting as a drag on me. I think that this is what I think: that this is a wonderful place for any woman who writes. So long as—So long as it doesn't replace living in the world most people live in.—Puritan. Stupid Puritan.

What would men have written in the log-book of Cedar Cottage? I do wonder. The sweet gratitude and pleasure of the women who have stayed here flows like honey from the horn. Take my dear cabin, it is yours, they all say. I was happy, be happy, they say. I wrote, they say— Write!

DAY 7, 26 April.

Noon.

Woke and lay and storydreamed till 6:40; got up and wrote and wrote and came to an end—which may or may not be the end—of the story I began my first full day here, which I'm calling "A Man of the People." Walked up to the Dark Tarn and round down to the herb garden, where I pencil-sketched Deer Lagoon. It's grey and rather chilly.

Last night A., L., and J. read their work, and we sat around till past eight in the farm parlour. B. put on her Vampire Teeth. They were all going to go to the Dark Tarn to howl at the full moon when it came over the trees; but if they did I didn't hear them. [Later: they all said they did.] I was luxuriating in the sleeping loft and had no wish to howl.

At two this afternoon I had a shower in the lovely bath house, that work of art, and coming back spoke to Nancy, who was chopping wood. Linda came by soon after for a cup of tea and to talk—about writing something about Hedgebrook (i.e., this journal)—we were not very conclusive. At four Nancy and Trece Greene arrived, and Nancy took us on her Woods Walk, showing me a couple of amazing places in the Labyrinth that I never had discovered or suspected: some cedars snaking themselves strangely along from a central root-source and then rising up straight; and a lovely fir grove. Back by Otter Pond and the great old cedar on the east side of it, to Cedar House. Trece had tea and I had whiskey, till we walked down to farewell dinner. Lots of rice and laughing. A. gave us all frog stationery she has drawn and printed. So back through the still, mild, chill, grey evening to Cedar House, to pack, and sleep one more night.

I should think that any stay here would be important in one way or another to most women; and a long stay could be a crossroads to a young woman; an utter blessing to any woman in genuine need of solitude to write or to complete a spiritual passage. My week here (that seemed so long at the beginning, and now seems both very long and very short)—the importance of it to me lies, I think now, mostly in the great beauty and peacefulness of the house and the forest and the farm—a place apart, "enisled"—seclusion, freedom, luxury, rest, and the touching beauty of it above all.

If I had not found a story to write, I wonder how it would have been? I worked, I worked, the joy of my life. So all the beauty, the sunlight, the rabbits, the deer, the walks, the good fellowship of the younger women, the sweet deep silence of the nights, and the waking to see the treetops through the tulip window of the loft in the first light—all that was gravy.

But, if I had not been here, in all probability I would not have written this story. It took the whole week; and it was a response to considerable pressure: "I am here to write, I brought this empty notebook—I need a story!" So Cedar House, Hedgebrook, gave me the story.

And the gravy.

Trece is to come by to drive me home at eight tomorrow morning. *Chau mi casita querida!*

Acknowledgments

The publication information for the book reviews in this collection is as follows:

Margaret Atwood, *Moral Disorder*. Published in the *Guardian*, September 2006.

Margaret Atwood, *The Year of the Flood*. Published in the *Guardian*, July 2009.

Margaret Atwood, *Stone Mattress*. Published in the *Financial Times*, September 2014.

J. G. Ballard, *Kingdom Come*. Published in the *Guardian*, July 2006.

Roberto Bolaño, *Monsieur Pain*. Published in the *Guardian*, January 2011.

T. C. Boyle, *When the Killing's Done*. Published in the *Guardian*, April 2011.

Geraldine Brooks, *People of the Book*. Published in the *Guardian*, January 2008.

Italo Calvino, *The Complete Cosmicomics*. Published in the *Guardian*, June 2009.

Margaret Drabble, *The Sea Lady*. Published in the *Guardian*, July 2006.

Carol Emshwiller, *Ledoyt*. First published by the *Women's Review of Books* in 1997; revised in 2002.

Alan Garner, *Boneland*. Published in the *Guardian*, August 2012.

Kent Haruf, *Benediction*. Published in the *Literary Review*, February 2014.

Kent Haruf, *Our Souls at Night*. Written in 2016, not previously published.

Tove Jansson, *The True Deceiver*. Published in the *Guardian*, December 2009.

Barbara Kingsolver, *Flight Behavior*. Published in the *Literary Review*,

December 2012.

Chang-Rae Lee, *On Such a Full Sea*. Published in the *Guardian*, February 2014.

Doris Lessing, *The Cleft*. Published in the *Guardian*, March 2007.

Donna Leon, *Suffer the Little Children*. Published in the *Guardian*, April 2007.

Yann Martel, *The High Mountains of Portugal*. Written in 2016, not previously published.

Chine Miéville, *Embassytown*. Published in the *Guardian*, April 2011.

China Miéville, *Three Moments of an Explosion*. Published in the *Guardian*, July 2015.

David Mitchell, *The Bone Clocks*. Published in the *Guardian*, September 2014.

Jan Morris, *Hav*. Published in the *Guardian*, June 2006.

Julie Otsuka, *The Buddha in the Attic*. Published in the *Guardian*, December 2011.

Salman Rushdie, *The Enchantress of Florence*. Published in the *Guardian Unlimited*, July 2014.

Salman Rushdie, *Two Years, Eight Months, and Twenty-Eight Nights*. Written in 2015, not previously published.

José Saramago, *Raised from the Ground*. Published in the *Guardian*, October 2012.

José Saramago, *Skylight*. Published in the *Guardian*, June 2014.

Sylvia Townsend Warner, *Dorset Stories*. Written in 2006. Not previously published.

Jo Walton, *Among Others*. Published in the *Guardian*, March 2013.

Jeanette Winterson, *Stone Gods*. Published in the *Guardian*, August 2007.

Stefan Zweig, *The Post Office Girl*. Published in the *Literary Review*, March 2009.

About the Author

Ursula Kroeber Le Guin was born in 1929 in Berkeley, and lives in Portland, Oregon. As of 2017, she will have published twenty-three novels, twelve collections of stories, five books of essays, thirteen books for children, nine volumes of poetry and four of translation. Among her numerous honors and awards are the Hugo, Nebula, National Book Award, PEN-Malamud, Library of Congress Living Legend, and National Book Foundation Medal. Recent publications include *Steering the Craft*, *The Found and the Lost: The Collected Novellas*, and *Late in the Day: Poems 2010–2014*. Her website is ursulakleguin.com.